WITHDRAWN

Writing Women's Literary History

Writing Women's Literary History

Margaret J. M. Ezell

The Johns Hopkins University Press
Baltimore and London

© 1993 The Johns Hopkins University Press
All rights reserved
Printed in the United States of America on acid-free paper

The Johns Hopkins University Press
701 West 40th Street
Baltimore, Maryland 21211
The Johns Hopkins Press Ltd., London

Part of chapter 2 appeared as "The Myth of Judith Shakespeare,"
New Literary History 21 (1989–90): 579–92. Reprinted w/permission.

Library of Congress Cataloging-in-Publication Data

Ezell, Margaret J. M.
  Writing women's literary history / Margaret J.M. Ezell.
    p.   cm.
  Includes bibliographical references (p.   ) and index.
  ISBN 0-8018-4432-0
  I. Title.
PR111.E94   1992
820.6'00082 – dc20   92-9227

22993

Contents

Acknowledgments

I have many friends, students, and colleagues to thank for their help in the several stages of researching and writing this book. First, the librarians at the Huntington Library, the Clark Library, the Bodleian Library, and the Cambridge University Library helped to make research for this project a constant pleasure. A Faculty Development Leave from Texas A&M University provided the time off needed to complete the manuscript; my students there, in particular my graduate students in the feminist criticism course, provided the incentive to write this book in the first place.

I am furthermore heavily indebted to my associates on the NEH—Brown University Women Writers Project (Susanne Woods, Elizabeth Kirk, Stuart Curran, Patricia Caldwell, Elizabeth Hageman, and Elaine Brennan). Working on the project has offered an unparalleled opportunity to explore the process through which "lost" texts are recovered utilizing computer technology and rediscovered in the classroom.

The development of the issues in this text was encouraged by the atmosphere of lively inquiry into the nature of historicism created by the lecture/colloquium series sponsored by the Interdisciplinary Group for Historical Literary Studies at Texas A&M between 1987 and 1989. I am obliged not only to the speakers from outside the university who shared their time and attention in discussions, including Jerome McGann, Marilyn Butler, Laurence Buell, J. Paul Hunter, and Ralph Cohen, but also the members of the Group itself, who kept my project alive with their interest and through the example of their own research. In particular, the members of the steering committee of IGHLS, Katherine O'Brien O'Keeffe, Jeffrey N. Cox, and Larry J. Reynolds, have been a constant source of support, advice, and encouragement. This book could not have been written without them.

Finally, I dedicate this text to Peter Laslett, a historian whose studies of the past and analyses of the nature of history and the duties of the historian opened the door for me as a graduate student, and who has continued to inspire me ever since.

Writing Women's Literary History

Introduction

Patterns of Inquiry

But what I find deplorable . . . looking about the bookshelves
again, is that nothing is known about women before the
eighteenth century. I have no model in my mind to turn about
this way and that. — Virginia Woolf, *A Room of One's Own*

Re-vision — the act of looking back, of seeing with fresh eyes, of
entering an old text from a new critical direction — is for women
more than a chapter in cultural history: it is an act of survival.
Until we can understand the assumptions in which we are
drenched we cannot know ourselves. — Adrienne Rich, "When We
Dead Awaken: Writing as Re-Vision"

British and American feminist scholars from Virginia Woolf to the
present traditionally have been concerned with historical issues in
women's writings, in recovering lost texts and traditions. Such efforts have resulted in what is being hailed as the new feminist literary
history: Elaine Showalter opens her 1985 anthology of current feminist literary theory by announcing that since the 1979 publication
of Sandra Gilbert and Susan Gubar's *Madwoman in the Attic*, their
basic insights into women's literary lives in the past have been
"tested, supplemented, and extended," resulting in a "coherent, if
still incomplete, narrative of female literary history which describes

1

the evolutionary stages of women's writings during the last 250 years."[1]

In making such statements, critics such as Showalter are asserting the coming of age of a new academic discipline, one that presents itself as different from and oppositional to the traditional patriarchal institution of literary criticism. However, as feminist theorists on both sides of the Atlantic have long pointed out, having institutional status brings the risk of losing that difference of perspective which being outside the institution offers. The question has already been raised to what extent feminist literary theory has benefited from its growing institutional reputation, from its appropriation and redirection of traditional literary criticism, and to what extent it has itself been appropriated and "domesticated" to fit within existing modes of patriarchal, institutional academic thought.

The question thus arises, how different is this evolutionary narrative of women's literary past from the traditional perception of literary history? For example, if the current model of women's literary history now offers a coherent narrative of women's literary lives for the last two hundred and fifty years, what was happening before 1700 and why is it not part of this narrative? Do the existing literary histories of women's writing, which first enabled the serious study of women's literature, paradoxically exclude or obscure significant blocks of early texts through the choice of certain models of historical progress?

In order to create a coherent narrative, any type of history must necessarily be selective in its choice of materials and in its presentation. This is as true for literary history as for social, for women's literary history as well as for accounts of the traditional canon — it is as true for this study as for those it analyzes. The question about the writing of women's literary history then becomes, what are the principles of selection and exclusion in the current women's literary history and to what extent are they manifestations of unquestioned assumptions about women's texts, about historical periods, and about the nature of authorship? In short, is it possible to uncover and recognize the assumptions under which we as feminist literary critics have labored in producing our analyses of the past?

My call for a reconsideration of the direction of feminist literary history by those interested in "early" (that is, written before 1700) women's texts may seem unnecessary, given the increasing numbers of critical studies and editions of medieval and Renaissance women writers in the last five years. Those who study early women's texts can point with pride to the growing number of studies devoted to the analysis and presentation of pre-1700 women's writings. For example, recent critical studies of early women's texts, such as Elaine Beilin's *Redeeming Eve: Women Writers of the English Renaissance* and Elaine Hobby's *Virtue of Necessity: English Women's Writing 1649–88*, collections of essays such as Mary Beth Rose's *Women in the Middle Ages and the Renaissance: Literary and Historical Perspectives* and Margaret P. Hannay's *Silent but for the Word: Tudor Women as Patrons, Translators, and Writers of Religious Works* have joined anthologies of early women's writings such as Katharina Wilson's *Women Writers of the Renaissance and Reformation*, Betty Travitsky's *Paradise of Women: Writings by Englishwomen of the Renaissance*, and Elizabeth Alvilda Petroff's *Medieval Women's Visionary Literature* to mark clearly the emergence of a new area of critical endeavor. Works such as Patricia Crawford's checklist of women's publications between 1600 and 1700 in Mary Prior's *Women in English Society 1500–1800*, Dale Spender's *Mothers of the Novel: 100 Good Writers before Jane Austen*, and Janet Todd's *Dictionary of British and American Women Writers, 1660–1800* provide the essential archival data for future studies as they document bibliographically and biographically the existence and the activities of a large number of early women writers so recently rediscovered. Important scholarly editions of the works of Lady Mary Wroth, the Countess of Pembroke, and Lady Elizabeth Carew, to name only a sample, are in production even as this is being written; in addition, we are now witnessing the creation of electronic data bases of women's texts, bibliographies, and critical studies by groups such as the NEH–Brown University Women Writers Project, the Women Writers Bibliography Project at the University of Oklahoma, and the Arizona Center for Medieval and Renaissance Studies at Arizona State University, which is creating a data base of secondary source materials.

With this growing body of critical materials suggesting the increasing scholarly interest and institutional support for study in the area, there is certainly occasion for celebration among those interested in women writing before 1700. Lack of serious, scholarly attention to this subject is no longer the issue. And yet, despite such activities, when one turns to the accounts of feminist literary history and discussions of feminist theory analyzing "the tradition" of women's writing in English, to a striking degree women writing before 1700 are still not part of the "tradition" as it is currently formulated. That is to say, although we have increasing numbers of excellent studies of individual figures, the theoretical model of women's literary history and the construction of women's literary studies as a field rest upon the assumption that women before 1700 either were effectively silenced or constituted in an evolutionary model of "female literature" an early "imitative" phase, contained and co-opted in patriarchal discourse.

As I discuss in subsequent chapters, the marginalization of early women writers in the Anglo-American tradition is in part the result of the early emphasis in feminist studies on nineteenth-century texts. But, as I hope to demonstrate, it is also the result of certain models of historiography which have been imported into women's studies, without a careful scrutiny of the assumptions they contain about the nature of authorship and about the generation of literary history. In general, the main focus of attention by feminist scholars studying pre-1700 writers has been on the essential task of the recovery of these lost texts, asserting their existence and making available a body of women's writings. The emphasis, thus, has not been on questioning whether one can, for example, as is commonly found now, use the same critical framework and vocabulary to describe and analyze women's texts produced for the commercial nineteenth-century market and those written within a seventeenth-century coterie circle, whether the rhetoric created to depict nineteenth-century literary practices is indeed suitable to analyze the literary productions of earlier periods. For example, we frequently find the label "private" or "closet" writings used to describe female authorship; yet the question is typically not asked whether "private" writing or "closet" authorship is really the same phenomenon in the seventeenth and nineteenth centuries, given the historical condition of two very different modes of literary production. While studies and anthologies of medieval and Renaissance women writers clearly and definitely refute the premise that the tradition of women's writing must begin some two hundred and fifty years ago because before then women did not write in sufficient numbers or produce works of sufficient merit or interest, they typically do not engage either the categories or vocabulary provided by the model of women's literary history put forward by Virginia Woolf and her twentieth-century theoretical elaborators, Gilbert, Gubar, and Showalter.

Simply put, for some scholars, the problem of the marginalization of pre-1700 women's writing would be solved if only there were more women in the medieval and Renaissance sections of *The Norton Anthology of Literature by Women*—the apparatus of their presentation, the overall model of the progress of women's writings, could remain in place unchallenged. There are, I believe, still more issues at stake than the numerical question of how many women wrote before 1700. For me, questions remain about the very terms we use to describe, categorize, and analyze early women's lives and texts: Where did we get our model of the past and how do we construct its history? This study's purpose is, using Rich's term, to "revision" women's literary past and to reveal some of the assumptions embedded in the current model of feminist historiography concerning the connections between gender and modes of literary production and about historical conditions of authorship. The questions of why feminist literary history lost so completely a very sizable number of women writers from periods before 1700 and what the explanations by Woolf and her twentieth-century followers for this literary void reveal about our critical assumptions concerning gender and authorship, gender and genre, remain open to investigation, even as work continues in the area of recovering and analyzing medieval and Renaissance texts.

As one way of exploring these questions, I examine the construction of a particular model of the past. Although my observations could apply to Anglo-Saxon and medieval texts and their treatment as well, for the purposes of this study, I have focused on the historiography of British women's writings during the Renaissance and seventeenth century, my particular area of interest. (No doubt a similar analysis could—and should—be performed on my study to reveal the assumptions about even earlier texts which I have unconsciously embedded in my presentation of the Renaissance.) To analyze the historiography, I look specifically at the presentation of women's writings during these periods in several different types of critical studies composed between 1660 and 1990. In this broad chronological sweep, I make no claims to absolute inclusiveness, but instead attempt to uncover the critical assumptions behind the patterns of presentation, whether biographical or bibliographical, Marxist or Whiggish, in these studies. My focus is not, therefore, on any individual critic's work or any particular critical orientation; this study should not be read as an attack on any "school" of criticism but as an investigation of the presuppositions that link even seem-ingly estranged critical points of view when women's writings from before 1700 are analyzed.

In this study, by "women's literary history" I mean the meth-odological approaches found in works that deal directly with the formation of a literary history, such as Ellen Moers's *Literary Women* and Showalter's *Literature of Their Own*, which study individual authors in a historical context, attempting in the process to establish a theory of women's writings. The new feminist literary history is also manifest in the ideology underlying the construction of an-thologies of women's writings. These texts arrange materials in a historical sequence and include in introductions and notes accounts of the writers' lives and times. In addition to the short literary lives in the anthologies, full-length biographies of women writers such as Ruth Perry's *Celebrated Mary Astell*, Angeline Goreau's *Recon-structing Aphra*, and Sara Mendelson's *Mental World of Stuart Women* rely on the existence of an evolutionary narrative history of women's writing practices in retelling their subjects' lives as authors.

Finally, by this phrase I also mean that unspoken sense of the history of women's socio-literary environments found in so many texts devoted to period studies. Texts such as Mary Poovey's *Proper Lady and the Woman Writer*, Nancy Armstrong's *Desire and Do-mestic Fiction*, Dale Spender's *Man-Made Language*, and Gilbert and Gubar's *Madwoman in the Attic*, texts frequently discussed as representative of feminist literary history, base their analyses of a particular period or group of texts on assumptions about the cir-cumstances of writers in preceding periods and on assumptions con-cerning the connections between generations of women writers. I am, therefore, not engaged in a critique of individual readings of particular works or authors, but in an examination of the theoretical principles underlying the construction of the historical model which are implicit in such readings.

The aim of my study is to suggest that feminist literary history has reached the level of critical development and self-confidence necessary to examine its own hidden assumptions as carefully as it has done those of the orthodox critics. In no way should this project be interpreted as expressing a lack of confidence in feminist literary criticism in general—on the contrary, it arises from a commitment to take this critical process seriously. The problems to be dealt with in this attempt are whether or not we can uncover such presuppositions in the first place and whether or not we can "re-vision" early periods in a manner that is not as restrictive and coercive as the one it seeks to challenge. That is, we hope not simply to substitute one monolithic critical model for another. In an attempt to avoid this, I intend this book to be a provocative and polemical study rather than one offering an expanded list of authors to supplement the existing model or imposing a "new" theory of the "tradition."

This study not only explores old materials in a different context, but also attempts to suggest means of future recovery, since many of the early women writers still are "lost." Although I discuss the critical treatment of specific Renaissance and Restoration women writers in chapters 1 and 2, I am attempting not to define the canon for those periods (for no doubt I have left out the reader's own favorite examples in including my own) but rather to suggest ways in which the academic study of early women writers can itself be studied. Indeed, the aim is to suggest questions that can be asked of women writers in any period not included in our current notion of the "tradition," including, for example, medieval women writers whom I do not discuss. Rather than offer a simple substitution of one evolutionary narrative for another, I wish my text to open the field up, to expand the possibilities of women's literary history by suggesting—for example, in my final chapter on early Quaker writers—some ways in which new patterns of inquiry might function.

By unconsciously permitting our perceptions of the past to be shaped by unexamined ideologies, perhaps unwittingly carried over from certain privileged texts or theories, we may have infused the values and standards of those texts and theories in our constructions of the past. The result could be that we have unintentionally marginalized or devalued a significant portion of female literary experience. The purpose of this study is in part to recover texts and authors and in part to analyze the agencies through which they have been lost, using an approach that intentionally seeks to make the literary past unfamiliar through a steady questioning of the ways in which we have previously organized and categorized it.

In the attempt to discover the assumptions embedded in current models of literary history, I draw on the practices of two schools of critical methodology sometimes presented as being unsympathetic or insensitive to feminist investigations of the past. As I discuss in later chapters, I find in the practices of both French feminist literary theory and new historicism techniques of interpretive reading which can be used to illuminate new possibilities for analyzing the historical past. In their own ways, each of these rather amorphous critical positions is concerned with recovering "difference" and attempting to let it speak, conscious always that the critic's voice necessarily joins in the presentation.

French feminist theory is often dismissed by Anglo-American critics as "essentialist" and totalizing and therefore not at all useful for a social, historical mode of analysis (although this charge is also routinely denied by those who practice it). In its quest to reveal and encourage the "difference" of the "other," however, French feminist writing can offer the willing historicist strategies for recognizing histories that homogenize the literary past as a triumphal evolution of aristocratic male writers into successful middle-class professional male writers, histories that have in effect silenced women writers' voices. In its very nature, recent French feminism demands that one question one's basic assumptions about the ways in which experience is ordered and presented. To make use of this advantageous position from which to regard the past and our own practice of writing about it does not entail adopting a caricatured essentialist stance, resulting in a monolithic, transhistorical reading of the nature of universal "WOMAN." Instead, we can use this position to see through various configurations—those of the past and the present, patriarchal and feminist—which block our view of women's activities in the past by forcing us to focus on a predetermined pattern and prevent us from appreciating the multitude and variety of texts by individual women at particular historical moments which constitute the history of women's writing.[2] To make use of French feminist thought means that we admit the possibility that it has something of value to say to us about recognizing and appreciating difference, not just in our time or in a transhistorical, timeless state, but also in the historical past.

French feminist celebration of difference across gender lines and roles is not that estranged from the historicist desire to celebrate difference through time, the insistence that, as far as possible, one let the past be the past rather than exist only as a forerunner to our own situation. As the editors of *The New Eighteenth Century* observe of the "new historicism" of the essays in their collection, the disparate pieces do not authorize a monolithic view of a period but instead are united through their "commitment to critical and political self-consciousness, to the unspoken of their texts, to the fore-grounding of theoretical assumptions."[3] We can only hear the "un-spoken," however, if we become aware of our received assumptions, and the reading strategies of French feminist theory (estranged as it is from Anglo-American) and new historicism can together operate to make us more aware of the ways in which we have configured the literary past and gender. More specifically to the topic at hand, this same recognition of the difficulties in exploring the past through a present-day lens appears in Elaine Hobby's conclusion to her ground-breaking study of individual seventeenth-century women writers, in which she observes, "In many ways we find in the past what we look for: by and large, we only come up with answers to questions we think to ask."[4] This type of self-conscious historicism intentionally makes us re-vision what we think we know about the past and the ways in which it has been transmitted to us.

Likewise, although several leading French psychoanalytic femi-nist critics have announced a lack of interest in pursuing literary history—believing that the process often leads to a validation of past practices by reconstructing it[5]—the disparate branches of their the-ories also can contribute to the ways in which we define and handle the problems encountered in the historiography of women's litera-ture. The very tone and nature of French feminist discourse—often personal, conversational, and utopian and so different from Anglo-American academic discourse—has been a bone of contention among feminist critics; such difference, however, could be used to explore familiar ground with a new map. French feminist writing in general forces the reader to be conscious of the control that patriarchal discourse can exert over perceptions of the subject matter, which in turn could be helpful in uncovering assumptions about literary his-tory which more familiar modes of academic discussion tend to smooth over.

Thus, in general, the approach to be found in this study has two key ideals: to "historicize" ("always," as Fredric Jameson would have it) self-consciously and to "gender" history. Historicism—new historicism, cultural materialist historicism, feminist historicism—enables us to begin to glimpse a past separate from our perceptions of it. Feminism, and certain schools of French feminism in particular, enables us to begin to glimpse women writers in earlier periods by becoming self-consciously aware of our received preconceptions of the sex. Together, these two strategies can help us to interrupt the flow of ideologies which streams between us and women writing in the past, to jam the airwaves, so to speak, to create a break in the steady static which will enable us to hear, even momentarily, a different voice from the past.

In the first chapter, the focus is on the present status of women's literary history that discusses "early" women's writings and on the creation in the twentieth century of a theory of literary history specifically for women's writings. The goal of this chapter is the examination of the underlying assumptions about genre, about the nature of authorship, and about history itself implicit in accounts of the woman's "tradition" and their treatment of Renaissance and seventeenth-century women's works in this context. In the second chapter, the discussion narrows to an exploration of the formation of a canon of women's writings in twentieth-century anthologies and the ways in which the materials presented shape our expectations concerning the nature of early women's writings. In the third chapter, the emphasis is on the tradition behind the twentieth century's historiography, an examination of eighteenth- and nineteenth-century literary biographers' and anthologists' use of earlier women's writings in the process of formulating their theories of a female aesthetic. The fourth chapter continues the process of exploration of women's literary past and the sources of our assumptions about early women's writings by analyzing the formation of the canon in eighteenth- and nineteenth-century anthologies of women's verse. These four chapters are linked in their study of eighteenth-, nineteenth-, and twentieth-century constructions of a female poetic and of these periods' attempts to formulate a canon of women's writings. Running through these chapters is an analysis of the construction of two powerful images of women writers, both of which have post-1700 sources: Judith Shakespeare and Clarissa.

Judith Shakespeare is the literary creation of Virginia Woolf, attempting to imagine the fate of a talented woman contemporary of Shakespeare. Her lot is to be denied an education, to rebel against paternal authority, to attempt and fail to earn a living in a commercial setting, and to self-destruct. Clarissa is the creation of the ideal eighteenth-century woman writer by Samuel Richardson, a bourgeois eighteenth-century male novelist. She is a well-educated, middle-class girl, whose talents and abilities are going to be sold by her family to a wealthy suitor. Her writings are designed for no audience but herself, except when they are pleas for liberty and justice. She writes constantly in private, but her written texts have no effect since they are not "published" until she is dead, when all who read them are moved. In our current theoretical models, we are thus offered two paradigms for the early woman writer. She can forfeit all social respectability to enter the arena of male commercial literature and be crushed, or she can suffer injustice privately without challenging the rules of social decorum and be vindicated through her posthumous publications.

The final chapter is different in its nature but not in its aim, being an application of the call for re-visioning of critical assumptions in a case study of a particular group of early women writers lost to us at the present time in current models of women's literary history, the Quaker women writing between 1650 and 1672. As I argue in my analysis of twentieth-century women's literary history, there has been a tendency to push for conceptualization of the past before archival and textual studies; in this final chapter, I extend the argument that existing assumptions about modes of literary production and about historiography can be challenged and that important texts by women writers can be recovered by a re-visioning of the literary past. In examining not only the disappearance of these writers from the realm of women's literary history but also their exclusion from the canon of Quaker literature, we begin to see how early women writers can be lost or diminished in the very historiography designed to celebrate women's accomplishments. The chapter suggests *one* possibility of what "re-visioning" could accomplish in critical practice.

From this summary of the contents it is clear that while this study has the single purpose of being a polemical investigation of presuppositions, it uses several methods to uncover and discuss them. In addition to investigating secondary criticism from a historicist, feminist perspective, this study introduces historical materials not currently in wide circulation in the field, resulting in a mixed mode of literary history and feminist theory. The sections focused on the presentation of earlier materials are done in the awareness that when Rich speaks of "entering an old text from a new critical direction," "new" does not mean "at long last the only correct one" or "one that escapes political ideology." The "new" direction underlying these sections is simply *my* direction, which is fundamentally one interested in the historically specific, in the particularity of the past, rather than an essentialist one searching for "the" woman. I take as my starting point the view that critical studies should enable and enhance future studies, should enlarge opportunities for discovery and interpretation, not negate or erase possibilities. Scholars interested in texts by women writers before 1700 have certainly been successful, especially in recent years, in producing studies of them, but the task has not been easy in part because the established critical perception of the tradition has obscured the possibilities for study — outside the circle of Renaissance specialists, the response to the announcement that one works on early women writers is still likely to be surprise that there were any women writers on which to work. Given this situation, an archeological approach — one that not only analyzes critical presuppositions but brings forward materials for future consideration as well — seems the more valuable approach to take for this project.

In her essay "What Do Feminist Critics Want?" Sandra Gilbert suggests that what we want is room to define ourselves within a rapidly and explosively changing social and critical environment. What the profession wants from feminist criticism, she suggests, "are rigorous and responsible revisions of ourselves, our texts, our traditions."[6] It seems to me that these two desires meet in writing women's literary history: What is needed now is a consideration of our historiography and a reconsideration of the patterns of inquiry which will determine the future direction of women's literary history.

At the present time, there is the opportunity for and interest in developing a feminist historicism — historicist in its insistence that one must self-consciously seek to preserve and present the "pastness" of the past and to struggle against the totalizing effect of the bland imposition of the present over it, feminist in its insistence on the very possibility of there being a significant feminine presence — not only masculine — in the past.[7] The project of this mode of writing women's literary history is to recognize our own preconceptions and assumptions as well as those of past historians and, while acknowledging the presence of ideologies, not to let them silence earlier women's voices. French feminist ideologies certainly impose problems of their own on reading and narrating the past, but using French feminist theory forces Anglo-American historicists to consider the configurations of our own ideologies; it is not so much the answer to our problems as a position from which to reconsider matters of history which, as we shall see, have all too often been decided for us in advance by previous generations of historians and critics.

At the same time, while occupying this space, we wish to preserve our ability to hear multiple voices of women writing in the past, not simply a universal female voice, and not to insist on continuity where diversity flourishes. As Teresa de Lauretis has observed of feminist studies in general, she sees this shift from a view of "woman defined purely by sexual difference (i.e., in relation to man) to the more difficult and complex notion that the female subject is the site of differences; differences that are not only sexual or only racial, economic, or (sub)cultural, but all of these together, and often enough at odds with one another."[8]

Feminist critics cannot escape ideology any more than can others, but by attempting to enter into a self-conscious study of the past, we become aware of the shaping forces at work on our literary histories as we receive them from previous generations, and as we write our own, we become aware of the presence of difference between past and present. We can adopt several strategies to aid us—for example, Jane Marcus's notion of "still practice,"[9] an attempt to quiet our noisy preconceptions in order to hear others; or the opposite approach, to make ourselves what the early Quakers and others referred to as "tender," that is, hypersensitive to our own acts and thoughts so that we do not casually, unself-consciously mistake the territory of ourselves for that of the past. Both have as their goal the attempt to let the past exist as different from the present; this, indeed, may be an impossible goal to achieve completely, but I believe it is essential to strive for it if one is truly committed to writing women's literary history.

A Tradition of Our Own

Writing Women's Literary History in the Twentieth Century

> With a few rare exceptions, there has not yet been any writing
> that inscribes femininity; exceptions so rare, in fact, that,
> after plowing through literature across languages, cultures, and
> ages, one can only be startled at this vain scouting mission. It
> is well known that the number of women writers . . . has always
> been ridiculously small. — Hélène Cixous, "The Laugh of
> the Medusa"

In Adrienne Rich's observation about the necessity to "re-vision"
women's writings and women's studies, she voices a central tenet
of all feminist scholarship. Indeed, her concept of "reading as re-
vision," the desire to reveal the unconscious assumptions about
gender with which previous generations of readers and critics have
read women authors, transcends methodological differences among
feminist critics. This goal of challenging the received tradition concerning women writers and uncovering the hidden structures of
society which have preconditioned our perceptions seems to me to
have common methodological ground with a mode of critical inquiry
often believed to be insensitive to feminist issues in its analysis of
power and class — "new historicism." As Judith Newton suggested
in a recent essay on feminism and new historicism (which, as we
shall see, significantly for this study cites only feminist studies of

nineteenth-century literature as examples of feminist literary history), the two modes of critical inquiry overlap in their practices but not as of yet in their perceptions of the importance of gender in any account of historical change.[1] This opens the door to a cooperative exchange, in which both critical modes would be enriched, so to say. Both new historicism and Rich's call for "re-vision" draw our attention to the degree to which our understanding of the past is shaped by largely unconscious acceptance and inculcation of present-day ideologies in our narratives of history.

Writing women's literary history has been compared to doing archaeology, to receiving an inheritance, and to replanting a mother's garden. In writing this book, I am obviously starting with the belief in the value of this activity, however it is characterized. What concerns me in my reading of contemporary feminist theory is that the structures used to shape our narrative of women's literary history may have unconsciously continued the existence of the restrictive ideologies that initially erased the vast majority of women's writings from literary history and teaching texts. That is, there appear to be several underlying assumptions about gender, genre, and historical progress which link together even the well-recognized divisions within feminist criticism. Such historiographical structures, although they have in fact enabled the serious study of women's texts in the university, privilege certain genres and periods; the effect has been that those of us interested in earlier women's writings find ourselves continually explaining the existence and significance of the texts we work with in much the same way as the pioneers of women's studies did.

There is, for example, a clear difference in the attitude toward writing literary history taken by many Anglo-American feminists and that voiced by some French theorists. Hélène Cixous, the inspirational voice of French feminist theory, appears in her criticism to negate the enterprise of writing women's literary history, while Elaine Showalter, the doyenne of women's literary history in America, feels that recent feminist critical texts have provided the essential framework for the establishment of a coherent narrative of the last two hundred and fifty years of women's writing. Cixous dismisses the past in part because "the number of women writers . . . has always been ridiculously small," and in part because the texts that do exist are not *l'écriture feminine*. Showalter invokes the past because she believes enough women writers have already been recovered to construct women's literary history; on the other hand, her narrative dismisses the past before 1700. Adopting different theories of women's writings and of history, both writers share the belief that women's writing prior to 1700 lacks significance in the overall scheme of women's literature.

But how did we arrive at this conclusion? And what exactly is meant by "writing" in such analyses—the production of *l'écriture feminine*? How do we know women were not producing such texts, except through the traditional channels of orthodox literary history? Cixous's dismissal of the past and Showalter's abridgment of it are in one sense based on a shared received understanding of what that past was and on the model in which women's literary history has been written, indeed, in which all literary histories have been written.

Janet Todd recently devoted a short, witty treatise to the defense of writing Showalter's style of women's literary history; "as historical critics we probably have to accept some chastisement from French theory," she admits, but nevertheless, we must "[hold] onto a belief in materialism," by which she means the very possibility and value of writing a coherent and "true" narrative of the past.[2] The two schools thus are held at odds, at a distance. I am in agreement with Todd in her assessment that the French feminist theories can benefit the American socio-historical school of criticism by destabilizing assumptions about reading and writing, by making texts "familiar, familial, and alien all at once." But I am not so sure that such theories must serve as "a critique not a complement" to literary history. I am not so sure, for example, that what is termed *l'écriture feminine* exists only in the future of women's writings; perhaps we have simply been looking for it in the wrong places in the past, or our construction of a historical narrative has hidden it from sight. Many American and British feminist literary historians will not agree that the primary task of feminist criticism is to reveal a mode of writing which is "a feminine textual body," or be comfortable with its depiction as a literature manifesting a "real capacity to lose hold and let go . . . [which] isn't predictable, isn't knowable and is therefore very disturbing," but one that is ultimately undefinable.[3] But, even those engaged in archeological pursuit of women's texts can profit by an awareness of this other delineation of women's writings, with its valorization of difference, because it can expand what we see in the past and how we describe it.

My goal is not to duplicate Todd's work, defending either side. Nor do I intend to cite Cixous, Luce Irigaray, or Julia Kristeva with the end of offering an analysis of the body of their thoughts on history and the history of women's writings, or to suggest that the ultimate goal of feminist literary history is to recover *l'écriture feminine.* Indeed, admirers of this disparate school that goes under the label "French feminist theory" may well be dismayed by my lack of specific attention to the differences each individual critic stresses; admirers of an essentialist philosophy of feminism may well be dismayed by my refusal to valorize certain types of texts by women over others.

Instead, I wish to use the provocative insights into the nature of the "feminine" and on the act of interpretive reading provided by these ahistorical, psycholinguistic feminisms to produce sparks off the seemingly iron facade of Anglo-American feminist literary history. I will, in short, use them to generate questions we can ask about feminist historiography and which might help to illuminate that period called the "Dark Ages" of women's imagination, the periods before 1700.

In her ground-breaking essay "Dancing through the Minefield: Some Observations on the Theory, Practice, and Politics of a Feminist Literary Criticism," Annette Kolodny called for a "playful pluralism" in feminist literary criticism. As I have noted, it may seem peculiar that I have chosen two modes of critical inquiry which are reputed to be hostile to the very enterprise of analyzing early women's texts, the typically ahistorical French feminism and the seemingly hostile "masculinist" new historicism. On the other hand, both of these schools of criticism offer critical reading strategies that can be of enormous use in re-visioning what we think we know. New historicist critics, such as Jerome McGann, have insisted that we become conscious of the nature of the ways in which we order, label, and describe phenomena, of the ideology that shapes even the questions we ask about the past; the questions raised by such an approach lead to reconsideration of the very project of recovering and analyzing early women's texts. French feminist theorists, such as Julia Kristeva, who refuse to accept a single definition of "woman" or of "female expression," ask us to listen for a multiplicity of voices, to be aware constantly of the fluidity and sheer abundance of possibilities attached to the search for "difference" when it is not defined as being rigidly dichotomized or competitively hierarchical. Critics such as Cixous ask the reader to enter a state of *"démoïsation,"* the art of the spectator in a theater, "the state without me, of dispossession of the self," in order to hear "the desire of all the others . . . the desire of all the characters, the audience's desire, the actors' desire, the director's desire . . . the desire of the others that are us."[4]

Together, these two interpretive modes urge the reader on the one hand to become highly conscious of the assumptions in which, as Rich says, we are drenched, highly conscious of the factors influencing our perceptions, while on the other hand, to attempt to approach the past willing to hear a multiplicity of voices where before we expected either to hear none, or to hear only a particular type. Thus, while new historicism demands that the reader be conscious of the political nature of the act of reading and interpreting, French feminism asks for a suspension of those preconceived categories and values in order that difference can be fully expressed and heard.

In this chapter, I examine the presuppositions about women's history and about literature in general on which the current Anglo-American model of feminist literary history is based. Rather than focus on any one "school" of feminist criticism or one genre of criticism, I seek the linking assumptions that bind different feminist criticisms together in their representation of women's writing before 1700. In the next chapter, I look at how the theoretical framework established in these important critical texts is put into operation in the construction of popular and classroom texts such as anthologies. Throughout, I invoke the critical strategies of uncovering controlling assumptions and exploring the possibilities of different voices, different readings.

In women's literary history as it has been and is being written, we find two central theoretical assumptions about literature and gender, regardless of whether it is American or British literature. The first is the assumption that there is a "tradition" of women's writings to be recovered; the second is that this tradition reveals an evolutionary model of feminism. These two assumptions shape not only the ways in which recent women's writings are discussed, but also the ways in which the Renaissance and seventeenth century are presented and analyzed.

Women's literary history has had as one of its stated goals the recovery and establishment of what Showalter labels a "female tradition." There are several interesting features in this mission as it has been pursued. First, the use of the term "tradition" implies the existence of common ground and continuity in literary works—in terms of subject, genre, style—and in the authors' lives, their education, social class, and literary activity. Even those who question the timing of writing a definitive women's literary history—who believe the drive to conceptualize overran the textual and archival research needed to support it—nevertheless seem to agree with this assumption.[5] Germaine Greer, who declared in 1982 that the field of women's studies was not yet ready to make generalizations about women's writings, sees as the ultimate goal of the project the delineation of similarities of past and present. By careful study of individual authors, she believes, we will eventually be able to "grasp what we have in common with the women who have gone our chosen way before us."[6]

Those who have ventured where Greer warns us not to tread, writing women's literary history, do encounter the problem of scarcity of texts and critical studies which Greer cites. To solve this problem and to establish common ground over a historical line, diachronically, the solution has been to investigate using a linear cause and effect analysis, either to start in the past and work forward in time, looking for development and searching for patterns of influence, or to read backward, starting with the present and looking for predecessors, a sort of literary genealogy. Because, until recent years, it was extremely difficult to obtain materials by and about women writers before 1800 (the causes of which are analyzed in chapters 3 and 4), the tendency has been to read backward. The starting point for establishing commonality and for generalizing about women's writing and women's lives as authors has been either from the present or from the nineteenth century, defined by Moers as the "epic age" of women writers. Because of this choice, as we shall see, recent critical assumptions about earlier women's writings and about patterns of female authorship have tended to be based on nineteenth- and twentieth-century examples.

In its search for a commonality through which to create a female literary tradition, women's literary history has scanned the biographies of early women writers. We seek to relate to the past through shared life experiences or shared responses. As Alice Walker phrased it, we search for our mothers' gardens: in describing the composition of "The Revenge of Hannah Kemhuff," Walker observed:

In that story I gathered up the historical and psychological threads of the life my ancestors lived, and in the writing of it I felt joy and strength and my own continuity. I had that wonderful feeling writers get sometimes, not very often, of being *with* a great many people, ancient spirits, all very happy to see me consulting and acknowledging them, and eager to let me know, through the joy of their presence, that, indeed, I am not alone.[7]

This metaphor of the female literary family is frequently found in studies of women's literary history. Moers's landmark study of nineteenth-century women writers makes use of this image of the literary community as a family of women to emphasize its stabilizing effect on the female author, the confidence given by the possession of predecessors. While modern women writers have more educational opportunities than their restricted Victorian ancestors, Moers argues, they, too, "appear to benefit still from their membership in the widespreading family of women writers."[8]

Ultimately, one can see the attempt to write women's literary history as having the same goal as the original one of genealogy. One very great need expressed in this search for the tradition is to provide literary ancestors; ancestors document the legitimacy of current women's literary activities. The re-creation of a female family of authorship also suggests that it will provide the emotional security and support lacking in society at large.

The danger in searching out one's relatives, however, is whom one might find. For ideological reasons this search is an important step in reclaiming significance for women's history, which then helps to enable future study. But are we actually seeing all that there is to see in the past, meeting all our relatives, in our genealogical sweeps? Or are we so concerned with establishing continuity that our vision of the life of a woman writer, before 1700 in particular, is exclusive and selective? Have we, to use Jerome McGann's terms, gerrymandered the past in order to support a particular present concept of the woman writer?

The possibility of such a selective shaping of the past is clearer when one considers the topics of the existing body of critical studies on women's writings. As Todd noted, the emphasis in American feminist criticism has been on the nineteenth century.[9] The majority of the literary histories about women writers and the key texts in

Anglo-American feminist study, such as *A Literature of Their Own, Literary Women, Madwoman in the Attic,* Nina Auerbach's *Woman and the Demon,* are primarily concerned with this "epic age" of nineteenth-century women writers, and the past is primarily invoked to explain that particular period. The scholars who have dominated the field of women's literary history in America, and whose analyses of texts are based in a scheme of historical context—Showalter, Kolodny, Moers, Auerbach, Gilbert, and Gubar—work mostly on nineteenth-century materials. Even though disagreeing in their interpretations of goals and methods in feminist criticism, critics such as Dale Spender, Catharine Stimpson, and Mary Jacobus also primarily use nineteenth-century writers—Mary Shelley, the Brontës, George Eliot, Emily Dickinson, and Elizabeth Barrett Browning—to illustrate their discussions of women's literary environments in the past. In short, not only are the examples cited concerned with the nineteenth century, but the data base for the majority of studies of women's literary history has been a nineteenth-century one as well.

A feminist/new historicist approach to this particular construction of the past raises several issues. Given the heavy dependence on nineteenth-century women's literature in the construction of a theory of female authorship, one must question the extent to which the image of the woman writer in earlier periods has been made to conform to a Romantic or Victorian concept of the artist. One must also wonder about the extent to which the analysis of pre-1700 literature in critical studies is based on a nineteenth-century model of literature as a commercial activity.

Thus, I find myself agreeing with Todd, whose own work focuses on the eighteenth century, that one of the central problems in existing women's literary history is the critics' lack of familiarity with early texts, that "we avoid listening to a past that might be annoying through its resolute refusal to anticipate us" (p. 46). However, I do not believe her assertion that this lack of familiarity is a characteristic of "the early phase of feminist criticism in general," a phase now supposedly superseded. I believe it arises in part from the insistence on women's literary history following a nineteenth-century model of narrative historiography. Narrative history is a linear mode of organization, which, in its ordering of events, concentrates on locating events on a time line to discover cause and effect solutions, on defining separate periods to serve as the bases for comparison and ranking, on finding "origins" and significant turning points in an evolutionary pattern that leads up to and explains the contemporary situation.

For example, the assumptions about the evolutionary nature of the technology of authorship permeate the very questions we bring to texts written before 1700. As we shall see, even studies on seventeenth-century women writers, such as Jacqueline Pearson's analysis of women dramatists in the Restoration and Goreau's reading of Aphra Behn and Lady Falkland, tend to adopt a nineteenth-century construction of the practice of authorship and the nature of literature as being the norm against which earlier practices are ranked. As I suggested in the Introduction, while the last decade has seen a rise in the number of studies of women writing before 1700, it has not yet seen a systematic challenge to the original conceptualization of an evolutionary pattern of female authorship proposed by Virginia Woolf in *A Room of One's Own*, which has been elaborated by Showalter, Moers, Gilbert, and Gubar into a theory of female creativity.

Instead, accounts of early women's writing have tended to push back the dates on the time line without questioning the system behind it. This adherence to a linear narrative of women's literary history has directed the type of questions we ask about early women writers. Thus we now debate whether Mary Astell or Jane Anger was the "first" English feminist, a debate that can only be decided by ranking the earlier woman's "feminism" against the latter's; likewise, Mary Sidney now contests with Aphra Behn for the title of "the first woman in the period who sought a clear literary vocation" without a question being raised concerning the point of this competition. Being "first," of course, establishes the model against which others are measured, but it also indicates a more rudimentary accomplishment—being the first is not usually equated with being the best.

And the current theoretical model of women's literary history is very much concerned with who wins, who is better than another. Not only does Showalter's model of the evolution of women's texts from the feminine, to the feminist, to the female rank the different periods in ascending order through chronological history, but studies devoted to Renaissance and Restoration periods adopt the same narrative strategy as well. When we study women writing in the Renaissance as a group, the ultimate question posed is, "is there evidence of evolution, both for the individual and for the group? Unsurprisingly, they write better the more they write; surprisingly in so small a group, each poet surpasses her predecessor"; we are offered an immediate cause and effect explanation in the scheme of the linear progress of women writing in the Renaissance: "Time would allow women to evolve poetically because once there was one published woman poet, other women would not only start practicing, they would realize that women could be poets without sacrificing their character."[10]

The problem with this type of linear historiography that focuses on unique events—whether it is involved in identifying the first feminist, or the first woman with a "true" literary vocation, or a more general event such as middle-class women beginning to write commercially, which Woolf cites as the turning point in women's history—is that it has an unstated notion of evolutionary progress built into it. Events are interpreted as they lead up to or follow a major event. As a result, this history can easily negate those events preceding the chosen significant one on the time line; for example, women who do not fit the pattern of development signposted by the special events get labeled "anomalies" or are defined as doing something different and less important (writing "closet" literature), or, as we shall see in the case of the late seventeenth-century Quaker women writers, they are simply left out.

The importance of nineteenth-century studies in the construction of women's literary history is also suggested in a much larger theoretical issue—the tension between concepts of "female" and "feminism" based on androgyny versus those based on "difference." In her analysis of the writing of women's history, Linda Gordon identified the nineteenth century as a period in which feminism in general was swinging from an androgynous stance to an emphasis on difference, a shift she feels is recurring in feminist studies this century. In Gordon's words, in the eighteenth century, feminist writers such as Wollstonecraft viewed "difference" as imposed on women as "part of a system of subordinating, constricting, and controlling them . . . [reducing] their capacities as well as their aspirations."[11] In contrast, according to Gordon, in the nineteenth century, feminists found that in stressing difference they gained "a moral superiority," citing female nurturing against male aggression, with motherhood as "the fundamental defining experience of womanhood" (p. 27).

One finds the same split occurring in feminism today. Ann Snitow has written in "Pages from a Gender Diary: Basic Divisions in Feminism" how confusing and how essential the uncertainty is. Describing a meeting of a consciousness-raising group, Snitow records one woman's joy: "[because of the movement] now I can be a woman; it's no longer so humiliating. I can stop fantasizing that secretly I am a man, as I used to before I had children. Now I can value what was once my shame." The author records her own shock: "Sitting in the same meetings during those years, my thoughts were roughly the reverse." Her feminism let her say: "Now I don't have to be a woman anymore. I need never become a mother. Being a woman has always been humiliating, but I used to assume there was no exit. Now the very idea 'woman' is up for grabs. 'Woman' is my slave name; feminism will give me freedom to seek some other identity altogether."[12]

American feminist literary criticism is deeply rooted in political and social activity, and therefore it is hardly surprising to find this same split reflected in feminist literary texts, even in those attempting to recover literary ancestors. Referring to feminist literary critics, Alice Jardine confidently asserts that "we perceive and conceptualize the world differently from men." But feminist critics' response to this difference has split into three types of reactions. Some feminist critics exalt difference

> by embracing a certain biology—and a certain eroticism. There are also those who deny it, or rather, who seek to defuse the power of difference by minimizing biology and emphasizing cultural coding: on some level these responses are saying, "Woman would be the same as . . . if only." A third strand states . . . that women are indeed different from men, but for feminist reasons they add: women are also better than men. This group's reasons would not be biological but sociocultural: as outsiders and nurturers, women do things differently from, and better than, men.[13]

The way one defines feminism today—androgyny or difference, or an uneasy compromise of the two—strongly affects one's perceptions of women's lives and writings in the past.

On the one hand, the search for female predecessors and the desire to establish a continuum can be seen as an indication of a belief in difference, that men and women are fundamentally different in their emotional responses, expression, and goals because of biological factors. The emphasis on separating women's writings from men's suggests that what women's literary histories and anthologies of women's writings are attempting to do is to define the nature of the women's "difference" through seeking similarity in women's writings. On the other hand, however, these same anthologies and literary histories strongly stress the repressive nature of being defined as "different," and of society's power to silence women through culturally maintained inhibitions, trapping the creative woman in a web of repressive definitions of "femininity."

The representation of women's writings before 1700 is strongly marked by this last view. Critical studies emphasize pre-1700 women writers' lack of the educational opportunities and publication outlets compared with those possessed by men. They stress the degree to which these women's activities were controlled by a definition of female "modesty," and the resulting fear of public attention. Such readings would seem to agree with twentieth-century feminists who advocate androgyny, who see traditional configurations of the feminine as repressive and distorting. In discussing past literature, critics of this school sometimes imply in their presentations that early women writers would have been "as good as" contemporary male, if their opportunities had been equal. Any woman who did write under such conditions is automatically ranked as an underdog on this literary scorecard. As we shall see in the next chapter, these texts lament the oppressive effects of society on early women writers, using the potent myth of Judith Shakespeare to represent the tragic fate of talented women. Society, this theory maintains, silenced women, and where it could not, it drove them mad and characteristically infused their writings with bitterness and anger.

In this model of women's literary history, anger is an identifying characteristic of the "female" (biological) reacting to the "feminine" (socio-cultural). It also is a linking mechanism in the chain of female literary ancestors. Moers cites Virginia Woolf as "the most brilliant of all critics of women's literature, and the most sensitive to its womanly quality of rage."[14] As Toril Moi pointed out, Gilbert and Gubar establish "anger as the *only* positive signal of a feminist consciousness."[15] For Gilbert and Gubar, the character of the madwoman in women's writings is "usually in some sense the *author's* double, an image of her own anxiety and rage . . . [created] so that female authors can come to terms with their own uniquely female feelings of fragmentation, their own keen sense of the discrepancies between what they are and what they are supposed to be."[16] Drawing heavily on Virginia Woolf, Gilbert and Gubar thus characterize the female writer in earlier periods as an individual at odds with her society and with herself because her creative drives require her to resist accepted "feminine" roles.

Interestingly, this image of the angry and alienated female artist arises from—and has in fact been explicitly tied to—a nineteenth-century male image of authorship. In another essay, Gilbert argues that women writers as a class are kin to the alienated Romantic figure: "dispossessed by her older brothers (the 'Sons of God'), educated to submission, enjoined to silence, the woman writer—in fantasy if not in reality—must often have 'stalked apart in joyless revery,' like Byron's heroes, like Satan, like Prometheus."[17] Likewise, Catharine Stimpson also argues that women writers in general have always had to fight to overcome a devaluation of themselves as producers of "public culture"; they have had to face their works being trivialized and being exiled to "empty fields" and the "despised forms" such as letters, diaries, and children's stories.[18] The imagery of such depictions of authorship suggests the female artist as outcast, a notion made concrete in the title of Nina Auerbach's study of nineteenth-century fiction, *Romantic Imprisonment: Women and Other Glorious Outcasts*. As we shall see, the criterion of female wrath and this image of the woman writer as Romantic outcast are reflected in the construction of anthologies of women's writings.

In addition to assuming that women writers share the emotional responses of anger and alienation, American and British literary historians have assumed that women writers in the sixteenth, seventeenth, and eighteenth centuries also shared certain innate values and desires with women in the nineteenth century and with us. "Many of the same configurations of power I have examined in this book still characterize American society," wrote Poovey in her study of Wollstonecraft, Austen, and Mary Shelley.

> Perhaps more important, many of the same values and inhibitions persist, sedimented deep in the layers of our culture and our unconscious. The psychological experience of many women still replicates the patterns I have observed in the lives and styles of these three women.[19]

Not only have women's literary histories confirmed the continuity of female experiences, but they have also tended to assert that emotional responses to landmark human experiences such as giving birth and psychological responses to social stress such as isolation or injustice have remained constant. Loneliness is loneliness, and anger is anger, we have assumed, whether it was felt by a thirteenth-century nun or a twentieth-century professor.

This belief in a uniform female response to life, then, enables us to identify with early women writers and to achieve a sense of a female literary family. Such a belief also results, at its crudest level, in a lamentable tendency to judge the "feminism" of earlier generations as it meets our standards. This is most noticeable in the treatment of women living and writing before 1800. We worry whether our literary forebears were "good" feminists. The Renaissance and the seventeenth century are particularly troublesome periods: Gilbert and Gubar comment on Renaissance women writers' "protected quality as well as their apparently greater docility" without defining what is meant, but strongly suggesting that what this period lacks is an angry Mary Wollstonecraft.[20] Some of the most widely known seventeenth-century women writers, such as Margaret Cavendish and Mary Astell, have extensive apologies offered up on their behalf for their "conservatism" or are dissected as not being sufficiently feminist. "To write of [Astell] as a feminist is to create a special version of her—almost to reinvent her—with her collaboration and the aid of historical hindsight," writes Perry; but she warns that "whoever reads Astell carefully will not find a feminist heroine of the past with whom it is easy to identify. The stamp of her ultraconservative attitudes are impressed on everything she wrote."[21] Here again, we see in this desire for continuity, for a maternal link, the expectation that the past should be similar to the present and that the value of studying the past is to find someone or something with which to identify.

Other early women writers suffer harsher criticism for not being ideologically sound or being too acceptable to the male establishment. Katherine Philips's appeal is rather diminished when Pearson declares that she was one of the few women "fortunate enough to find favour with the male establishment. . . . She led a blameless life, avoided risqué subjects, did not explicitly question conventional notions of women, and above all did not seek for publication. Consequently she . . . seemed unthreatening to men and thus retained their respect."[22] In this presentation, however, she loses ours.

Likewise, Margaret Cavendish, another "celebrity" author during the seventeenth century, tends to have an ambiguous slot in twentieth-century feminism. She is included in an anthology of feminist writings despite her sharp words concerning silly females, but her place there is qualified: "In keeping with her class, the Duchess of Newcastle's primary motivation was the improvement of her own individual situation."[23] Cavendish is denounced elsewhere as "not a true champion of her sex, but an egoist who happened to be of the female gender. . . . When balked in her quest for male privileges she adopted a feminist perspective. But instead of wishing to see her female contemporaries raised from their 'dejected' position, her real desire was to shine above all rivals."[24] While we lament the scarcity of women writers from earlier periods, there is a tendency to devalue or even to "reinvent" those who do not conform to our criteria of "good feminists."

It is particularly interesting to consider the implications behind the vocabulary used in the writing of these lives of early women authors. Astell becomes the "collaborator" in her own "reinvention" and "creation" of her as "an Early English Feminist." Aphra Behn is likewise the "creation" of her biographer, who laboriously binds scattered pieces of biographical data together with speculations in *Reconstructing Aphra.* But have these women been reassembled to create different creatures than their originals? Has the search for commonality and shared emotional response erased significant historical differences and led to an inadvertent silencing of these Renaissance and seventeenth-century women? As we shall see in chapter 5, the treatment by history of the most prolific group of women writers during this period suggests that we have indeed lost a chorus of powerful voices from the past.

The second key feature of recent literary histories is the adherence to an evolutionary narrative of literature and feminism. As Showalter summarized it, we have created a model

> which describes the evolutionary stages of women's writing . . . from imitation through protest to self-definition, and defines and traces the connections throughout history and across national boundaries of the recurring images, themes, and plots that emerge from women's social, psychological, and aesthetic experience in male-dominated cultures.[25]

Here we see the types of female authors emerging: the illiterate medieval woman, the silent, docile Renaissance woman, the modest coterie Cavalier female, the independent professional Restoration playwright, the emerging female novelist, the mad Victorian, and the culmination in our own time's self-conscious and self-critical pilgrim in search of female identity.

Obviously, this evolutionary model has little appeal for scholars working on periods before the Restoration, that time *NALW* refers to as the "Dark Ages" of the female imagination.[26] It is most frequently used by those constructing literary histories focusing on the novel, in particular the nineteenth-century novel. However, since the bulk of writings about women's literature in a historical context has concerned itself with this epic age, it is this view of the past which is most widely published in women's literary history. While these studies offer insightful critiques of nineteenth- and twentieth-century texts, their assumptions about earlier women writers are often misleading and are perpetuated in texts dealing with earlier material.

For example, an excellent recent study of eighteenth-century women novelists by Jane Spencer has an important position implicit in its title. *The Rise of the Woman Novelist* indicates not only its Marxist heritage with its emphasis on the development of the middle class, but also the belief that prior to a certain period, women writers occupied a less elevated position than that achieved by the female novelists of the eighteenth century. A more ambitious and theoretically complex reading by Nancy Armstrong links the "history of a specifically modern form of desire that, during the early eighteenth century, changed the criteria for determining what was most important in a female" with what she terms "the rise of the domestic woman" and the "rise of the novel"; she thus integrates Foucault's sexual historiography with Marxist social history. Like Spencer, Armstrong retains, however, the defining categories of Ian Watt's classic literary history. "I know of no history of the English novel that can explain why women began to write respectable fiction near the end of the eighteenth century," states Armstrong; "yet that they suddenly began writing and were recognized as women writers strikes me as a central event in the history of the novel."[27] This may well be so, but it strikes those of us working in earlier periods that Armstrong's history of the "rise" of the novel, like Watt's, does not include any reference at all to Aphra Behn's and Delarivier Manley's earlier popular prose fictions.

In a sense, studies such as these define the ground of their arguments through a negation of a previous period. There is one type of the evolutionary view of the past which uses the sixteenth and seventeenth centuries as prestages or primitive versions of a later and more significant literary era, when it even acknowledges that significant activities *were* occurring. As we have seen, even critical studies focused on Renaissance women writers have carried over this organizing period structure, whereby authors are fit into categories depending on where they fall on the time line—early or late, imitative or self-defining, feminine or feminist.

Such evolution-based narratives have several identifying features in their treatment of pre-1700 women's writings and lives. First, like Cixous, these critics believe that before the Restoration, women writers were isolated and unusual creatures. Pearson's study opens with the premise that "published women writers first appear in any numbers and first exert a real influence on English literature in the Restoration and early eighteenth century."[28] Before that time, women thus were not really "authors." According to Pearson, since "publication was usually the barrier beyond which it was felt a good woman must not go," women before the Restoration were exiled into "private and informal literary modes like letters and journals" (p. 12). Mary Mahl and Helene Koons in their introduction to *The Female Spectator* assert of the Restoration literary scene that there were "few competent writers" among the women of the leisured classes to which literature was supposedly confined. Aphra Behn was "an exception . . . driven to write by the necessity to be self-supporting."[29] While Behn is frequently cited as the first female professional writer, critics of this school also warn us not to be misled by her: In the view of one, "it was not until the nineteenth century that women writers existed in any numbers as professionals, and even as hacks."[30]

Jane Spencer's more extended description of the female literary population during this earlier period likewise suggests it could be conveniently counted on one's fingers: "Seventeenth-century women writers included a number of aristocrats dedicating their leisure hours to literary pursuits, and less well known but also important, several middle-class women writing on household, medical and religious matters."[31] "Before the 1690s," she continues, "they were maverick figures, hesitant or bold according to individual temperament, with little sense of group identity" (p. 41). The argument of her book rests on the premise that the eighteenth century saw the "rise" of a new literary life for women. Previous women writers lacked the opportunities to write provided by the market for fiction; of equal importance in this view, writing by women was seen as an infringement on the male sphere during the earlier periods. By the end of the seventeenth century, "the traditional notion of woman's proper silence was being challenged, then, and in particular there were feminist writers who, by their emphasis on women's intellectual capacities and the need for education, fostered a view that women's learning and women's writing were the instruments of struggle against male domination" (p. 22). The evolution of women's writing is thus directly tied to a growing, published "feminist" voice.

Moira Ferguson's anthology of feminist writings spans from 1578 to 1799 and also stresses the changing economic status and the "domestication of women" in her opening narrative of the literary history of the period. Writing is depicted as a dangerous occupation before 1740, attracting "only the most audacious of women, for being paid to write fell into the same category as writing at all: society frowned upon it and only those who were both bold and desperate dared, or those whose privileged status allowed them to dispense with society's sanction of their activities."[32] Female dramatists in particular "suffered for their courage" in using "forms generally viewed as exclusively male" (p. 18). Apart from the terrifying world of drama, there was poetry, "an escape from endless 'leisure' for many aristocratic and middle-class women, for whom self-expression was tacitly vetoed" (p. 19).

This image of the pre-1700 woman writer as either an aristocratic dilettante or one of a tiny group of embattled publishing writers is also at the heart of Poovey's theories about the "proper lady." In her section titled "The Situation of Women Writers," Poovey establishes as the historical norm that "marriage was virtually the only respectable 'occupation' for women (and both learning and writing were frequently seen as threats to domestic duty), but writing catapulted women directly into the public arena, where attention must be fought for, where explicit competition reigned."[33] Moreover,

Writing for publication . . . jeopardizes modesty, that critical keystone of feminine propriety; for it not only "hazard[s] . . . disgrace" but cultivates and calls attention to the woman as subject, as initiator of direct action, as a person deserving of notice for her own sake. Taken to its logical extreme, to write is to assume the initiative of creator, to imitate *the* Creator; and, as Sandra Gilbert and Susan Gubar have pointed out, it is to usurp the male instrument of power, the phallus that the pen may symbolize. (p. 36)

Her example of this dilemma is Lady Mary Wortley Montagu (a key figure in chapters 3 and 4, where eighteenth- and nineteenth-century receptions of her writings are examined). In Poovey's view, Lady Mary was one of those "respectable women who wrote primarily for their own or their friends' amusement," the amateur aristocrat of Spencer's and Ferguson's literary landscape. Lady Mary "allowed her unpublished writing to be circulated privately among her social peers . . . she published political or critical writing anonymously. Both practices were widespread through the century. . . . Both allowed women an indirect, disguised entrance into the competitive arena of literary creation" (p. 36). Studies such as these collapse creativity into publication; it is implied that publication and commercial success of some degree are inherent goals in writing. Literary activity thus becomes confined to public competition in a print format.

In discussions of the evolution of women's writing, another key assumption found in these critical studies concerns the relationship between genre and gender. The emphasis in twentieth-century feminist literary history is on women novelists. Rosalind Miles put it bluntly: "When we say 'women writers,' then, the phrase is generally taken to mean 'women novelists'. For reasons only recently being addressed by feminist criticism, women have yet to make any substantial impact in large numbers on any other literary form."[34] The novel is the characteristic genre in what we have seen described as the golden age of women's writing—the nineteenth century.

Such studies privilege the novel as a true female genre. The form of the novel is supposedly particularly suited to women's circumstances. The novel, it is maintained, did not conventionally identify the speaking voice as male. "[The novel] was a logical extension of women's role," writes Spender, being derived from women's letter writing practices; letters "are a good medium for exploring emotions and maintaining relationships." In the eighteenth century, women writers began to draw "on the strengths they had been allowed and transformed their private literary indulgence into a public paid performance, and in the process they gained for themselves a voice and helped to create a new literary form."[35]

The novel also satisfies all of Virginia Woolf's criteria, being the literary form in which women have received the most commercial success and critical acclaim. Woolf noted at the end of her survey of women's literary history,

> there is no reason to think that the form of the epic or of the poetic play suits a woman any more than the sentence suits her. But all the older forms of literature were hardened and set by the time she [the female author] became a writer. The novel alone was young enough to be soft in her hands. . . . it is the poetry that is still denied outlet.[36]

Showalter, summarizing Woolf's position as it is used in recent feminist studies, states that women writers "excluded by custom and education from achieving distinction in poetry, history, or drama" turned to the novel as an area open for female endeavors. In this view, at least in the novel, women writers did have significant impact on the development of the form and did in fact end up dominating the field in the eighteenth and nineteenth centuries.[37] However, by this logic, women writers before this new form was available would suffer from a disadvantage, since the forms in which they worked supposedly would be less accepting of a feminine voice.

Such assumptions that privilege the nineteenth century in these important recent critical studies are pervasive in accounts of literature written before 1700. It is assumed that in the earlier period the act of a woman writing was viewed as subversive; therefore, as we have seen, it is asserted that women were restricted to "private" literary forms such as letters, diaries, and poetry which "remained" unpublished, intended either for a small uncritical audience or for none at all. Bridget Hill defines pre-Restoration literary activity by women as a "private expression of their thoughts in spiritual diaries, letters and poetry."[38] Such activity does not measure up in conventional definitions of "authorship" as significant literary activity capable of having any influence in a wider sphere. We shall see in the next chapter how this definition of authorship has dramatically defined the contents of the canon of women's literature.

The argument that women were intimidated from writing because of the aggressive competitive nature of publication is convincing — for the later eighteenth and the nineteenth century. Attitudes toward print and authorship during these later periods were formed in an environment in which there was a financial incentive to publish and therefore to write for the widest possible audience. By the nineteenth century, publication and critical commentary had become the hallmark of literary legitimacy as opposed to dilettantism, which might condescend to the vanity press, or the amateur's inability to get anything printed.

This view, however, as I have argued elsewhere, obscures the existing conditions in a preprofessional literary environment; to publish was the exception for both men and women, and the most common practice was the circulation of manuscript copies, a mode of distribution recently labeled "scribal publication" by Harold Love.[39] The concept of "public" and "private" literary forms is a construction based on a nineteenth-century commercial literary environment. Showalter explicitly states in *A Literature of Their Own* that she is interested only in the tradition of women writing for pay. Critics such as Pearson and Spender argue that Renaissance and seventeenth-century women were restricted to the "private" and "informal" literary genres of letters and diaries while men monopolized the "public sphere" of commercial print. The sense in these studies of women being restricted to a "private audience" may also stem from the perception of continuity in women's experiences: Then, as well as today, it is asserted, "the taboo is on women's public writing."[40]

The definition of letters and diaries as "private" is very much the product of nineteenth- and twentieth-century experiences. For example, the whole concept of a "letter" was different in the seventeenth century than in the nineteenth century. Letters were an established literary form in the Renaissance and seventeenth century and were not "private" in the sense of personal domestic correspondence. They were highly conventional public forms of address, "epistles" on weighty matters written to display the author's rhetorical graces and intended to be circulated. A quick scan of titles published between 1600 and 1700 reveals that among the most popular titles were "An Epistle on" and "Letters to." Their forms and style could be studied in helpful books such as Davies's *Writing Schoolmaster* or Guez's *Collection of Some Modern Epistles*, which also offered models for imitation. Rather than being a despised literary form, the letter as a genre commanded much attention and respect. As we shall see in chapter 5, the epistles of the early Quaker women writers were designed as public declarations of their beliefs, crafted with rhetorical sophistication to meet the needs of different audiences.

In the same fashion, diaries in the seventeenth century were most commonly kept by those in quest of spiritual improvement. Their function was not only to enable the author to examine his or her own life, but also to provide examples to other Christians; thus, spiritual autobiographies became one of the most widely published of all literary forms during the period. As with letters, there were model texts and formal conventions to be followed in diary writing. Neither the letter nor the diary occupied the same literary place in the Renaissance and seventeenth century as it did in the nineteenth century, when, indeed, the forms tended to be the private modes of expression which we use today.

The common argument that we find evidence of early women writers' intimidation in their use of pseudonyms or anonymous publication is likewise based on a sense of the ways in which nineteenth-century women used these conventions. For Showalter, the use of a male pseudonym "like Eve's fig leaf . . . signals the loss of innocence . . . [a] radical understanding of the role-playing required by women's effort to participate in the mainstream of literary culture."[41] Stimpson extends this shrewd observation to cover women's experience of literary life in general; she cites only the Brontës, however, as her example of a woman writer forced to trade "the recognition of her female birth for the chance to express herself publicly."[42] Poovey also sees the use of pseudonyms and anonymous publication as an attempt to shield the female writer from the discovery of her sex by her readers: "The rapid demise of literary patronage after 1740 meant that a woman *could* publish anonymously, without having either to solicit the interest of a patron . . . or even to acknowledge her own sex."[43] Pearson emphasizes the use of "fanciful pseudonyms" as a protective device, and Spender also stresses the notion that in the past "women understood that they got a 'better hearing' if it was thought they were males."[44] Interestingly, continuity of past and present women's experiences is again asserted: Spender ties this nineteenth-century practice to twentieth-century academic writing, suggesting that "seeking publication while concealing one is female (as in scholarly journals) is another attempt to pre-empt the operation of the double standard which has been used to ensure that women are not encouraged to address themselves to men" (p. 197).

Given the strength of this condemnation, it is not surprising, therefore, that accounts of earlier women writers cast a pitying glance on the practice of using pseudonyms: "Women knew quite well that if one woman signed her work with her own name," Louise Bernikow's anthology asserts, "she opened herself to moral and social abuse."[45] Pseudonyms and anonymous publication are seen as protective strategies because they effectively hide the author's sex and enable her to simultaneously preserve her "modesty" while receiving a fair hearing.

However, in the sixteenth and seventeenth centuries, unlike the nineteenth century, we do not find women using pseudonyms to hide their sex. The pseudonyms chosen — Orinda, Astrea, Ardelia, Ephelia, Corinna — clearly signal the writer's sex. Nor was the use of this type of pseudonym a marginal literary practice — we have Poliarchus (Sir Charles Cottrell), Philaretus (Robert Boyle), Thyrsis (Rochester), and Damon (a favorite for several men, including even the sober John Locke). The use of a pseudonym did serve to create a literary persona, but in the Renaissance and seventeenth century, one finds these names are gender specific. As will be seen in the next chapter, the process of exchanging pseudonymous verses creates and confirms relationships within a separate, self-contained literary world. Given the nature of manuscript circulation, in which the author and reader were members of a social group, the attempt to hide one's sex would have been as futile as it was unnecessary.

Even anonymous publications did not always try to mask the sex of the author. When one scans the lists of printed works before 1700, the label of "written by a Lady of Quality" is a frequent assertion, as is the use of initials with a feminine title, such as "Mrs. H" or "Lady L." Some writers who published anonymously also included clear references to their sex in their titles, such as Astell's *Serious Proposal to the Ladies . . . By a Lover of Her Sex.* While the use of pseudonyms and anonymous publication undoubtedly was a strategy to disguise gender in the later eighteenth and the nineteenth century, it was not necessarily so in the preprofessional literary periods of the Renaissance and seventeenth century.

The related belief that literary activity has as its goal publication is also an assumption based on a nineteenth-century literary environment. Critics such as Pearson deny influence to women writers who did not print. Critics such as Poovey, Ferguson, Spencer, Gilbert, and Gubar, for example, devalue Lady Mary Wortley Montagu's mode of literary production, which was to circulate pieces in manuscript. "Women who wanted to publish continued to encounter — or fear — the persistent prejudice against learned ladies," maintains Poovey.[46] Cora Kaplan's introduction to her anthology stresses that "the difficulties, psychic and social, of writing and publishing poetry made women peculiarly self-conscious about their endeavors."[47] What is implied in this view is that all authors wish to be in print, and therefore something must be preventing these women from publishing their writings.

Poovey states that manuscript circulation among one's peers was a female strategy, in effect an insincere effort to conform to social standards of female modesty and to avoid infringing on male turf. Lady Mary "allowed" her works to be read in manuscript, an "indirect, disguised entrance into the competitive arena of literary creation" (p. 36). However, while such statements may be perfectly valid in a nineteenth-century literary environment, they show a lack of understanding of the workings of manuscript tradition as it existed in the Renaissance and seventeenth century. As we shall see in the next chapter, such assumptions about coterie writing strongly affect the presentation of early periods in teaching texts.

Furthermore, such beliefs equate literary creation with the competitive commercial market, a market not available until the ready accessibility of print in the eighteenth century. Gilbert and Gubar's anthology applauds the Restoration as a period when women entered "the literary marketplace," as though the existence of a commercial market was somehow a liberating condition for women writers.[48] Again, we can see how unsuitable this approach is in understanding the literary life of the sixteenth and seventeenth centuries (when literature as we generally define it was not a commercial activity, but a social one) by thinking of the careers of male authors such as Thomas Traherne, Henry King, and the Earl of Rochester. All of these writers followed patterns of literary creation identical to that of Lady Mary Wortley Montagu, circulating their works in manuscript and occasionally publishing an anonymous piece that was usually attributable to them given their wide readership in manuscript.

This assumption of the supremacy and desirability of print is ironic in the context of the literary history of early women writers. Coterie literature is devalued as the "leisure" pastime of aristocratic ladies, or a disguised means to break into serious literature, but this is only true when an alternative literary environment is well established. Before the eighteenth century, coterie literature was the most common form of literary exchange. To accept it as a legitimate literary outlet for women before 1700, as it was for men, however, would mean dropping the image of the "maverick" female writer.

Manuscript circulation is social and noncompetitive in nature; works circulate in manuscript inviting additions and corrections, with no need for the author to establish ownership or copyright. As I discuss in the next chapter, coterie literature does, in fact, provide that literary "family" so desired by Moers and Showalter in their studies. Because of our concept of the literary environment as a nineteenth-century competitive, commercial one, we have over-looked or excluded a literary world before 1700, one in which men and women participated together and, as I discuss in chapter 3, in which women were represented and depicted as being "competitive" with men.

The nineteenth century has had unusual influence in our construction of a literary history for women writers. When one considers a range of feminist criticism which represents female authorship before 1700, it becomes clear that underlying seemingly disparate critical approaches are strong preconceptions about genre, gender, and authorship. Ironically, in both the images of the female author and the definition of what types of writings will make up our "tradition," one finds assumptions about the past which operate well for establishing continuity between the nineteenth and twentieth centuries, but which break down for earlier periods; models that in fact enabled the growth of women's studies by challenging traditional literary histories paradoxically have acted to marginalize texts by earlier women writers. Because of the way we have defined authorship, audience, and literature, we have effectively silenced a large number of early women's voices in our very attempts to preserve and celebrate women's writings.

The Myth of Judith Shakespeare

Creating the Canon of Women's Literature

in the Twentieth Century

The arts are our storehouses of recorded values. — I. A. Richards, *The Principles of Literary Criticism*

The forthcoming *Norton Anthology of Women's Literature* [*sic*], edited by Gilbert and Gubar, . . . will establish a feminist canon for the next generation. — Elaine Showalter, "Women's Time, Women's Space: Writing the History of Feminist Criticism"

In the last few decades, while some feminist critics have concentrated their efforts to enlarge the boundaries of critical discourse about women's texts by developing theories of the female poetic and the female tradition, others have sought to expand the opportunities to study women's literature by making the primary texts more easily available. As typified by the work of Virago Press, a good deal of energy has gone into the retrieval of the actual texts themselves in an attempt to revive interest in long out-of-print novels by women authors. Still other critics have focused their attention on presenting women's writing in a format that would permit it to be integrated into a standard college curriculum. In American feminist critical practice in particular, this drive to apply the new-found perceptions and feminist theory finds powerful expression in the classroom through women's studies programs and courses.

Obviously such new courses need texts to teach: This decade has brought the appearance of a scholarly anthology purporting to delineate "the tradition in English" of women's writing, a text hailed as presenting the canon for the future. This production, which unites the search for a female poetic with the retrieval of lost texts, offers the chance for feminist scholars themselves to stop to consider the direction women's literary history is taking and the conclusions drawn from this new canon of women's literature. Whether or not one approves of the concept of a canon, or shudders at the thought of anthologies, the phenomenon they embody deserves attention as an indication of the wider, popular concept of women's writings.

The flagships of the drive to establish a working, workable body of literature which represents women's writings in English throughout history are the anthologies. An anthology by nature is primarily a popular or teaching text: It is designed for readers who lack familiarity with the subject matter. It is the introduction, however, to more than the texts themselves. Anthologies as a form also help to create and to confirm canons: Their selections signal to the reader what the critical community considers to be worthy of study and also the dominant critical framework in which the texts are to be read. By their selections, anthologies thus invite readers to consider particular critical issues or questions concerning social context and literary history in addition to questions about specific authors. In short, they are the mechanisms of diffusion for the evolutionary narrative theory of female creativity we have seen constructed in the critical studies of early women writers.

Anthologies of women's writings have appeared in increasing numbers over the last twenty years. Certainly such endeavors have opened up many valuable opportunities for the study of heretofore "lost" women writers. Again, as we have seen in the previous chapter, while on the one hand such texts enable the study of women writers, on the other, ironically, they block our perception of many women writing before 1700. What gets lost in the process of preserving, given the "tradition" behind the writing of the history of women's literature in this century and the formation of a canon from such efforts?

In the anthologies of women's writings produced in the last two decades, one finds, as in the theoretical texts, that too often the twentieth century's perceptions of works by Renaissance and seventeenth-century women rest on a set of anachronistic and restrictive presumptions. We find the models structured on a set of assumptions about literary practice, production, and genre. Too often the presentations of the literature are supported by an unquestioning use of an evolutionary "Whig" interpretation of English society. Texts such as those edited by Katherine Rogers, Joan Goulianos, Bernikow, Goreau, Fidelis Morgan, Gilbert and Gubar, and Greer et al. project a seemingly clear and unambiguous sense of literary history which is narrated by the entries they include.[1] These anthologies, like the critical studies discussed previously, share certain critical assumptions about literary history and about women's participation in it. While they continue the drive to make forgotten, inaccessible works available, these texts also perpetuate the view that—with the exception of anomalous and isolated figures such as Aphra Behn during the Restoration—the women of the sixteenth and seventeenth centuries did not write for an audience, if indeed they wrote at all.

Perhaps the most powerful of these anthologies is *The Norton Anthology of Literature by Women: The Tradition in English,* a true landmark on the path to establishing women's studies as part of a standard university-level curriculum. Carrying the stamp of intellectual authority bestowed by its editors' reputations in feminist theory and the seal of approval of one of the largest publishers of college texts, this anthology, in both its contents and commentary, will have tremendous power in shaping the point of view of the next generation of scholars and the college-educated reading public. Therefore, it is of no small concern to both feminist literary historians and literary critics working in the pre-Romantic periods to discover that "the tradition in English" of women's literature before 1800 occupies only 172 pages out of 2,390.

The view of early women writers implied by this selection is stated explicitly in other anthologies. "The eighteenth century shows the oppression of women traditional in our culture, but it also marks the first period, in English, when they found a voice in literature," begins one anthology published in 1979.[2] Commenting on Aphra Behn, another anthology appearing in 1974 declares that "such a voice had not been heard in English literature before. . . . It invented itself without precedent out of the life of the woman who owned it."[3] In a similar vein, "Aphra Behn was the first Englishwoman to become a professional writer," announces a frequently reprinted selection from a critical literary biography; "though she did not and could not know it then, [she] would signal a turning in feminine history, [and] augur a whole new spectrum of possibility for her sex."[4] Even in anthologies devoted to seventeenth-century female authorship, it is steadily maintained that women writing before the eighteenth century were rare and eccentric creatures, the exceptions, not the norm. "If a woman managed to overcome obstacles of inadequate education or self-doubt and succeeded in publishing her writing, she could expect to be mocked, jeered, flouted, and attacked by critics," announces a 1985 anthology; seventeenth-century female authors are depicted as "*guerrilleras*, untrained, ill-equipped, isolated and vulnerable," in Greer et al.'s 1988 text *Kissing the Rod*, and their primary audience was the fireplace where "most of the poetry written by lonely women in the seventeenth century probably ended [up]".[5]

This reduction of seventeenth-century authorship and the determination to begin the tradition in the eighteenth century arises in part from a second assumption the anthologies share with much of the narrative of literary history discussed in the previous chapter. As we have seen, unlike French feminist theory, there has been a tendency in Anglo-American feminist literary studies to focus on common and continuing patterns in women's writings.[6] Anthologies of women's writings demonstrate in their selections their belief in the continuity in female experiences as well as writings, that such experiences transcend history. Furthermore, these anthologies suggest that one should always read women's texts as autobiographical documents, and the unstated goal of many of these texts is to provide "appropriate" role models for women writers and readers.

The underlying design in an anthology published in 1973 is to determine "what it may have meant, what it still may mean, to be a woman writer."[7] *NALW* opens its preface with Virginia Woolf's statement that "women's books continue each other," and, significantly, the editors describe the contents of the anthology as a means of "documenting" Woolf's thesis of continuity.[8] In short, the anthologies have suggested that one important agenda in formalizing a historical canon is to establish commonality in female experience throughout history, not difference, what Jane Marcus describes as Virginia Woolf's ability to "think back through her [literary] mothers" and to provide for the reader a "collective identity" for female writers and readers.[9] However, as discussed in the previous chapter, this constructed identity is essentially a contemporary one, with the anthology thus acting as the reader's mirror.

To summarize the position on early women writers as presented in the existing anthologies, sixteenth- and seventeenth-century Englishwomen, having "neither the experience of public life nor the expectation of an audience that would foster creativity," were effectively silenced. If they refused to remain mute, they were left isolated from those "literary communities comparable to the loosely organized groups of male writers who supported and encouraged the works of artists like Marlowe."[10] Recent anthologies start the tradition in the eighteenth century with "the emergence of productive, publishing women, who began to form a unique tradition of their own" (*NALW* p. 1). By emphasizing professional publication as the indicator of the start of a unique female tradition, such texts as Gilbert and Gubar's, Greer's, and Goreau's imply that the most interesting questions about the earlier periods are how and why women were silenced. The issue suggested by the anthologies to the scholar and student alike to solve is "why weren't there any female Shakespeares?" and the answers focus on the means of repression, not the modes of production.

Virginia Woolf and her influential book *A Room of One's Own* seem to be the inspirational source for this fundamental question asked by twentieth-century anthologists. "It is a perennial puzzle why no woman wrote a word of that extraordinary literature when every other man, it seemed, was capable of a song or sonnet," Woolf mused. She answers her own question by asserting that given the social conditions for women during the Renaissance and seventeenth century, "no woman could have written poetry."[11] Thus, Woolf and her followers view the canon as having been historically defined through silence or absence. *NALW* is simply the most eloquent and complete statement of Woolf's assertions about early women writers.

Obviously, for those of us who study and teach the Renaissance and seventeenth century, there are several disturbing features in such a presentation of the female "tradition" and in the resulting canon. Recent bibliographical studies add fuel to the fire: Patricia Crawford's checklist of women's writings published between 1600 and 1700 reveals the names of nearly three hundred women authors and more than eight hundred first editions.[12] As discussed in the previous chapter, however, our evolutionary narrative effectively blocks most of them from inclusion.

From the point of view of those interested in the earlier stages, there are two basic problems with the current literary history of female authorship and the resulting canon of women's literature. First, and most obvious, the "canon" was assembled before we fully knew the extent of women's writings in the Renaissance and Restoration. Second, the canon created has been constructed in general using the definition of literary hierarchies found in the male canon — poetry, drama, fiction, and belles lettres — and, as we have seen, privileges some forms above others, the novel being depicted as a uniquely "feminine" literary form. By doing so, this canon highlights continuity, but at the expense of crucial differences, historical differences in patterns of authorship and in modes of production of women's writings in societies that were in the transition stages in the developing technology of print.

Interestingly enough, the initial model of the silenced, alienated Renaissance woman presented in the anthologies may have been the attempt by a twentieth-century writer to create a voice for her. Our concept of the beginning of the unique tradition as found in the eighteenth century is a product of our perception of history, in particular women's lives in earlier times. The image that these anthologies perpetuate is derived largely from Virginia Woolf's fictional creation "Judith Shakespeare." No single theoretical text has had as much impact on shaping both the contents and the vocabulary of existing anthologies and teaching texts as Woolf's lecture series to the students at Newnham and Girton.

In *A Room of One's Own*, Woolf created the character of "Judith Shakespeare" to represent the experience of a talented female in early modern English society. In seeking to answer the question why there had been no female Shakespeares, Woolf became frustrated by the historical blank representing the life of the average woman of that period: "What I find deplorable," she observed to the young ladies of Girton and Newnham in 1928, "is that nothing is known about women before the eighteenth century" (p. 43). To fill this gap, Woolf imagined the lot of Shakespeare's sister, which is not a happy one. In Woolf's story, Judith is denied a formal education, discouraged from wasting her time scribbling, betrothed in her teens, and beaten by her father; she runs away to London, is rejected by the theater world, becomes pregnant, and finally kills herself "one winter's night and lies buried at some cross-roads" (pp. 49–50). Needless to say, Shakespeare's sister was not a commercial, publishing author, much less a successful, celebrated, or self-sufficient woman.

Woolf's use of this episode in the rest of her analysis of women's literature is nearly as interesting as the story itself.

> This may be true or it may be false — who can say? — but what is true in it, so it seemed to me, reviewing the story of Shakespeare's sister as I had made it, is that any woman born with a great gift in the sixteenth century would certainly have gone crazed, shot herself, or ended her days in some lonely cottage outside the village, half witch, half wizard, feared and mocked at. For it needs little skill in psychology to be sure that the highly gifted girl who had tried to use her gift for poetry would have been so thwarted and hindered by other people, so tortured and pulled asunder by her own contrary instincts, that she must have lost her health and sanity to a certainty (p. 51).

Here, fiction is claiming the force and authority of fact. In the absence of facts, Woolf asserts, who can deny that this is the likely pattern of experience for a woman writer in the earlier centuries? This myth of Shakespeare's sister is so compelling that Woolf begins her next chapter with this flat assertion: "That one would find any woman in that state of mind [to produce a work of genius] in the sixteenth century was obviously impossible. . . . no woman could have written poetry then" (p. 61).

Woolf's analysis of the literature of the seventeenth century and Restoration period is built on this conclusion. When discussing the Countess of Winchilsea, Woolf again returns to the novelist's world and she "imagines the sneers and the laughter, the adulation of toadies, the scepticism of the professional poet." Woolf concludes that "she must have shut herself up in a room in the country to write, and been torn asunder by bitterness and scruples" (p. 63). On the Duchess of Newcastle, Woolf likewise exclaims, "What a vision of loneliness and riot the thought of Margaret Cavendish brings to mind!" (p. 65). Continuing her survey, Woolf dismisses Dorothy Osborne because "letters did not count" as literature. Finally, Woolf concludes with the figure with whom most anthologists start, Aphra Behn: "With Mrs. Behn we turn a very important corner on the road. We leave behind, shut up in their parks among their folios, those solitary great ladies who wrote without audience or criticism, for their own delight alone" (p. 66). Literature, for Woolf, was the process by which one could gain an economic independence, a financial respectability through one's own labors, which these isolated amateurs, she believed, could not attain.

Woolf's vision of women writers before Jane Austen is one of isolated, embittered, or embattled creatures. In her vision of history, if women did write, it was over opposition and discouragement, and their writings were never intended to be read. Woolf's selections of seventeenth-century female authors emphasize the destructive effects of the literary life on women, torn between the forces of genius and social demands.

As we have seen, links between Woolf's analysis, her image of the woman writer in the Renaissance, and the contents of current women's literary history are direct and striking. *A Room of One's Own* is cited repeatedly to gloss historical texts, and its impact is clearly seen in the anthologies of essays on feminist literary theory. Showalter's anthology opens with the declaration cited at the beginning of the Introduction that *Madwoman in the Attic* established Woolf's vision of the past. Armstrong's analysis of the "rise" of the domestic female novelist both opens and concludes with a quote from *A Room of One's Own* identifying the appearance of the middle-class female author as a turning point in history. Woolf's myth of Renaissance silence permeates the collection of critical selections published by Mary Eagleton. In Jane Marcus's volume of essays, *Art and Anger: Reading like a Woman,* Woolf is offered to us as "an example of how to be a literary critic" and *A Room of One's Own* is described as "the first modern text of feminist criticism, the model in both theory and practice of a specifically socialist feminist criticism."[13]

One sees the power of her narrative most clearly in the structure of existing literary anthologies: Almost every anthology that deals with a historical perspective on women's writings cites Woolf's theory of the isolated, self-destructive female artist. An anthology on Restoration women playwrights uses Woolf's description of Aphra Behn as the woman responsible for "freeing" the mind of women writers.[14] Another anthology opens with a passage from *A Room of One's Own* as its epigraph and cites this "very beautiful, very personal essay" as being "full of clues" in unraveling the situation faced by such women writers as the Countess of Winchilsea.[15]

Finally, not only does *NALW* use Woolf's theory of continuity in women's writings as its framework of selection, but it also uses her as a critical source on individual authors of the earlier periods. The background section on the seventeenth and eighteenth centuries begins with an episode from *Orlando* and continues with references to *A Room of One's Own* concerning the significance of the transition to publishing professionals during the period, the "emergence" of women who could "form a unique tradition of their own" (p. 40). The biographical section on the Duchess of Newcastle starts with the quotation cited earlier concerning "the vision of loneliness;" the one on Katherine Philips makes references to Philips having "a room of her own" (p. 72, 81). The section on Aphra Behn closes with a quote from Woolf exclaiming, "All women together ought to let flowers fall upon the tomb of Aphra Behn for it was she who earned them the right to speak their minds" (p. 88). Needless to say, Woolf is again involved in the section on the Countess of Winchilsea, used to establish Finch's "anger and bitterness" (p. 100). In short, *NALW* proceeds in its early sections to present selections that fulfill its opening declaration to "document" Woolf's vision of the past.

The majority of twentieth-century feminist literary historians, like Woolf, see the transition from a system of patronage to that of the paid professional writer as the turning point in women's literary history. Recent anthologies are solidly based on this notion, constructed using a "great figure" scheme of history. This is why Aphra Behn has assumed such importance in the canon—she was supposedly the first "professional" woman writer, the first to make her living independently, unabashedly, by her literary productions. The "solitary ladies" mentioned by Woolf who "wrote for their own delight" are not, in this view, as significant in the development of women's writing and its "tradition" as the professional.

This insistence on commercial viability as the hallmark of literary activity is striking when it is put in the context of the "other" canon. Alexander Pope is certainly noted in traditional anthologies as the author who managed to break the mold as far as patronage is concerned, but this recognition does not devalue his predecessors such as Thomas Traherne and Sir Philip Sidney who did not publish their works or make their living by writing. Certainly, we are not encouraged to fling flowers at George Wither and Francis Quarles, the authors whose books were listed by seventeenth-century book vendors as "best sellers."

Yet, the reason for women's celebration of professionalism in these anthologies is not hard to see. For Woolf, the professional woman writer was the one who *could* be independent of men, who earned her keep by means other than performing menial labor or being a dependent wife. "I think that you may object that in all this I have made too much of the importance of material things," she acknowledges at one point; "you may say that the mind should rise above such things." For Woolf, however,

> intellectual freedom depends upon material things. Poetry depends upon intellectual freedom. And women have always been poor, not for two hundred years merely, but from the beginning of time. Women have had less intellectual freedom than the sons of Athenian slaves. Women, then, have not had a dog's chance of writing poetry. That is why I have laid so much stress on money and a room of one's own. (p. 112)

Money could, in Woolf's view, procure that "lock on the door" which male writers seem to possess as a right. Money, in short, enabled women to write, as long as it was independently obtained.

Likewise, Woolf's view of women's literary history ascribes the boom in female authorship in the eighteenth century, a change "of greater importance than the Crusades or the Wars of the Roses," not to the power of the new technology of print, but to economics.

> The extreme activity of the mind which showed itself in the later eighteenth century among women — the talking, and the meeting, the writing of essays on Shakespeare, the translating of the classics — was found on the solid fact that women could make money by writing. Money dignifies what is frivolous if unpaid for. (p. 68)

Commercial readership, or at least the opportunity to write for commercial outlets, can thus be seen as the validation of female authorship in Woolf's presentation of the literary past.

In our current formation of the canon, the literary profession has come to represent an escape from social roles and norms, whether the escape is complete, as in the case of Behn, or partial, in the simple attainment of a quiet room. The opportunity to be a *professional* writer in the current canon "freed" the mind. Being an amateur or coterie writer in the Renaissance or seventeenth century, it appears, did not. It is implied that if a woman was still dependent on male relatives for financial support, she would therefore necessarily be constrained or "co-opted" in her writings. Given this assumption, even Jane Austen and the Brontës can be viewed as questionable members of the tradition.

The links between Woolf's theories on the continuity of feminine experience and the current dependence on her by the compilers of twentieth-century anthologies bring up two further considerations. What was the source for Woolf's image of the life of Shakespeare's sister – the isolated, betrayed, and self-divided woman writer – and what is the effect of the emphasis on professional commercialism in setting the parameters of a female "canon"?

If one reads the source critically, it is clear that the life of Judith Shakespeare is based on rather interesting historical material shaped by a particular notion of historical progress. Having failed to uncover books specifically on women's history in the British Museum, Woolf in her account turned to "one of the latest" general histories, George Trevelyan's *History of England*. There she found under "Women, position of" her accounts of wife beating and child marriages. Woolf notes that ironically, while women occupied a prominent spot in the literary imagination of the Renaissance, Trevelyan's account of the actual lives of Renaissance Englishwomen depicts them as being "locked up, beaten and flung about the room" (p. 45).

This grand masterpiece of Edwardian historical narrative, a view of history as an account of the "significant" forces in terms of bills passed, wars fought, and kings crowned, is the basis of the myth of Judith Shakespeare. However, since the 1920s, social historians have changed the focus and the findings of history dramatically. The pioneering, if controversial, use of demographic reconstruction by Peter Laslett and E. A. Wrigley of the Cambridge Group and by Lawrence Stone has destroyed the notion of teenage marriage as the norm in English society, raising the average age at marriage for both sexes into the mid-twenties. Peter Clark, Valerie Elliott, and David Souden's work on the growth of cities and migration patterns in early modern England shows that women moved from the country to the city and between parishes in the same fashion as did men and did not stay rooted at home, as had been supposed.[16] Finally, no longer are social histories written only about the urban upper classes; important studies by Ann Kassmaul, Margaret Spufford, and Sandra Clark focus on servant life and the daily round of small rural communities.[17]

This is not the world imagined by Virginia Woolf. She is a great novelist, an inspired analyst of the process of literary creation – but she is not a great historian, and it is unfair to demand that she act in such a role. She was bound by the limitations of the historiography of her day. We, on the other hand, have taken a text designed to be provocative and to stimulate further research into women's lives in the past and canonized it as history. One could object here that Woolf's historical accuracy or lack of it is irrelevant, since publications by women before 1750 are indeed a small fraction of all those produced. But that leaves the question unanswered: What were women writing and how in the sixteenth and seventeenth centuries?

The practice of coterie literature as a whole raises issues not only of literary production, but also of literature and social class. As cited before, Woolf tends to dismiss the isolated aristocrats as serious writers or part of the tradition; Judith Shakespeare is resolutely middle class and in search of an income from her literary labors. In this line, *NALW* compares English Renaissance women writers unfavorably with "the independent bourgeoise Christine de Pisan": They did not publish, as de Pisan, nor, the editors believe, did they write with her anger over social conditions. Instead, in its presentation of this group, the anthology emphasizes "their protected quality, as well as their apparently greater docility" (p. 14). The presentation of the women included in the section (Julian of Norwich, Margery Kempe, Queen Elizabeth, Mary Sidney Herbert, and Amelia Lanier) neutralizes them by depicting them as amateurs, merely aristocrats amusing themselves with scribbling: "Although they wielded some power as patronesses, these English women of letters were almost always economically dependent on church or state. . . . Thus, unlike the independent bourgeoise Christine de Pisan, they seem for the most part to articulate conventional pieties, as if to prove their loyalty to the system that supported them" (p. 14). Although these early women's writings are thus preserved as part of the canon, such commentary automatically lessens their value and significance in the "tradition."

In such presentations, social rank is equated with economic dependence, and, even though it provided the necessary leisure from hard labor required, aristocratic rank is depicted as pulling whatever fangs these ladies might have dared to show. The implication is that even though such women wrote, what they wrote was co-opted by a patriarchal society, leaving us with an interesting vision of the Countess of Pembroke as a sort of a "running dog lackey" of patriarchal cultural imperialism. Perhaps even more damaging, however, than the effects on the individual reputations of the women chosen to represent what the editors refer to as "the so-called Dark Ages" of the female imagination is the general impression of female authorship. Implied in this narrative is that only aristocrats and nuns wrote and that the fate of a middle-class girl would be Judith Shakespeare's, whose story the editors summarize to complete the introduction to the Renaissance section (p. 15).

Rogers' *Before Their Time* likewise presents the view that early women writers were "exceptions" who were "protected" by "high social rank" but who, as a result, confined their efforts to "academic plays and translations" rather than serious literary endeavours in their effort to uphold their positions as "lad[ies] and aristocrat[s]." In *The World Split Open*, Bernikow characterizes the "English Renaissance lady" as one who "lived quashed in a double bind." Aristocratic ladies, in order to be ladies, "had to be modest. . . . more poets have been lost to "virtue" than to death in childbirth or early starvation or disease in factories and mines."[18] Paradoxically, Bernikow illustrates this theory with an extended passage from Elizabeth Carew to show how "virtue" silenced Renaissance women writers, not discussing how Carew managed to escape being intimidated into silence. Bernikow concludes that "women knew quite well that if one woman signed her work . . . , she opened herself to moral and social abuse. To become anonymous was the only way to survive the social order, if one cared to survive" (p. 20).

More recently, Greer et al.'s *Kissing the Rod* is not so severe on its aristocratic women writers. It recognizes literary activity among aristocratic coteries, although as the editors point out in the introduction, "no one who was or aspired to be 'of the quality,' that is, unsullied by commerce or manual labour, could write too seriously or too well" (p. 4). In short, the overall view of Renaissance and seventeenth-century women's literature is that aristocratic rank enabled women to write, but also simultaneously thwarted possible serious literary endeavors and compromised quality.

The choice of the adjective "unsullied" in Greer's account of coterie verse is particularly interesting in light of the theory expressed by Bernikow and by Goreau in *The Whole Duty of a Woman*. Goreau's anthology depicts seventeenth-century women as strongly desiring to appear in print, but "modesty," which Goreau equates with "chastity," prevented them. This definition of modesty is a gender consideration that cuts across class lines. She cites Dorothy Osborne's seven-year-long epistolary correspondence and Katherine Philips's "illness" over the publication of her verses as examples of how women's fears for their sexual reputations could block their literary ambitions; "feminine modesty and making one's thoughts public" is in Goreau's reading clearly "irreconcilable" for the early woman writer (pp. 13–15).

Even the important study of early women's writing by Elaine Hobby, *Virtue of Necessity*, which demands that we question our relationship with the past and explore new genres and literary forms, uses the conventional vocabulary to depict the shrinking-violet female author. Even while making the crucial point that our view of writers such as Katherine Philips is distorted by an anachronistic dismissal of manuscript circulation as type of "publication," Hobby describes the typical early woman writer as one who "dared to go into print in her own name." Such intrepid women found "back door" methods "into the public world," and "to have a few songs or poems appear anonymously or under a pseudonym in a miscellany carried minimal risk to a woman's modest reputation."[19]

The other underlying assumption in many anthologies concerning coterie writing and the publication of editions either pirated or posthumous is that the women involved in these literary activities were essentially passive after penning the poems in question. The assumption seems to be that the women had to be either dead or "violated," as were Anne Bradstreet and Philips, in order to appear in print. In *Kissing the Rod*, the preservation of manuscript copies is seen as an act of fate rather than an authorial intention. "The survival of [Hester Wyat's] poem we owe to the fact that another of her friends thought it worth copying and keeping," the introduction asserts (p. 7). Interestingly, men are presented as the active agents; "a male relative might without prejudice publish the works of a gentlewoman under her own name after her death," and before she died, the coterie literary lady in this vision was "only too grateful when a properly educated male of [her] acquaintance agreed to correct [her] work" (p. 7). The female coterie or manuscript writer is too often presented as the docile victim of a patriarchal literary system.

Gilbert and Gubar's image of the frustrated middle-class female desiring a commercial platform, Greer's view of the dilettante aristocrat seeking male help and approval, and Bernikow's and Goreau's theory of the control of literary publication by social definitions of feminine "modesty" are undoubtedly correct as elements in women's literary lives in the past. But what these seemingly disparate theories of women's literary history do is erase coterie literature as a means of serious "public" expression entirely, whether it is the aristocratic daughters of William Cavendish or the middle-class circle of Constance Aston Fowler or Mary Barber. The lower classes are routinely assumed to have been completely illiterate, which has blocked any perception of writings by groups of women such as the early Quakers from being considered as part of the tradition. Such assumptions have effectively silenced a significant group of female voices from the sixteenth and seventeenth centuries.

The appearance of Greer's anthology does free one from the necessity of continually asserting to doubting readers the inaccuracy of Woolf's belief that women did not produce songs or sonnets in significant numbers before Behn. More than four hundred pages of selections from forty-five women writers testify that at least one of our basic assumptions about women's literary lives on which we have founded our "tradition" is incorrect.

However, even this audacious anthology opens, as we have seen, with the depiction of these early women writers as "isolated and vulnerable," words recalling Woolf's image of the silent Renaissance female and the solitary mad poetess. Even though mention is made of the different modes of production in the seventeenth century, that is, manuscript copy, this alternative literary practice is presented as "private." The editors have no hesitation in stating authorial intention for these early women writers: "Most of the poetry written by lonely women in the seventeenth century probably ended as Wyat expects hers to, in the fire, burned by their authors if not by the people they addressed" (p. 6).

This statement is obviously not true of the forty-five writers featured in the anthology, many of whose manuscripts were carefully preserved, in beautiful calligraphy, in bound volumes to ensure later readership. Such fair copies, whether in their own volumes, copied onto blank sheets in printed books, or kept in a single sheet form, I would argue, were produced with the aim of preservation and with an audience in mind. These are not rough or working drafts, but fair copies, sometimes done by the author, or her friends, but also done by professional scribes. Many exist in multiple copies, and most, certainly, are not single, unfinished drafts.

The mode of production and preservation of these scripts, I would argue, implies a readership. Moreover, during the Renaissance and seventeenth century, as Greer noted about the Restoration, circulating one's works in manuscript did not prevent one from having a "public" reputation as a poet, without a poem ever being published. Donne and Sidney again come to mind as examples of this phenomenon, but, as Elaine Hobby notes, Katherine Philips, too, knew that so many copies of her poems were in circulation that the fact that the pirated printed edition of her verse did not use her name on the title page would not hide her identity from the reading public (p. 129). One thinks, too, of Anne Bradstreet and Anne Killigrew as examples of women writers who established reputations as poets through manuscript circulation before their works were printed. As Greer pointed out, publication often followed fame during the Restoration.

Furthermore, if one examines the posthumous editions of women's works, such as those of Killigrew and Mary Monck, it becomes clear that seventeenth-century women did indeed participate in literary circles. The posthumous edition of Monck's *Marinda* indiscriminately includes poems written to her as part of verse exchanges as well as her own poems, revealing in its contents that Monck was part of a literary group that exchanged works, not an isolated individual writing never to be read. The same is true of the Quaker poet Mary Mollineux; the preface to the printed edition of her poems establishes that her work was circulated in manuscript among Quaker groups long before its publication. Although Killigrew, Monck, and Mollineux state they have no desire for worldly applause, neither do they object to others reading and criticizing their verses.

Such evidence as revealed in the prefaces of posthumous works encourages one to look for further activity of manuscript circles involving women. Katherine Philips's circle is the best known, but why do we believe that she was unique in this activity? The Tixall papers of the Aston family during the mid-seventeenth century offer yet another good example of the mechanics of women's involvement in group literary activities. None of the letters or poems was published during the group's lifetime, but Constance Aston Fowler was the controlling center of a literary group that included Lady Dorothy Shirley, Katherine Thimelby, and Gertrude Aston, in addition to Fowler's brother Herbert Aston and the Cavalier poet Sir Richard Fanshawe.

The gap between the twentieth century's assumptions of what constitutes writing for an audience in an age of print technology and authorship in the sixteenth and seventeenth centuries, still in the transition stage between modes of literary technology, is wide and is part of the confusion in the delineation of the tradition of women's writing. Likewise, our assumption that professionalism yields a higher quality of literature might seem to have grounds, given the scornful attitude generally held about professional writers ("the last profession that a liberal mind would choose," observed one weary eighteenth-century author). But it does not seem relevant if one's goal is to establish a "tradition" based on an accurate historical overview of women's literary activities and productions, and any canon formed on this basis must by necessity exclude the majority of early women writers.

It is clear from even a cursory examination of manuscript groups and multiple copies that women writers were not producing these pieces with the anticipation that no none would ever see or comment on them. It is also clear that they wanted control over their audience, but this does not mean they necessarily sought an uncritical readership. Women writers' manuscript circles included men as well as other women, professional writers and critics as well as brothers and in-laws. Pope admired the Countess of Winchilsea's poetry before it was printed, as well as that by Lady Mary Wortley Montagu before it was about him. Dryden knew Anne Killigrew's work and also Anne Wharton's in manuscript copy. Manuscript works in this period cannot be dismissed as being either private or unpolished with a readership of this caliber.

The objection that works produced in such a manner are in a sense co-opted by the patriarchal system and therefore an invalid part of a female tradition perpetuated in the anthologies is at once both a more complex and a simpler issue. It is simple in the sense that if "feminist" consists of a self-consciousness of oneself as a woman writer and a conscious concern with the condition and roles of women in society, the works written by women during the Renaissance and seventeenth century do exhibit a high level of concern over roles allotted to them as females in society and as authors within a certain social class. For example, Elizabeth Carew's *Mariam*, it has been persuasively argued, uses the very conventions of the "closet" drama to consider the nature of female power within the system; likewise, the female voice in Lady Mary Wroth's sonnet sequence is acutely conscious both of the literary convention in which she plays her part and of the part assigned to women in sonnet lore.[20] In addition, as I have argued elsewhere, manuscript circles and epistolary networks could act as a mechanism for women writers to enter into the male intellectual and literary institutions of the time. There is no indication that modern critics view Mary Astell's beliefs constrained or compromised because of her correspondence with John Norris, which resulted in publication. Nor is there any indication that Astell herself devalued her poetry sent in a handsome manuscript copy to Bishop Sancroft.[21] One does not sense that Elizabeth Burnet felt constraint against publishing her correspondence with Locke and Stillingfleet or her diary; one senses, instead, a complete lack of interest in commercial enterprise that Woolf believed validated authorship. It is not publishing but profit these women disdained.

One also finds in coterie networks a bonding together of like minds against an ideologically or a politically divided society. The pseudonyms in Philips's circle as well as in Aston's did not hide gender but created cohesion through a shared literary identity, a secret, closed community. Coterie literature could, as with the male Cavalier tradition, be used to confirm shared ideology. Here the criticism that such writing is not truly "feminine" but a co-opted form of imitation of male models could be advanced, for in the manuscript writings of Lady Elizabeth Brackley and Lady Jane Cavendish, for example, one does find a strong Royalist vein; however, side by side with their defense of king, church, and country is a satiric portrayal of courtship and wedding practices told from a decidedly female perspective.[22] Likewise, there is the example of the vicar's daughter, Marie Burghope, writing in 1699. In a poetic description of the Bridgewater family seat, Ashridge, surely an emblem of power and patriarchal patronage, she opens with a ringing polemic against men's attitudes toward women's education.[23] So, in a sense, these women are indeed writing within a social system, but it does not seem to have stopped them from engaging in independent literary pursuits or commenting directly on their perceptions of women's status within the system. Before their writings are dismissed, they need to be more closely examined, and, certainly, their sense of literary community needs to be represented in teaching anthologies.

A further difficulty in including manuscript literature in current anthology formats comes from our implicit belief that authorship is an individual act of creation which can be identified and documented. The nature of manuscript circulation, however, is a social one. The writer is part of a group, both in circulating her or his pieces and in receiving and transcribing the works of others. The emphasis placed by twentieth-century literary history on assigning unique authorship to pieces and defining literature as the product of a single creative mind is not a feature of earlier literary practice. Collaboration was common and pieces circulated unsigned. Manuscript circulation was a socially acceptable literary practice and, in short, is the opposite tradition from that of isolation, alienation, and competition.

What would be the effects of the inclusion of manuscript pieces in presenting the tradition of women's writings? First, it would break the chain of continuous commonality which we have believed linked women writers. It would require readers to perceive and accept differences as well as similarities in women's literary activities in the past and present. It would explode the notion that women writers before 1800 were isolated and unread. It would force us to rethink that vision of female authors as being traditionally at odds with their society and with themselves simply because of the activity of authorship itself, as opposed to having a polemic content in their writings.

Likewise, it would free our perceptions of women's literary activities in the past from the restrictive notion of genre which has caused so many Renaissance and seventeenth-century women writers to be marginalized. There are large numbers of women writers in the Renaissance and seventeenth century who wrote in forms that Woolf declared did not count — epistles, religious treatises, prayers, advice books, and prophetic writings — who had a clear expectation of an audience, although they did not expect or desire worldly profit for their writings. As with manuscript writing and coterie circles, we have carried over certain assumptions about genre and tradition into our creation of the canon.

Admittedly, some anthologies do include materials not normally found in traditional canonical texts except as secondary materials, such as letters and diary excerpts. But even though the anthologies of women's writings include such materials, it is interesting to see how they are presented. Letters and memoirs are seen as literary refuges for women, "entirely private forms of writing . . . dealing with what limited experience might come within the circumference of a lady's life."[24] "Voluminous letters" were available to early women writers "to relate their feelings and experience," states another anthology, but it insists that not until the mid-eighteenth century was "women's experience . . . enlarged, and they were encouraged to think their minds worth developing."[25] In short, even in anthologies devoted to women's writings, such materials retain their status as secondary literary documents.

In addition, the hierarchical value structure of the genres in the recent feminist anthologies resembles that found in traditional male canonical collections. Verse forms such as ballads, limericks, and "minor lyrics" tend to be grouped together in separate sections at the end of periods in texts such as *The Norton Anthology of English Literature.* In anthologies of womens' writings, these "minor" genres tend to be left out entirely. With the exception of one piece by Lady Griselle Baillie in *Kissing the Rod,* there are no examples of women writer's early experimentation with dialect verse and certainly no sense of there having been a tradition of female balladeers, such as typified by Isobel Pagan, Lady Anne Lindsay, and Caroline, Lady Nairne. Attention has been focused instead on literary forms leading to the "rise" of prose fiction in the eighteenth century, which, as discussed in the previous chapter, is seen as offering a new genre more suited to the female voice.

Essentially, then, the earlier periods of women's literary history have been caught between seemingly conflicting perceptions. On the one hand, there is the assumption that women were silenced, that they did not write. On the other, there is the assumption that because of the literary practices followed or the forms used, the writings that were produced were not a legitimate part of the "tradition" that "blossomed" in the golden age of the nineteenth-century female novelist. Instead, it is asserted, such pieces were merely "imitations" of masculine literary expressions and not a separate tradition.

Once again, a statistical analysis of bibliographical data on women's texts raises some interesting questions. Crawford found that of women's publications between 1600 and 1700, the categories of "fiction" and "literature" combined make up only 171 of the 822 editions produced. By far the largest number of editions by women were religious materials, with Quaker women producing double the number of texts of any other group. It cannot be argued that they were "closet" authors: as I discuss in a later chapter, Quaker women in particular were adept at changing styles and formats to fit different readerships. These women also had a strong sense of a "female tradition" of authorship of which they believed they were a part. Like the coterie manuscript writers, these seventeenth-century Quaker women also wrote collaboratively, a feature of women's literary production our tradition and anthologies have not yet encompassed or questioned in their presentations of past literary activity.

Having spent a good part of this chapter analyzing the effects of *A Room of One's Own* on current assumptions about women writers in the Renaissance and seventeenth century, I shall attempt at this point to formulate some generalizations about the status of the female canon by returning to Woolf's vision. While pondering the lack of books on the subject of women's lives in earlier times, Woolf muses, "It would be ambitious beyond my daring, I thought, looking about the shelves for books that were not there, to suggest to the students of those famous colleges that they should re-write history" (p. 47), suggesting, of course, just that. It is equally daring, perhaps, now to suggest that we must rethink, re-vision, the grounds on which we have so laboriously and with great pains established the tradition in English of women's writings.

Woolf had the courage to say frankly that her generation was ignorant, that books needed to be written and perceptions of the past revised. Although our knowledge has increased dramatically since she scanned the bookshelves, there is much we simply do not know about life in earlier times and much we do not know about what people wrote and why. We must therefore ask ourselves if the formation of a canon of women's literature is still premature. As Greer stated concerning women's writing in general, "The rehabilitation of women's literary history is a huge undertaking, for there are literally thousands of women writers whose life and work are . . . imperfectly understood."[26]

We also must ask ourselves whether the canon of women's literature, whenever it is constructed, should simply be a replica of the male tradition as defined by literary history. While much valuable work has been done to recover "lost" literary texts by women, much more remains to be done. More also remains to be done in terms of the questions we bring to the texts written by women and our sense of how genre is important in the analysis of a female literary tradition.

If in our anthologies we no longer impose modern literary hierarchies on women authors in the past, we open up the possibility of a new concept of women's literature. We open up for exploration a literary environment that apparently was collaborative, with open-ended texts created in an intimate community defined in part by shared values and in part by shared literary languages, whether that of pastoral pseudonyms or ecstatic prophecy. If we accept manuscript and coterie authorship and nontraditional literary forms as part of the female tradition, the canon of women's literature in the Renaissance and seventeenth century will no longer be silenced, but will speak with many voices.

Indeed, the multiplicity of the voices in the choir may raise the whole issue of the need to establish a traditional restricted "canon" at all. As Marilyn L. Williamson pointed out in writing about traditional canons, "Study of the canon, even for feminists, concentrates attention on women's failures."[27] The canon purposed by *NALW*, although hailed as ground breaking and affirming, is also constructed upon the notion of the early woman writer's silence or absence. Moreover, in its format, as Lillian S. Robinson pointed out, "from its subtitle on, *NALW* is presented as 'the' tradition of literature by Anglophone women, producing the implication of an unchallenged (indeed, unassailable) canon, parallel in many ways to the other canon, with which, indeed, it may overlap."[28]

The overlap exists and reveals further interesting assumptions about women's writing in the Renaissance and seventeenth century. The names one finds in these sections are also the ones most frequently cited by the orthodox critical establishment. Of the fifteen women included in the section given to the seventeenth and eighteen centuries in *NALW*, Jane Lead, Lady Mary Chudleigh, Mary Rowlandson, and Charlotte Smith are newcomers in anthologies, but few readers of seventeenth- and eighteenth-century literature would be surprised to see the names of Anne Bradstreet, Margaret Cavendish, Katherine Philips, Anne Killigrew, Aphra Behn, Anne Finch, Mary Astell, Lady Mary Wortley Montagu, and Mary Wollstonecraft. Bradstreet, Cavendish, Philips, Killigrew, Behn, Finch, Astell, Montagu, and Wollstonecraft can be read in mainstream anthologies, including The Norton; Broadbent's *Signet Classic Poets of the Seventeenth Century*; Tillotson, Fussell, and Waingrow's *Eighteenth-Century English Literature*; Witherspoon and Warnke's *Seventeenth-Century Prose and Poetry*; Meserole's *Seventeenth-Century American Poetry*; and even in the charming World's Classic *English Verse* series edited by W. Peacock.

In fact, these mainstream anthologies include numerous other female authors from the periods in addition to those used by *NALW*. In the mainstream anthologies, one can read Ann Collins, Lady

Katherine Dyer, Jane Barker, "Ephelia," Anne Wharton, Sarah Kemble Knight, Jane Elliot, Isobel Pagan, Anna Letitia Barbauld, Lady Anne Lindsay, Lady Nairne, and the most famous woman playwright of her generation, Joanna Baillie. The obvious question arises: How is it that these women appear in traditional anthologies but not in women's literary traditions?

It would appear, as we have seen, that certain female experiences are not considered as valuable in constructing a tradition as others. In the evolutionary narrative of women's literary history, structured on a "great woman" or "turning point" linear model, we have labeled winners and losers; one of the goals of the anthologies is to present the "best" examples of women's writing. The "best," of course, depends on the criteria of the compilers. For the majority of the anthologies discussed in this chapter, the best are texts that provide a mirror for us to see ourselves, that is, a view of the past as being very like the present. Under these conditions, we are encouraged to read the selections as autobiographical statements about the author's personal experiences as a woman, to evaluate her responses as if she were our contemporary.

In terms of the distribution of the content, the emphasis on nineteenth- and twentieth-century literature in *NALW* may simplify teaching the materials as well as document Woolf, but it has an impact on our perception of the past as a whole. As Barbara Herrnstein Smith noted of canons in general, "The repeated inclusion of a particular work in literary anthologies not only promotes the value of that work but goes some distance toward creating its value, as does also its repeated appearance on reading lists or its frequent citation or quotation by professors, scholars, and academic critics."[29] Value as embodied in literary canons, in Smith's view, demonstrates that "all value is radically contingent, being neither an inherent property of objects nor an arbitrary projection of subjects but, rather, the product of the dynamics of an economic system" (p. 15). In short, she concludes, "what are commonly taken to be the *signs* of literary value are, in effect, also its *springs*" (p. 34).

What are the "personal economics" governing the value of the texts included in the feminist canon as it is being formed? Are there elements in either the construction of the anthologies or in the materials presented which are mentioned so repeatedly that even though no theoretical position has been articulated, an underlying ideology can be understood? In the recent anthologies of women's writings there seem to be two related, yet seemingly contradictory, factors in operation. One is embodied in the format, or physical presentation, of the texts, and one in the selection of individual items by particular writers.

It seems paradoxical that texts that declare themselves to be in revolt against existing patriarchally constructed canons are so very similar to them in form and style. In addition to a duplication of authors, the orthodox canonical anthologies and the canon of women's literature as constructed by *NALW* follow almost identical formats, not only in presentation of individual authors, but also in the presentation of different genres. *NALW* is divided into the conventional literary periods — the Middle Ages, the Renaissance, modernist literature, contemporary literature — by century, but also by literary movement as defined by the orthodox academic institutions. The implication is that women's literary history thus fits within the existing literary framework. And given the selections, it does.

Within the sections, the emphasis is similar to that found in the conventional anthologies. As we have seen, space, and therefore value, is given mostly to nineteenth- and twentieth-century literature. The overall balance of materials is also heavily slanted toward particular genres. Although literature before 1800 commands only one hundred and sixty pages, three novels are included in their entirety — Jane Austen's *Love and Friendship*, Charlotte Brontë's *Jane Eyre*, and Kate Chopin's *The Awakening* — and occupy more than five hundred pages.

The other selections reflect a valuing of polemical essays on women's roles, short fiction, and the traditionally defined "high" poetic genres that fit within literary labels such as "modernist." Letters and diary materials also are included. In conventional canons, such materials are usually presented as secondary materials, texts useful in understanding key literary works, but not in themselves a significant form. In the specific case of women's anthologies, while such materials are given a larger proportion of space, the material is still usually presented not as "literature," but as examples of stifled literary ambition: Dorothy Wordsworth's journal selections are introduced with the observation that critics have viewed her sparse poetic production as "troublesome," but "perhaps, as Virginia Woolf was to speculate in *A Room of One's Own*, she turned her talents to prose because 'the poetry' is often 'denied outlet' in women" (pp. 195–96).

The construction of the canon of women's literature, therefore, owes much to the institution it sets out to redefine, sharing certain assumptions about literary genre, value, and the format of presentation. As we have seen, however, there is good evidence that the conventional categories do not accurately reflect the nature of the literary *activities* of women writing before 1800. The point that canons are a cultural creation in terms of the selection of items to be included is not a new one. What appears to have escaped general discussion is the extent to which the very categories within which canonical pieces are placed reflect a particular critical agenda. In the current canon, novels and short stories rank above diaries or prophetic discourse in terms of the "tradition" of women's writings, because prose is, to return to Woolf, the best venue for a woman's voice since women "have not had a dog's chance of writing poetry" (p. 112).

Characteristically, canons search for "the best," and one by-product of this search is the need to impose hierarchies, both in literary merit and literary form. In constructing a feminist canon of women's literature, however, do we wish to construct it using the indentical categories, hierarchies, and critical values that have determined the existing male canon, even though women were writing in very different genres, under very different historical circumstances?

The other key area in which the recent anthologies of women's literature share assumptions with the traditional canon is found in the criteria of excellence. Given the move toward the formation of a canon of women's literature at present, one finds an interesting unspoken competition. Often what is implied in the construction of the anthology is that male canonical figures and texts are the appropriate measure of excellence. We are constantly reminded that we are seeking "Shakespeare's" sister, after all, not Shadwell's. The implied attitude behind the phrase "Shakespeare's sister" is that there might be female equivalents, women "as good as" Shakespeare, Milton, or Donne. We seem to be trying to match individual authors; the presentation of early women writers constantly brings before us the questions, as good as Samuel Richardson? As good as Ben Jonson? As good as Congreve? The intent behind some of the collections seems to be a desire to be able to answer yes—yes, women wrote novels or lyrics or Restoration comedies as good as any written by male authors and thus these women deserve our study, too.

Is this type of question, however, the best one on which to found a tradition? How do we determine who are the "best" women writers to make up a tradition? The entries in NALW imply that the values used to construct the male canon that has graciously included women writers come into force—as we shall see in the next two chapters, Lady Mary Wortley Montagu, Anne Finch, and Katherine Philips have never been completely "lost" although they may have been thoroughly patronized. Enduring critical notice, therefore, even negative, seems to be one unacknowledged criterion of "value." Women writers such as these have, in Samuel Johnson's terms, pleased many and have pleased long, male and female reader alike.

Obviously, however, although the selection of authors included overlap, there seems to be a sharp difference in what anthology editors have found pleasing in women's writing. As discussed in the previous chapter, Woolf and modern critics such as Gilbert, Gubar, and Showalter define women's literary history as "evolutionary" in nature, moving from imitation of male forms with an internalization of patriarchal values, to protest against standards (the feminine phase), arriving finally at "self-discovery" (the feminist phase), in which the turning inward frees the individual from constantly de-fining one's self in opposition. This vision of the nature of women's literary history clearly underlies the selection and presentation of materials in *NALW*; it can also be felt in Rogers and Greer, although not with such a powerful theoretical framework explicitly stated.

This "economy," to return to Smith's terms, thus values protest. Anger, as discussed in the previous chapter, is defined as the char-acteristic mode of feminist writing—not to be angry indicates that the individual has been co-opted or assimilated into the values of the dominant culture. The materials in the existing anthologies certainly give evidence that there were many angry young (and not so young) women writers, but the earlier periods are depicted as lacking this elemental feminist ire. As we have seen, women writers of the Renaissance are depicted as "docile," not angry enough and therefore compromised.

Again the questions are raised: Is this emphasis on anger as the defining element of historical feminist writing really a re-vision of the literary past which will create that sense of literary community and tradition for women writers? By excluding those women not deemed sufficiently feminist, has one simply switched from one restrictive framework to another? These models, based on *exclusion*, do not seem best suited to this stage of feminist literary reconstructive history. Instead of opening doors, liberating voices, or offering a new vision of women in the past, they in one sense confirm the presentation of women writers as "not good enough" to be part of any canon by, as Williamson suggested, dwelling on failure.

What would be alternative structures, should indeed a canonical anthology be attempted? What could such a text do to ensure that implicit assumptions about what belongs in a tradition did not by accident lose either the author or the literary forms found in women's writings before 1700?

One solution would be to redirect the current emphasis on the individual as an isolated figure. Anthologies now present each woman in a discreet block of text as though she and her work were created and existed in a vacuum. Renaissance and seventeenth-century women's poetic literature was by and large a collaborative effort, sometimes between women, as in the case of the Aston-Thimelby circle, sometimes between men and women, as in the case of Katherine Philips. Women's polemical and prophetic writings were designed to address particular social circumstances; they, too, often form part of a dialogue with other printed texts rather than standing as a discreet document. Instead of organizing the material and thus focusing attention on the individual, perhaps one could organize the entries around the mode of production and the intended audience, approaches that would invite fresh questions about the past rather than silencing its answers.

The most important feature of any attempt to anthologize or canonize the writings of women in the Renaissance and seventeenth century, however, is that in the pursuit of continuity, we do not diminish or dismiss that which is disparate or diverse. The threads of continuity which literary historians have used so convincingly to bind together women writers of the nineteenth and twentieth centuries inadvertently may be strangling those women who lived and wrote in centuries when the technology and the ethos of authorship were significantly different than in later times.

The Tedious Chase

Writing Women's Literary History in the

Eighteenth and Nineteenth Centuries

That one would find any woman in that [free and unimpeded]
state of mind in the sixteenth century was obviously impossible.
One has only to think of the Elizabethan tombstones with all
those children kneeling with clasped hands; and their early
deaths; and to see their houses with their dark, cramped rooms, to
realise that no woman could have written poetry then. — Virginia
Woolf, *A Room of One's Own*

These volumes are perhaps the most solid compliment that can
possibly be paid to the Fair Sex. They are a standing proof that
great abilities are not confined to the men, and that genius often
glows with equal warmth, and perhaps with more delicacy, in the
breast of a female. — George Colman and Bonnell Thornton,
"Preface," *Poems by Eminent Ladies* (1755)

If one believes, as I do, that Virginia Woolf wrote her narrative of
women's history in good faith, our attention then must be drawn
to the materials available for her study, the bases of her assumptions,
and the narrative strategies behind the portrayal of female authorship
in a historical context. We have seen how Woolf's perceptions of
social history were affected by the historiography of her day — is the

same true with the literary reference sources available to this Edwardian critic? What presuppositions about gender, genre, and audience did eighteenth- and nineteenth-century editors and literary biographers bring to the materials? How have subsequent feminist literary historians treated these eighteenth- and nineteenth-century reference sources?

When Woolf's narrator in *A Room of One's Own* went to research her Cambridge lectures, she tells her audience she found no early women writers on the shelves and no mention of women's texts in the standard authorities. She thus assumed, as we see in the passage that opens this chapter, that there were no early women writers, and concentrated her energies on explaining their absence. As we have seen in the previous chapters, many recent scholars, following Woolf's example, have also assumed that there were few women writers of note prior to 1700; even as women writers during these earlier periods are recovered, however, they are assumed to be writing within the hostile environment imagined by Woolf. That is, even as we find more and more women's texts written during the sixteenth and seventeenth centuries, we continue to interpret them within the framework of Woolf's historical narrative. Thus, the study of early women's texts is encrusted with several layers of assumptions which must be dug through before their works can be re-visioned. The question we begin with is how Woolf and those who followed her came to perceive early women writers as silenced or without audience or influence. Part of the answer lies in the history of the reference works and critical accounts of women's writings and of the "feminine poetic" available to Woolf.

Traditionally, biographical dictionaries or encyclopedias have been basic sources for those in search of general knowledge about a subject area. As a form, they contain in addition to information the general and widely accepted views of their subjects — the content is likely to be aimed at a broad readership and not likely to be strikingly eccentric in perspective or on the cutting edge of critical reassessment. Like anthologies, they serve as introductions to the student and the lay reader alike, and it is likely that the shelves consulted by Woolf contained numerous volumes of this nature. The question is whether there were any studies specifically focused on women's literary lives and works and whether dictionaries and encyclopedias of literature in general included early women writers. Woolf's response quoted above suggests to us that such texts were not available and that general reference works did not give much space or attention to women's writing from the earlier periods.

We have, of course, no way of knowing for sure what reference books, if any, Woolf might have consulted while composing her talks for the students (surely the *Dictionary of National Biography*!). Unfortunately, what has also been lost to us, as it apparently was to Woolf, is an early tradition of anthologizing women's verse and recording women writers' works and lives. There has been no modern critical discussion of the contents of such volumes or of how the narrative presentation of these early women reveals information about the contemporary status of Renaissance and Restoration women writers.[1] Nor, obviously, has there been any discussion of changes in the selection and presentation of women's authorship contained in such texts, changes that might suggest explanations for the barren shelves found by Woolf. In this chapter, I focus on the early attempts in the eighteenth and nineteenth centuries to formulate a theory and present a narrative of women's literary history and to define the "female poetic" in these popular reference works, the literary encyclopedias, biographical dictionaries, and memoirs. What was the shaping ideology behind their formation and how has this material been transmitted and modified in subsequent readings of it? In the next chapter, I turn to an analysis of the specific pieces included in these early anthologies as they suggest shifts in the theory of a female tradition and in the definition of the female poetic.

Ours is certainly not the first century to be fascinated by questions concerning the relationship of gender and creativity. Nor are we the first to consider that there might be a distinct and different female tradition and female poetic. Although few individuals could rival the enthusiasm for women's writings shown by the Reverend F. J. Stainforth, whose collection of British and American women poets and dramatists required six days for Sotheby's to auction in 1867 and contained more than three thousand items, readers in general in the eighteenth and nineteenth centuries would have had access to a large body of writing by women and studies of women authors. Between 1675 and 1875, there were at least twenty-five biographical encyclopedias and anthologies specifically devoted to chronicling the lives and labors of literary Englishwomen. From the early accounts of "Women among the Moderns Eminent for Poetry" in Edward Phillips's *Theatrum Poetarum* (1675) to Jane Williams's *Lit-*

erary Women of England (1861) and Eric Robertson's *English Poetesses* (1883), curious readers could peruse the lives of female writers. Starting with *The Nine Muses* (1700) and Colman and Thornton's *Poems by Eminent Ladies* (1755 and 1780) up through Frederic Rowton's *Cyclopedia of Female Poets* (1848–74), they could ponder exactly what style, subject, or domestic circumstance were revealed as "feminine" in the selections of women's writing presented in these anthologies.

Establishing an ideology of the feminine is a key feature of all of these texts. The popular anthology and biographical encyclopedia reveal different information to the historian than the single author scholarly edition. Indeed, as we have seen with modern anthologies, this type of format is intended for the widest and most general audience. In this sense, the anthologies and biographical encyclopedias are good indications of the extent to which women writers of the Renaissance and seventeenth century were presented as part of the past literary landscape as well as how the general reader understood the concept of "female writing."

In addition to providing entertainment, a literary biographical dictionary or encyclopedia, like an anthology, functions not only to introduce the curious reader to the subject area but also to introduce what the compilers feel is critically significant. As we have seen in the previous chapter, beyond providing texts, anthologies and biographical collections also suggest the questions that we should ask, the critical framework in which the works are to be viewed. In these early accounts of women writers in particular, the compilers were extremely concerned with pointing out what was worthy of emulation.

The didactic function of these texts is an interesting factor when considering the extent to which such texts were intended for an eighteenth- and nineteenth-century female readership. Mary Hays's six-volume *Female Biography* (1803) has a specifically female audience in mind: Hays declared, "My pen has been taken up in the cause, and for the benefit of my own sex."[2] Because of this, the volume is composed differently than a traditional encyclopedia; women readers, Hays believed, "read not for dry information to load their memories with uninteresting facts, or to make a display of vain erudition," and she, as a woman writer, had "at heart the happiness of my sex, and their advancement in the grand scale of rational and social existence" (p. iv). Likewise, Mrs. Anne Elwood also designed her *Memoirs of the Literary Ladies of England* (1843) for "such of her own sex, who, not feeling themselves equal to profound and abstract subjects, can derive amusement and information from what is professionally too light for the learned, and too simple for the studious."[3] Despite such seemingly modest disclaimers, these nineteenth-century texts function as repositories not only for information about women writers' lives and productions, but also for the preservation of a female tradition and the creation of an ideology that shapes the definition of "feminine" during these periods.

The earliest reference guides to authorship during the seventeenth century focused on vast subject areas—Famous Authors from the Beginning of Time. During the Restoration, women poets found a place in such literary histories both by mingling with their male contemporaries and by occupying separate sections of these general literary works. In this format, the entries are usually quite short and quite laudatory. Edward Phillips contented himself in *Theatrum Poetarum, Or a Compleat Collection of the Poets, Especially the Most Eminent of All Ages* (1675) with a sentence or two giving the titles of the woman's writings and perhaps her ancestry. His list includes sixteen Englishwomen and eight Europeans; no distinction is made between literary form or social status, so that the entry on Anne Askew, the Protestant martyr, rests comfortably among those of Aphra Behn and the Countess of Pembroke. The praise is of a general nature and frequently indicates the source of the material or a reference to approval bestowed by another scholar on the woman's work: Elizabeth Weston, for example, is described as "an English Poetess of some repute in the esteem of *Farnabie*, who ranks her with Sir *Th. More, Alabaster, Drurie*, and other English writers of Latin Poetry."[4]

The practice of seventeenth- and early eighteenth-century editors such as Phillips of placing entries on women writers in separate sections than those of their male contemporaries suggests that women writers were already viewed as a group or a class of writers. At this stage in their historiography, however, the terms in which they were praised and criticized remain consistently within the general critical tenets of the time. Restoration critics do discuss poetry in terms of gender, but not in terms of there being a unified "Female" aesthetic of a different nature than the male one; it is not felt necessary to devise separate criteria with which to evaluate their writings. Nor is there a sense that the editors were interested in establishing or confirming a universal "Woman's" experience, as poets and mystics, translators and queens shared the pages together.

Perhaps against our expectations, Phillips does not overtly connect the women's private lives with their public writings, either in the matter of "modesty" or in defining a feminine voice. While Anne Askew is praised for her virtue and resolution in addition to her verse, Aphra Behn is not rebuked for being a commercial playwright, nor is it implied that her virtue is at question. Phillips does raise the issue of pseudonyms and anonymous verse in his preface, but he associates the practice with men. "Sorry I am," he admits, "I cannot pay a due respect to Mr. *Anonymus*, but he is the Author of so many Books that to make but a Catalogue of them would require a Volume sufficient of itself."

The critical distinction fascinating the compilers of these texts was not so much gender but the shift from the "uncouthness" of earlier English verse to "the smooth style of our present Language taken to be so much of late refined."[5] Giles Jacob, for example, felt that his volume would provide readers in the 1720s with the "Satisfaction of observing the Progress and Improvement of our English Poetry."[6] In terms of the writing of women's literary history, it is important to note that women writers were included in this larger scheme of the evolution of English verse as it moved from the crude to the refined, although at this point, gender was not specifically cited as a driving agent in this evolution.

In Dryden's letter to Elizabeth Thomas ("Corinna") in 1699 in which he responds to her sending him some of her poems, he lays out the critical distinctions in masculine and feminine writing as each was then defined. He calls her "Corinna" because of the quality of her verse; he explains the name refers to "not the Lady with whom Ovid was in Love, but the famous Theban Poetess, who overcame Pindar five Times."[7] He is distinguishing and complimenting her, therefore, not as the subject of great poetry, but as the author of verse that can successfully compete with the best of men's.

Her poems were, he wrote, "too good to be a woman's; some of my friends to whom I read them were also of the same opinion."[8] Restoration "women's writing" in Dryden's use, unlike the classical Corinna's, is characteristically different by being of poor quality verse. This inferiority, however, is not inherently tied to the sex. Dryden characterizes the feminine as a style, not necessarily a poetic: "They generally write with more softness than strength." Corinna, in contrast, lacks "neither vigour in [her] thought, nor force in [her] expression, nor harmony in [her] numbers," in which she compares favorably with Katherine Philips. These same terms of praise are, of course, also present in Dryden's eulogistic presentation of Anne Killigrew's poetry in his ode "To the Pious Memory of the Accomplished Young Lady Mrs. Anne Killigrew": "Her wit," declared Dryden, "was more than Man" and her verse displayed "Noble Vigour" (lines 70, 74).

Dryden's correspondence with Thomas also alerts us to the extent to which an author's gender was viewed as a factor determining the subject and style deemed appropriate. In another letter to Thomas, Dryden warns her of further pitfalls in female writing other than "softness" and lack of "vigour." He urges her to study "the best authors" to make herself "absolute Mistress of Poetry" but to avoid "the Licence which Mrs. Behn allowed herself, of writing loosely, and giving (if I may have leave to say so) some Scandal to the Modesty of her Sex."[9] It is not only females, however, who must be careful to observe decorum. In the same letter, he blames himself for having been "too much of a Libertine in most of my Poems," sounding a similar note to the complaint found in "To the Pious Memory of . . . Mrs. Anne Killegrew": This "barbaric and lubric age" has "Made prostitute and profligate the Muse, / Debased to each obscene and impious use, / Whose harmony was first ordained above / For tongues of angels, and for hymns of love!" (lines 58–61). Licence, at this point in Dryden's career, was not granted to either sex.

In the reference works and critical observations composed in the first half of the eighteenth century, one finds a position parallel to Dryden's: On the one hand, it is asserted that "women's writing" is recognizable by certain characteristics that make it less good than "masculine" verse; on the other, women are capable of competing successfully with male writers by writing in a "masculine" manner. In common with Cixous, critics and editors in the early eighteenth century believed that "to be signed with a woman's name doesn't necessarily make a piece of writing feminine . . . [and to be] signed with a man's name does not in itself exclude feminity."[10] Unlike Cixous, however, the eighteenth-century critics valorized the masculinity achieved by women writers. The vocabulary of critical praise is masculine. The literary standard of excellence so defined is attainable by either sex. For a woman writer, therefore, a type of androgyny was the literary goal—not to be perceived as a "woman writer," but simply as a "writer."

The editors of *Poems by Eminent Ladies* (1755) suggest this critical stance in the prefatory materials they include in the anthology. Mary Barber's poems are introduced by two letters, one from Jonathan Swift to the Earl of Orrery in 1733 and the other an extract of a letter from another poet in the volume, Mrs. Mary Jones, to the Honorable Miss Lovelace. Swift observes in recommending Barber's verses to Orrery that "they generally contain something new and useful, tending to the reproof of vice or folly. . . . She never writes on a subject with general unconnected topicks, but always with a scheme and method driving to some particular end."[11] In his estimation, Barber has "a true poetical genius, better cultivated than could well be expected, either from her sex, or the scene she hath acted in, as the wife of a citizen." He hastens to assure Orrery that her poetical activities in no way affected her usefulness to her husband "in the way of his business." In Swift's view, Barber's poetry is rational, didactic, and well organized and is not a reflection of her gender, social rank, or domestic activities. It is, in fact, entirely distinct from those factors governing her private life and as such praiseworthy.

Mrs. Jones repeats similar sentiments to Miss Lovelace. "I am always pleas'd with any attempts of this nature among my own sex," she writes, commenting on Barber's verse. She particularly likes Barber's poems: "[because] throughout the whole book, I don't remember to have met with an immodest expression; nor, what is more remarkable a word of that passion which has made so many female poets; I mean love" (1:7). Sounding much like Margaret Cavendish in "Epigraph to the Theme of Love" ("O love, how thou art tired out with rhyme! / Thou art a tree whereon all poets climb"), Jones, too, fears that love as the chief topic for women's verse leads to formulaic phrasing and cliched sentiment:

> Whenever I meet with a sister in print, I always expect to hear that *Corydon* has prov'd false; or that *Sylvia's* cruel parents have had the prudence enough to keep two mad people from playing the fool together, for life. (1:6)

"I've often wish'd, for the honour of our sex," she concludes tartly, "that these subjects had been exhausted seventeen hundred years

ago. . . . 'Tis pity that this passion alone should set us to rhyming."
In Jones's assessment of female literary history, the female poet's
fixation with the subject of the wrongs of love and the subsequent
restriction of the poet's scope is probably "one reason, why we so
seldom succeed in our poetical excursions."

Not all of Jones's contemporaries fell into the passion pit, and the
midcentury anthologists and encyclopedists found many to praise.
Like Dryden, Swift, and Jones, these editors and annotators use gender specific critical terms when evaluating verse. When Theophilus
Cibber comes to praise and blame women writers in *The Lives of
the Poets* (1753), he, too, uses a vocabulary of strength and vigor
and, like Phillips, is careful to include validation from other authorities. Citing Charles Gildon, Cibber defends Behn, for example,
on the grounds of her "great strength of mind and command of
thought."[12] Like the praise Dryden gives Corinna's poems, Behn's
works are described as ranking with any man's: In a comparison
with Durfey's productions, Cibber declares "there are marks of a
fine understanding in the most unfinished piece of Mrs. Behn, and
the very worst of this lady's compositions are preferable to Durfey's
best" (3:27).

In such accounts, the vocabulary of conventional praise presents
women writers of the Restoration and early eighteenth century as
rivals who could even outdo male authors.[13] The critical framework
in which their writings are presented invites the reader to consider
how well the writer transcended her social role and how well her
verse displayed male gender characteristics. Women writers could
"compete" with males by being more "masculine," by displaying
control over meter and rhyme, by being witty, and by having a strong
intellectual framework and content. Cowley's crowning praise for
Katherine Philips is to salute her "well-knit sense" and her "manly"
poetics, which compete successfully with the male poet's best efforts: "Ah! Cruel Sex, will you depose us too in Wit? / Orinda do's
in that too reign, / . . . / We our old Title plead in vain, / Man may
be Head, but Woman's now the Brain."[14]

In the Restoration and the first part of the eighteenth century,
the stress on "wit" and "sense" is a recurrent feature, not only in
the critique of male poets such as Shadwell in "MacFlecknoe," but
also in the presentation of women's writings. In the early days of
their relationship, for example, Alexander Pope found in Lady Mary
Wortley Montagu's portrait signs of the poet's "Heavenly Mind /

Where every grace with every Virtue's join'd / Learning not in vain, and wisdom not severe / With Greatness easy, and with wit sincere."[15] Giles Jacob likewise applauds Anne Wharton as "a Lady of excelling Wit and Sense."[16] "Philomusus" in his commendatory verse prefacing *The Nine Muses or Poems Written by Nine Several Ladies upon the Death of the Late Famous John Dryden* (1700) also chooses wit and sense as the aspects of their poems deserving praise: "In their Lines I feel that strength of Thought, / Which I could never reach tho' daily *sought*."[17] He, like Cowley, depicts the women as successful poetic rivals:

> Believe me, Friend, and think my Censure true,
> I feel the *Lover*, and the *Rival* too,
> Raptur'd with Joys which all my Soul possess,
> Yet could *almost* have wish'd the Pleasure less;
> . . . .
> Hence issues forth a most delightful Song,
> Fair as their *Sex*, and as their *Judgment* strong,
> Moving its *Force*, and tempting its *Ease*,
> Secur'd of Fame, unknowing to *displease*,
> In ev'ry word like *Aganippe* clear,
> And *close* its meaning, and its Sence *severe*,
> As virtuous *Thoughts* with chast *Expressions* join,
> And make 'em truly, what They feign, *divine*.

Sincerity is not the point of interest here. Whether or not the verses justified Philomusus's enthusiastic praise, or whether he is merely being unctuous, it is interesting to note what he and other commentators single out as praiseworthy in women's verse: What emerges is that the vocabulary of conventional plaudits applied to women's verse establishes a consistent pattern of praise for the traditionally "masculine" traits of strength, force, sense, and judgment.

Restoration and early eighteenth-century women writers joined in this chorus of praise which focuses on the intellect rather than the emotions. As we have seen, Mary Jones was a severe critic of female poetry. In her "Epistle to Lady Bower" she likewise observes, "How much paper's spoil'd! what floods of ink! / And yet how few, how very few can think! / The knack of writing is an easy trade; / But to think well requires — at least a head."[18] Elizabeth Carter praises Elizabeth Singer Rowe's "happy elegance of thought"; her poetry is "refin'd by virtue" and her "pow'rful strains . . . wake the nobler passions of the soul."[19] It is Aphra Behn's "strenuous Polite Lines" that first attracted "Ephelia," who also notes that Behn's verse contains that which "might be Envy'd by the wittiest Men."[20] Behn's poetry is successful in her analysis because of its "rare connexion of Strong and Sweet."

Behn's verse likewise drew for her the title "sole Empress of the Land of wit" from another of her anonymous female admirers. In this 1688 poem, the terms and the range of the praise bestowed involve almost all the critical elements found in discussions of women's verse in the first half of the eighteenth century. Poetry is depicted as an arena, where Behn has won the field: Behn is the poet

> To whom all conquer'd Authors must submit,
> And at thy feet their fading Laurels lay,
>
> . . . .
>
> The subject was Divine we all confess,
> Nor was that flame, thy mighty fancy less.
> That cloath'd thy thought in such a pleasing dress,
> As did at once a Masculine wit express,
> And all the softness of a Femal[sic] tenderness.
> No more shall men their fancy'd Empire hold,
> Since thou Astrea form'd of finer mould,
> By nature temper'd more with humid cold,
> Doth man excel —
> Not in soft strokes alone, but even in the bold.[21]

While we may find the tone excessive in such passages, our assumption that early women writers were unread and uninfluential in their contemporary literary environments is not supported by the terms of praise given to women such as Philips, Rowe, and Behn.

Philips's female admirers invoke her as their muse frequently. "Philo-Philippa" calls her "Thou Glory of our Sex, Envy of Men. / Who are both pleas'd and vex'd with thy bright Pen."[22] Philips's poetry forces the issues of gender and creativity for her eighteenth-century readers: In Philo-Philippa's view, "If Souls no Sexes have, as 'tis confes'd, / 'Tis not the He or She makes Poems best." Instead, true verse, like Behn's, is a uniting of the feminine with "Sense Vigorous and Masculine."

The Restoration dramatist who became a pious polemicist and John Locke's advocate, Catherine Trotter Cockburn, served as a similar type of inspirational muse to her female contemporaries. She,

---

too, uses familiar critical criteria in her advice to aspiring writers of both sexes in "Calliope's Directions How to Deserve and Distinguish the Muses Inspiration." In addition to stressing solid judgment, Cockburn insists: "Let none presume the hallow'd way to tread, / By other than the noblest motives led." For Cockburn, commercialism is corrupting:

> If for a sordid gain, or glitt'ring fame,
> To please, without instructing, be your aim,
> To lower means your groveling thoughts confine,
> Unworthy of an art that's all divine.[23]

The young writer must strive to avoid "uncouth thought," "glaring tinsel-shew," and "pompous empty sound." In their discussions of other women writers, female commentators, like their male contemporaries, insist on reason over sentiment, "sense" over sound.

Katherine Philips is the most frequently cited during the Restoration by both sexes as the exemplary androgynous author, combining as she does the gender characteristics found in the writings of both sexes. In his poem on Philips's death, Cowley repeatedly refers to the power of her "wit" which brought her to such poetic success. She stands alone, in Cowley's estimation, on the "Female coasts of Fame":

> Of Female Poets, who had Names of old,
> Nothing is shown, but only Told,
> And all we hear of them perhaps may be
> Male-Flatt'ry only, and Male-Poetry.
>
> . . . .
>
> The certain proofs of our *Orinda's* Wit,
> In her own lasting Characters are writ,
> And they will long my praise of them survive.[24]

Her verses, Cowley maintains, are excellent because they transcend the limitations of gender. In "On Orinda's Poems," Cowley declares,

> 'Tis solid and 'tis manly all,
> Or rather 'tis angelical
> For as in angels we
> Do in thy Verses see
> Both improv'd Sexes eminently meet;
> They are than Man more strong, and more than Woman sweet.[25]

Like that of Philomusus and Cockburn, such praise raises androgyny, or the combining of both sexes' characteristics, to the level of the divine or the angelic. Women poets could expect praise from critics of either sex for their wit, their "vigour," and their originality, but not for "softness" or sentiment unless it was allied with the masculine traits.

The references to women writers in the Restoration and early eighteenth-century biographical dictionaries are only one indication of the interest in female authorship. The entries for men and women in books such as Giles Jacob's *Poetical Register* (1719) and *An Historical Account of the Lives and Writings of Our Most Considerable English Poets* (1720) are intended more as a Who's Who than an analysis of style. However, as we have seen, Cibber, Colman, and Thornton point the way toward a discussion of the connections between gender and poetic genius and between a woman's life and her art within the larger scheme of the evolution of English poetry.

The most developed and subsequently influential presentation of early women writers is the eighteenth-century antiquarian George Ballard's *Memoirs of Several Ladies of Great Britain: who have been celebrated for their writings or skill in the learned languages, arts and sciences* (1752). In this text, which offers more fully researched and developed biographies of women intellectuals and writers, one sees the start of a shift in emphasis in the presentation of learned women. The depiction of women's writing as possessing masculine wit and sense and of poetry and drama as competitive arenas which characterizes the criticism of the early part of the century is shadowed into a more subtle and complex statement of what women writers can do and what they should do.

Students of women's literature owe an enormous debt to Ballard. Ballard is the key source for information about women writers in the Renaissance and seventeenth century for almost all subsequent biographical dictionaries including women writers, from *Biographium Faemineum* published in 1766 to the *DNB*. He is also a standard reference for biographical notices in anthologies of women writers beginning in the eighteenth century and continuing to *NALW*; he continues to be frequently cited in recent critical biographies of Mary Astell and Margaret Cavendish. In short, this one document has had enormous and diverse impact on several areas of women's studies; as Perry referred to it, this "landmark in the history of feminism" has served generations of feminist scholars as a guide for our voyage through the past.[26]

What is interesting from the point of view of this chapter is the use of Ballard's biographical materials by others in constructing an image of the female author and a literary history. We do not know if Woolf consulted Ballard, but it is abundantly clear that he is a privileged source for many subsequent studies. The authority granted to Ballard's work by eighteenth- and nineteenth-century anthologists and by twentieth-century scholars reflects, I believe, the belief that Ballard was an objective antiquarian, rather than a subjective historian or didactic biographer.

That Ballard was considered by his contemporaries an antiquarian there is no doubt. Long before he contemplated compiling data on the lives of British women distinguished for their learning, Ballard and his sister Elizabeth were mentioned in antiquarian circles as the collectors of rare Roman coins. Ballard knew Richard Graves, Thomas Hearne, Joseph Ames, and most of the other leading antiquarians of his time and, as Perry pointed out, used them for more than fifteen years to gather information to put into his volume. But unlike these men, Ballard was interested in collecting lives as well as artifacts of past cultures; I differ from Perry and other modern users of his text in seeing in the *Memoirs* not an antiquarian catalog but a highly rhetorical narrative of feminine accomplishment.

Recognizing the difference between Ballard's antiquarian activities and his production of the *Memoirs* seems to me to be important given the text's reception history, where Ballard's data is transmitted, often word for word, through several generations. Examining the entries on selected authors across the two centuries since its publication provides an insight into the ways in which Ballard's reputation as an antiquarian has affected the reading of his text and the ways in which this eighteenth-century biographer's views on educated women and literary ladies have been disseminated.

In her biography of Mary Astell, for example, Ruth Perry informs us that "according to tradition," Astell's uncle, a clergyman, was responsible for her early education.[27] A glimpse at Ballard's entry and those in subsequent biographical dictionaries reveals how such traditions are formed. Ballard states that "her excellent natural parts and great propensity to learning being observed by an uncle who was a clergyman, he generously undertook to be her preceptor."[28] In 1766,

Biographium Faemineum records that "her uncle, a clergyman, observing her excellent natural parts, and inclination to learning, generously undertook to be her preceptor."[29] Mary Hays's *Female Biography* (1803) informs us that "the proofs of acuteness and capacity, which she displayed in the early periods of youth, attracted the attention of her uncle, a clergyman, who requested her parents to commit their daughter to his charge, and allow him to become her preceptor."[30] By 1804, Matilda Betham's *Biographical Dictionary of Celebrated Women of Every Age and Country* simply opens with the announcement that "an uncle of the lady, who was a clergyman, having observed in her proofs of a superior capacity, generously undertook to be her preceptor."[31] Ballard's influence extended even to the American biographical accounts: Sarah Hale records in her concise *Woman's Record* (1854) that "her uncle, a clergyman, observing her uncommon genius, took her under his tuition."[32] It surely comes as no surprise to read Astell's *DNB* entry, which states, "Her uncle, a clergyman, observing her excellent abilities, undertook to educate her himself."[33]

Of the works cited, only Mary Hays and the *DNB* list Ballard as a source for information on Astell. We have in this small sampling an example of the way in which Ballard's entries have been used by subsequent scholars of women's lives: It is as though Astell's "early genius" had entered the realm of historical artifact along with the fact that her uncle was a clergyman, who obviously must have favored educating women.

I believe that Ballard's designation as an antiquarian rather than a biographer has permitted his work to be used in this word-for-word fashion without much comment. In the eighteenth century, "antiquarian" was a mildly derogative label. There is attached to the label the notion of the indiscriminate collector of physical artifacts, whether they be coins or copies of monumental inscriptions: Horace Walpole admits, "We antiquaries . . . hold everything worth preserving, merely because it has been preserved."[34] Furthermore, there is the implication that the collector is solely concerned with the physical gathering of artifacts and is incapable of seeing the larger significance of the items he or she catalogs. Johnson's *Dictionary* cites Pope in its definition, who suggests that in their zeal for accumulation, "with sharpen'd sight pale *antiquarians* pore, / The inscription value, but the rust adore."

In contrast, we have in the eighteenth century a celebration of the skills of the historian and the biographer, also students of the past; but instead of indiscriminately collecting it, they provide an interpretive and didactic framework for the improvement of their readers. History, in Johnson's *Dictionary*, is not a catalog or chronology but "a narration of events and facts delivered with dignity." In his famous *Rambler* essay #60, published two years before Ballard's *Memoirs*, Johnson applauds biography as the literary form most capable of "widely diffus[ing] instruction to every diversity of condition," and the type of biographer he criticizes is the one who only offers "a chronological series of actions or preferments" rather than a didactic narrative.

In short, the eighteenth century tended to rank antiquarianism a notch below the writing of history and, later, the writing of biographies. Antiquarian writers in this view merely collected facts, whether artifacts or dates. The inability or unwillingness to create a coherent, discriminating narrative structure on the past based on these facts was viewed by those such as Johnson as a limitation of the antiquarian pursuit.

Ironically, it is this very refusal to attempt to create a coherent pattern which has so recommended itself to modern readers of Ballard and made *Memoirs* a privileged text in the study of early women writers. Ballard's text has been mined as a repository of facts about women by biographers and anthologists of women writers throughout the last two centuries. Perry's introduction to it explicitly links Ballard's antiquarianism with the importance of the *Memoirs* to feminist scholars. "Despite his odd and innovative subject, Ballard writes like an antiquarian," Perry asserts.

> He is first and foremost a collector and does not show much interest in the charms of exegesis or analysis. He obviously felt he was a compiler, not an interpreter. . . . Ballard discovered, edited, and published original documents . . . he did not write sensitive and compelling interpretations.[35]

Given the current perspective of historical narratives as embodying ideology as well as data, Ballard's supposedly antiquarian text appears to Perry as "a unique repository of information," offered to us without "interpretation or analysis" (pp. 13, 28). Perry further consolidates this validation of Ballard's contents with her comments on Ballard's style, or lack of it; in her assessment, his character is that of the earnest and dedicated amateur, not the inspired interpreter or the mercenary hack writer. "Ballard monotonously and methodically detailed all the information he had been able to gather . . . clearly intend[ing] his memoirs to be informative rather than panegyric" (p. 28); in another study, she characterizes his biographies as "not so much stories as little collections of reprinted documents, data set out in one place, undigested and uninterpreted."[36]

While I do not question the value of this document, Ballard's commitment to the education of women, or the contribution of the editor in making it easily available for modern scholars, I do quail at the prospect of accepting the work as it has been up to this time — as a document that somehow escapes its historical context, one that is arhetorical and thus nonideological in its presentation of the past, a "repository" of pure fact. I wish to suggest the possibility that we have been confusing the nature of the content with the persona of the narrator; Ballard does indeed present himself and his activities as purely antiquarian, but the actual structuring and content of the text is a didactic narrative defining female excellence in specifically eighteenth-century terms. If we fail to note the effects of the rhetorical strategies and the ideology underlying the shaping of the narrative involved in Ballard's stated goal of preserving "from oblivion the memory of illustrious persons" and setting "their great excellencies and attainments in a true and proper light," we risk infusing our own attempts to reconstruct the past with Ballard's eighteenth-century didactic view of history and of women.

That Ballard would have been aware of the need to construct a persona of the detached man of fact while simultaneously seeing the need for the persuasive graces of rhetoric to implement the higher didactic goals of the biographer is clear from his unpublished correspondence. His friends such as Sarah Chapone (the mother-in-law of the bluestocking Hester Chapone) warn him of the scholarly community's disdain for his subject. She writes of her brother's visit to Oxford where "he heard a whole room full of [men] deny that a thing was or could be written by a woman."[37] Likewise, Elizabeth Elstob, the noted linguist who herself had cause to complain of neglect, wrote Ballard in early 1752 commiserating with him over the difficulty in getting subscribers:

> this is not an Age to hope for any encouragement to Learning of any kind. For your part I am sorry to tell you the choice you have made for the Honour of the Females was the wrongest subject you could pitch upon. For you can come into no company of Ladies or Gentlemen wher[e]

you shall not hear an open and Vehement exclamation against Learned Women.[38]

Beyond worries about subject matter, his friends also urged caution in the style of presentation. As early as 1744, parts of Ballard's book were being circulated in manuscript for comment and correction. Chapone conveyed Dr. Delany's approval of the scheme, but added that Delany urged Ballard to "apply to some ingenious friend to look over the whole, with a particular eye, to all peculiarity of expression, which are never so perceptible to an author, as to his readers."[39] The difficulties Ballard faced in finding subscribers, the repeated gloomy warnings of his correspondents, the stylistic suggestions that were offered, must all have combined to impress on Ballard the need to present his materials in such a way as to generate support and approval for his topic in a social environment openly skeptical of its significance.

Ballard's narrative persona is intrusive; he frequently interrupts the accounts of the women's lives to refer to himself and to his efforts in tracing materials. He is both self-effacing and defiant in his preface: He presents himself as the modest amateur, one "truly sensible of his incapacity to do justice to the merits of the past times, or to afford entertainment for the present" (p. 54); he concludes defiantly, however, by recognizing his critics and asserting that he expects this work to gain him no "character in the learned world; nor indeed is he solicitous about it" (p. 55).

His use of the first person in the lives generally acts as a disclaimer, further consolidating our impression of him as a disinterested, if bumbling, antiquarian. Of Elizabeth Dancy, Sir Thomas More's daughter, Ballard states that while More's biographers mention her scholarly attainments, "what she wrote or when she did I could never learn"; he also confesses that he is "at a loss . . . to ascribe" which of More's daughters authored a certain translation (p. 162). Likewise, who would not be disarmed by Ballard's candid opening to the life of Catherine Tishem: "I am entirely ignorant in relation to the birth, parentage, and time this learned gentlewoman died, and therefore don't know where to put her more properly than in this place" (p. 60). This practice of acknowledging antiquarian defeat at the hands of history has the obvious effect of boosting the reader's confidence in the accuracy of the materials Ballard does choose to present.

This persona of the antiquarian as the detached transmitter of verified relics of the past is clearly demonstrated in Ballard's treatment of Elizabeth, Countess of Bridgewater. Ballard opens with a lengthy explanation of her presence in this volume of learned ladies:

> Elizabeth, Countess of Bridgewater, has such an extraordinary character given of her in her monumental inscription that being come to that period of time in which she lived, I am unwilling to pass her over in silence. I have searched very carefully, though ineffectually, for some concurrent testimonies of her merit. But as I cannot add anything to the account given in her epitaph, so neither will it be thought much wanting in the opinion of those who are so candid as to suppose that inscription to have been drawn up with a view of doing justice rather than of honour to her memory. I shall therefore transcribe it as I find it printed in Sir Henry Chauncey's *History and Antiquities of Hertfordshire* and Mr. Collin's *Peerage*. (p. 266)

Ballard then proceeds to do just that, quoting the inscription's praise of her "winning and attractive behaviour," her "charming discourse," "her meek and humble disposition," her charity, and her "exemplary" devotion. He finishes the account by quoting her husband's epitaph.

Superficially, what could be more antiseptic than this treatment of historical fact? Ballard merely monotonously conveys word for word the contents of two inscriptions, graven in stone, and cited by two other authorities. He acknowledges his limitations and salutes the superior skills of the more established antiquarians.

However, what Ballard has decided, independently of these authorities, is to include the countess as part of what he repeatedly refers to as the "design" or "scheme" of his volume. The most powerful of all the strategies that Ballard employs in his drive to establish credibility for himself and his subject is not in the style of presentation, but in his principles of selection, which in turn effectively create a narrative of female experience. Unlike an antiquarian catalog that has a subject area but no shaping thesis, there is clearly a controlling design for this volume, a methodology behind its presentation, and a set of criteria for inclusion.

Although we have adopted his text as antiquarian, Ballard's stated purpose in the preface is closer to Johnson's description of the biographer. He avows as his goal to preserve "from oblivion the memory of illustrious persons . . . to set their great excellencies and attainments in a true and proper light, to inform us of those particulars in their lives and manners which best deserve our imitation, and to transmit to posterity even those peculiarities also, which afford us no inconsiderable entertainment" (p. 53). From his preface and the full title, one glimpses the skeleton of Ballard's design. First, only women "celebrated" for certain skills will be included—Ballard is not interested in unearthing unknown female authors and his presentation is characterized by its scrupulous documentation of references to his subjects in established scholars' works. This not only reinforces his persona as the disinterested speaker, but also ratifies the claim of these women to serious scholarly attention.

A closer look at these sources also suggests another principle of selection. Ballard relies heavily on standard church histories and biographies such as Bishop Tanner's *Bibliotheca,* Fox's *Acts and Monuments of the Church,* Strype's *Memorials Ecclesiastical,* Fuller's *Church History,* Bishop Burnet's *History of the Reformation,* and Wood's *Athena Oxoniensis.* All of these texts are concerned with larger issues than women's literary activities; where women are mentioned, it is usually in relationship to their male kinfolk's accomplishments or as exempla of Christian virtues. Even though Ballard's manuscript notes indicate his familiarity with Thomas Heywood's truly encyclopedic *Generall History of Women* (1657), where women poets share the pages with "women every way learned," including sibyls, prophetesses, witches, and "chaste women and wanton," Ballard does not draw on him as a source or a model.[40] There were certain celebrated ladies Ballard had no interest in chronicling.

There are no commercial female playwrights: Aphra Behn, Mary Pix, and Susannah Centlivre are within the time frame followed by Ballard, but noticeable by their absence. In addition, professional women writers such as Hannah Woolly, the popular author of domestic treatises, do not fit in his scheme. Ballard does not include any Quaker women, the most prolific publishers during the seventeenth century, which leaves the memories of Margaret Fell, "the Mother of Quakerism," and Anne, Viscountess Conway, the correspondent of the Cambridge Platonists, to perish in oblivion. While he does include the eccentric Lady Eleanor Davies, Ballard omits other equally prolific and influential women prophets such as Jane Lead, who founded the English Philadelphian society and published sixteen books. Finally, Ballard is also content to abandon to the void women writers such as Delarivier Manley, author of scandalous fiction, and Elizabeth Thomas, Dryden's Corinna, who ended up in prison.

None of these women were obscure figures during Ballard's lifetime. All had their lives documented in sources cited by Ballard, or had collections of their works published during the time Ballard was compiling his volume. They were the friends of leading religious figures of the day and the *amorosa* of leading literary lights, women whose names sparked public recognition. Perry notes the surprising homogeneous nature of Ballard's ladies; I believe it was achieved deliberately through Ballard's careful criteria of selection, which produced an ideal of the learned lady, a vision that, unlike Woolf's, excludes popular or commercial authorship and which is fundamentally based on the moral character of the subject rather than literary, scientific, or artistic merit.

This can be seen in his decision to include certain women as well as to omit others. In writing of Catherine Bovey, Ballard admits, "Notwithstanding that I am not positively assured that this worthy gentlewoman was either a linguist or writer, yet I cannot by any means think she ought to be omitted in these memoirs." Her character bares a striking resemblance to that of the Countess of Bridgewater mentioned before:

> Her extraordinary merit, her exemplary life, and the noble use she made of an ample fortune demand for her an honourable place among female worthies; her great genius and good judgment improved by the reading of the finest authors, and the wit and elegance of her own conversation, which has been so much admired and celebrated by the best judges justly entitles her to a character among the learned. And if she was not a writer, we at least wish that she had been so. (p. 377)

Perry does acknowledge that if "there is any narrative tendency" in Ballard, it is toward what she describes as the repetition of "idealized suffering" producing the "intellectual woman indomitable but without power, yet ultimately transcendent because of her superior knowledge."[41] I wish to expand Perry's qualified observation to suggest that Ballard, in true Johnsonian fashion, has carefully constructed a didactic model of the learned lady through his selection and presentation of these women's lives which we have absorbed in our perception of the past.

The significance of recognizing Ballard's biographical urges behind his antiquarian methodology is acute given the extent of Ballard's influence in shaping our view of women's activities in the past. Although we may have used Ballard as though his narrative were without art, the women Ballard chose to include, such as the countess, Bovey, and Elizabeth Walker, who "distinguished herself eminently through . . . her life in a most amiable and cheerful exercise of every Christian virtue," serve as perfect role models of feminine accomplishment that is within socially acceptable bounds.

The model suggests that authorship and education are upper- and middle-class activities, designed for the benefit of the writer and her immediate circle, not for a popular or commercial audience, and that, in fact, virtue and modesty are as important as literary success for women. These women's reputations are based on witty conversation supported by the reading of the finest authors; while they are universally loved for their virtues, they never transgress the bounds of propriety. They are modest and humble, preserving their virtue even in licentious ages. Given this concept of feminine accomplishments, it is easy to see why Anne Killigrew, the "young probationer, / And candidate for heaven," in Dryden's ode, has a place, while the much more prolific and popular Susannah Centlivre, whose comedies seemed to eighteenth-century critics to "encourage adultery, to ridicule the clergy and to set women above the arbitrary power of their husbands [and] to exert [women's] rights for the preservation of their lusts," does not merit preservation from oblivion.[42] Those who actively pursue fame or fortune through their talents are silently erased in Ballard's scheme.

Perhaps most striking, when one considers Ballard's entries as composing a didactic narrative of feminine accomplishment, is the close similarity between Ballard's role model of the patient, suffering literary lady and one of the eighteenth century's greatest literary creations — Clarissa. Sarah Chapone wrote to Ballard in 1750 that she could put him in touch with the author of *Clarissa*, noting that "a work of such great merit could not escape your notice."[43] Samuel Richardson ended up subscribing to the volume and offered to "assist Mr. Ballard in the choice of a Book-seller, Paper, etc." Clarissa, characterized by her deep piety, her daily exercise of Christian virtues, notably charity, her well-informed mind, and her charming conversation, leads me to say with Ballard that if she was not one of Ballard's celebrated ladies, we wish she could have been, so perfectly does she exemplify his model.

By unconsciously permitting our perceptions of the past to be shaped by a privileged text such as Ballard's, we have unwittingly infused the values and standards of it in our literary histories, an act that may have contributed to the silencing and marginalization of early women writers' voices. Ballard was indeed pro-female in his writings; he does indeed write eloquently in their defense and for the improved education of women—but only that they may fulfill certain social roles, ones agreeable to his skeptical eighteenth-century readers. His ideal woman in this volume—modest, middle-class, well-read, pious, and charitable—does not challenge her society in any direct way except to urge further educational activities. Women who do not fit this pattern are permitted to slip into oblivion.

The recognition that, while Ballard the man was an important antiquarian and source of information on women's lives, *Memoirs* has a rhetorical stance and a didactic purpose which converts the text from a simple repository of facts into a tribute to ideal womanhood. We may find this less helpful as we attempt to see how women lived their lives in earlier times, how and what they wrote, but one does at least have the satisfaction of knowing that Samuel Johnson would have heartily approved of Ballard's design to diffuse the example of the virtuous learned lady by showing her in her true and proper eighteenth-century light. Certainly the generations of biographers who followed him have accepted Ballard's didactic presentation of the past as an accurate antiquarian compilation of women's accomplishments in general.

Ballard's enormously influential text displays a different attitude toward women's writing than that found in critical presentations written during the Restoration. While earlier critics and commentators on women's writing essentially adopted an androgynous set of criteria, placing men and women in the same poetic "arena," Ballard presents women writers in a separate category and defined them by their differences from men—he sought his image of the feminine. Unfortunately for the fate of some women writers, his definition of the feminine—and that of many who used him as a primary source—emphasized the domestic, the melancholic, and the impulse for self-sacrifice over the public, the witty, or the defiant (not to mention the erotic) in women's writings. In providing one of the initial models of a separate sphere of women's writing, Ballard in a sense valorizes his subjects: He believes that women writers are worthy of study in their own terms, within their own tradition.

But, in that his definition of the feminine was highly restrictive, he also set the example of marginalizing or even erasing women writers who did not fit within his criteria.

Later commentators sympathized with this image of the female author and shared Ballard's didactic goals in their presentations. As Jane Williams, the author of *The Literary Women of England* (1861), declared, "In all biographies, the main things to be considered, both by the writers and readers, are, the training-ground of character, the arena of life's struggle, and subsequent results."[44] By the nineteenth century, as this quote suggests, the arena had changed from literature to character, and, following Ballard's lead, a very different picture of female authorship was presented from that found in the early eighteenth century.

Theophilus Cibber relies heavily on Ballard in his five-volume *Lives of the Poets of Great Britain and Ireland, to the Time of Dean Swift* (1753). His portrait of Margaret Cavendish, for example, is strongly derivative, stressing as does Ballard's account Cavendish's virtues as a wife, "a most agreeable companion to the marquis, during the gloomy period of exile, [who] enlivened their recess, both by her writing and conversation, as appears by the many compliments and addresses he made her on that occasion."[45]

Cibber is more interesting in his presentation of several women playwrights that Ballard does not include. As befits the son of the notorious apologist Colley Cibber, Theophilus tends to be sympathetic in his portrayal of them and defends them from charges of immodesty wherever possible. "The authors of the Biographia Britanica say that [Behn's] poetry is none of the best, and that her comedies, tho' not without humour, are full of the most indecent scenes and expressions."[46] He refutes the charges against her verse, as we have seen, on the grounds of its lively wit and solid understanding. The charges of "indecency" in her plays, he admits, are harder to disprove, but he offers as a defense, "Let those who are ready to blame her, consider, that her's was a sad alternative to write or starve; the taste of the times was corrupt; and it is a true observation, that they who live to please, must please to live" (3:26).

This condemnation of the Restoration period rather than the woman extends in the other portraits of women playwrights. Delarivier Manley is depicted as "a lady, who was born with high powers from nature, which were afterwards cultivated by enjoying the brightest conversation; the early part of her life was unfortunate, she fell a sacrifice to a seducer, who laid the foundation for those errors she afterwards committed, and of those sufferings she underwent" (4:18). Susannah Centlivre is also let off lightly: "From a mean parentage and education, after several gay adventures (over which we shall draw a veil) she had . . . as good success [in writing for the stage] as any of her sex before her" (4:59). While these women's morals are less than sterling (Manley's sense of virtue is depicted as "nodding, and she was ready to fall into the arms of any gallant, like mellow fruit, without much trouble in the gathering"), they are not stripped of their successes as writers competing in the arena of poetry and drama.

While Cibber is a defender of errant dramatists, his ideal literary lady, however, the author on whom he lavishes the most unconditional praise, fits Ballard's domesticated model to perfection. Elizabeth Singer Rowe (1674–1734) led a very different life than the Restoration female dramatists, and the terms used to describe her literary life and productions are also quite different. Cibber discusses her early poetic genius in tandem with her early piety. She is praised primarily in terms of her relationship with her husband, Thomas: "Mr. Rowe knew how to value that treasure of wit, softness and virtue, with which heaven had blessed him." Cibber asserts that the esteem Rowe felt for his wife never abated, "a circumstance which seldom happens, but to those who are capable of enjoying mental intercourse, and have a relish for the ideal transports, as well as those of a less elevated nature" (4:326). The summary of her virtues as a poet is strikingly like the model described in Ballard:

> She had few equals in conversation; her wit was lively, and she expressed her thoughts in the most beautiful and flowing eloquence. . . . In short, if the most cultivated understanding, if an imagination lively and extensive, a character perfectly moral, and a soul formed for the most exalted exercises of devotion, can render a person amiable, Mrs. Rowe has a just claim to that epithet, as well as to the admiration of the lovers of poetry and elegant composition. (4:341)

While Cibber extends the honors of authorship to the female dramatists among whom he was raised (and who obviously enjoyed intercourse other than purely intellectual), he nevertheless bestows the crown of female poetics to the woman whose private life seems most in keeping with the divine nature of her writings.

Another team of theatrical associates, George Colman and Bonnell

Thornton, combined to produce an anthology in 1755 entitled *Poems by Eminent Ladies*. The two-volume work was apparently a commercial success for it enjoyed three editions, being reprinted and revised in 1780. Colman and Thornton cite Ballard in the introductory remarks for individual authors and continue his assessment of the women; the preface to the anthology volume offers the first extended narrative overview of women's writing as a separate tradition and gives some indication of the grounds on which subsequent anthologists will approach their task.

The preface states that the anthology is "standing proof that great abilities are not confined to the men, and that genius often glows with equal warmth, and perhaps with more delicacy, in the breast of a female."[47] It is thus the intent of this volume to present women's writings as being as important and successful as men's. For this reason, Colman and Thornton frequently include the praise of their subjects by established male writers. "It is indeed a remarkable circumstance," the editors observe happily, "that there is scarce one Lady, who was not celebrated by her contemporary poets, and that most of them have been particularly distinguished by the most lavish encomiums either from *Cowley, Dryden, Roscommon, Creech, Pope,* or *Swift.*" By so doing, the editors ensure at least a measure of instant literary respectability.

The editors furthermore deny that the poems in the volume will be marked by any lessening of judgment or fancy found in similar collections by male poets. Indeed, they claim that the reader will find that "this collection is not inferior to any miscellany compiled from the works of men." They do acknowledge, however, that "most of these Ladies (like many of our greatest male writers) were more indebted to nature for their success, than to education" and that this lack of education does indeed hinder many women from competing in the poetic arena with men (p. iv).

In the preface and headnotes, Colman and Thornton thus combine two critical notions. They continue the tradition of praising women for successfully competing with and rivaling male poets in terms of their masculine abilities, but they also add the concept that women's writing, even that of genius, has a different nature than men's. As we have seen, in their choice of Restoration women poets to include—Mary Barber and Mary Jones—the emphasis is on women's writing being indistinguishable from that of men. However, there is also the implication in the preface that these women were writing under very different conditions than the males with whom they were competing. Unlike Dryden's criticism, moreover, there seems to be no desire to erase the difference that identifies women's writings from men's. There is the suggestion that the female genius, while having all the strength of originality of that found in males, may also have characteristically more "delicacy," a critical term discussed in the next chapter as it controls the contents of the anthologies of the period.

It is this emphasis on women's writing as "different" from men's in its nature, if not its quality, which is one of the distinguishing features of accounts of women's literary careers written after 1800. While the Restoration and early eighteenth-century critics were concerned with the evolution of English poetry from its uncouth stage to the polished couplets of Dryden and Pope, the Victorian encyclopedists and anthologists were concerned with tracing the evolution of human nature itself, with poetry acting as a "compendium of the knowledge of the age, a reflection of its manners, and the essence of its spirit."[48] Likewise, there is an even greater emphasis on the woman writer's private life and how well she serves as a female role model.

Part of the decline of the Renaissance and Restoration female author arises from the Victorian's low esteem for the eras in which they lived. Jane Williams lambastes the "long tyranny of pert mediocrity and profligate folly" which she sees as characteristic of the Restoration and attacks the generally accorded virtues of women writers such as Mary Monck and Catherine Cockburn simply for their existence in licentious times.[49] Monck's poems are "sullied by the vicious habits of her time, which so obscured the moral perceptions even of the pure in heart as to permit the familiar use of indelicate expressions" (pp. 144–45). Cockburn's celebrated moral tragedy *Agnes de Castro,* which she intended as her "part toward reforming the abuses of the Stage," is dismissed by Williams as containing indecorous allusions, which would not be tolerated either on the stage or elsewhere in modern times." In fact, "hence may be inferred the low standard of poetry in the year 1698, and the gross profligacy of an age which reputed this play to be a corrective model of propriety" (p. 182).

The women writers, it was felt, took their tone from the coarseness of the times. Very few of the women celebrated by the early anthologists and encyclopedists emerge unscathed by the steely glance of the Victorian watchdogs of feminine delicacy. Eric Robertson can hardly bring himself to discuss Aphra Behn: "It is a pity," he declares, "[that] mention should be made of so unsexed a writer as Mrs. Aphra Behn."[50] Even though "it is rather a fearful task for a modern critic's eyes to read through the corrupt plays which this woman put on stage," Robertson does acknowledge that she had wit. But this wit and ingenuity cannot overbalance his sense that "it is a pity that even such plots and such dialogue should suffice to preserve on any shelves the writings of so impure a pen" (p. 11). Behn can only be acceptable "in that doubtful society where anything is licensed that is savoured with wit."

In her history of women novelists, *English Women of Letters* (1863), Julia Kavanagh faces the charge that nineteenth-century novels suffer from overrefinement because of the domination of female authors. She turns to the history of the novel seeking solutions; like Robertson, Kavanagh warns her readers that "too much delicacy or refinement was not the sin of poor Aphra Behn, or of the times when she wrote."[51] Her wit was "sharp, boisterous and indelicate . . . [she] could scarcely write ten pages without coarseness" (1:20). Kavanagh does admit that Behn's plays, "though not worse than those of her contemporaries," revolt the Victorian reader by their lack of feminine traits. In attempting to compete with male writers, "the inveterate coarseness of her mind sullied Aphra Behn's noblest gifts; beauty, sincerity, wit, an eloquent tongue and a ready pen, perished in the wreck of all that is delicate and refined in woman" (1:7). The critical term "delicacy," which was used as a possible characteristic to differentiate women's writings from men's by Colman and Thornton, has evolved in Kavanagh's literary history to the primary standard of literary merit for women writers.

No longer is wit an acceptable "virtue" in feminine writing when the author's life does not serve as a model of feminity. Behn has been transformed in the critical presentation of her writings from the empress of wit, whose works transcend the limitations of separate genders by combining the qualities of each, into an "unsexed writer." Her very lack of "feminine" characteristics makes her such a failure—both as a female and as a writer. Indeed, in Robertson and Kavanagh, success in the second category depends primarily on success in the first.

Therefore, although Robertson does not like Katherine Philips's poetry, finding it "affected" and "not very interesting to the modern reader," it is nevertheless infinitely preferable to Aphra Behn's works in the chronicle of female literary history. Philips "exhibits as much command as any author of her time" (p. 4). Robertson furthermore believes that "the general looseness of both morality and of literary form that had been bred by the Restoration" may have driven this "pure-minded woman of talent" into her affected French style — "in short, she shines to us as she shone for those who surrounded her, a sweet woman in a corrupt society" (p. 3). Louisa Costello agrees in *Memoirs of Eminent Englishwomen* (1844), noting that "there is but little beauty" in Philips's friendship verse to other women and that "the affected adoption of romantic names, as well as an over-estimation of genius, particularly in females was a fault of the times."[52] In *The British Female Poets* (1848), George Bethune goes so far as to use Philips as a prime example of "how small a portion of talent then made a woman remarkable."[53]

On the positive side, although surrounded by depravity and living in a period perceived as having little literary taste or sensibility, Philips, Robertson asserts, never "once lower[ed] the dignity of her womanhood" (p. 3). In Robertson's estimation, in her poem on the death of her son, she is able to achieve "the simple expression of a tender and pure mother's heart" despite her society's corrupting effects (p. 7). As Jane Williams summarizes Philips, she "cannot be said to have been a woman of genius, but her verses betoken an interesting and placid enthusiasm of heart and cultivated taste, that form a beautiful specimen of female character" (p. 87). Bad verse, in this literary criterion, can be excused when appropriate "feminine" characteristics are manifest. As in Ballard's model of the learned lady, feminine morality has become more important than literary accomplishment, no matter how the latter is defined.

While Dryden and Edward Phillips may have celebrated the evolution of English poesy from uncouth to refined, in the Victorian critic's mind literature before 1750 was a "chaos of our past Poetry," and anthologizing it required a "tedious chase through the jungles of forgotten literature," as Dyce described it in 1824.[54] The American George Bethune goes even further in his 1848 anthology of British women's verse to declare that "nothing shows the superiority of women in our day to those of past centuries, more than a comparison of their writings" (p. v). In Bethune's view, "it will readily be seen how insignificant even 'the Matchless Orinda' is by the side of those least distinguished among her modern sisters" (p. v).

Ironically, such views are in accord with the twentieth-century presentation of the evolution of women's writings and the development of the "feminine" form resulting in the golden age of women's literature in the nineteenth century. In Bethune's assessment, literature has been in a steady evolution that shows the "progress of feminine talent." In his article on nineteenth-century poet Felicia Hemans in *Ladies Magazine and Museum* (1832), Robert Folkstone Williams opens by declaring that "in no period of history has female genius been so fruitful . . . no country can boast of so many talented women in existence, as those who are continually adding to the value of our modern literature."[55] Sounding remarkably like twentieth-century critics, Williams presents an evolutionary scheme of women's literary history, starting with the Renaissance, when intellectual women enjoyed a brief encouragement under Elizabeth, which died with her. In Charles II's court, women were celebrated for their beauty and wit, but not their writings: Between the sexes, "there existed but little sincerity in their mental intercourse, and less respect" (p. 14). Not until the eighteenth century did the female intellect start its "rapid" progress toward its nineteenth-century zenith. Dyce, too, feels that his trek through the Renaissance and Restoration wilderness will at least pave the way for future anthologies that will be "more interesting and more exquisite" because "the human mind, and above all, the female mind, is making a rapid advance" (p. iv–v). Human society itself is arriving at the pinnacle of "its moral advancement" as displayed in its literature.

Another American anthologist, Rufus Griswold, underlines the simultaneous progression of national manners and the rise of female poets. Women writers exist in his view to "soften and enrich the tumult of enterprise, and action, by the interblended music of a calmer and loftier sphere." For Griswold,

the most striking quality of that civilization which is evolving itself in America is the deference felt for women . . . it ought to be valued and vaunted as the pride of our freedom, and the brightest hope of our history. . . . in the absence from us of those great visible and formal institutions by which Europe has been educated, it seems as if Nature had designed that resources of her own providing should guide us onward to the maturity of civil refinement. The increased degree in which women among us are taking a leading part in literature, is one of the circumstances of this augmented distinction and control on their part.[56]

Although Griswold is speaking here of American women writers and the development of a specifically national literature, his view on the nature of women's writings and the importance of "femininity" in both the works and the life of the author is a notion transcending national boundaries. The implication in the Victorian anthologists' and biographers' presentations of women's writings is that feminity is deeply connected with the "spirit of the age." In their presentations of the Renaissance and Restoration, they imply that these earlier, less "civilized" periods did not value the feminine and seek to keep it "pure" and separate from masculine writing.

By the 1840s, we can clearly see taking place in the literary biographies the domestication or "clarissification" of the witty Restoration female author who competes with the men. No longer is solid sense or wit the crowning item of praise in these volumes; instead, "pure" and "unaffected" expression of feminine sentiments are valorized. Frederic Rowton, whose 1848 anthology was reprinted several times in both Britain and America, celebrates the potential of women and women writers; however, he is adamant in keeping the spheres of activity separate. "While Man's intellect is meant to make the world stronger and wiser," he observes, "Woman's is intended to make it purer and better. The reader will not fail to notice how rarely our Female Poets have addressed themselves to the mere understanding, and on the other hand how constantly they have sought to impress the feelings of the race."[57] In general, he summarizes, "Man arrives at truth by long and tedious study; woman by intuition. He thinks; she feels. He reasons; she sympathizes" (p. xvi).

Critical evaluations likewise seem to place less emphasis on the intellectual content of the verse or drama than on the sentiments expressed by its style, especially as it is seen as a reflection of the private life or the times of the author. In his justification of women's verse, Rowton asserts that while it may be that "woman's verse is less exciting than man's," it is only because the "coarser spirit" of Man has hitherto dominated literature. What he calls for is not the androgyny favored by the early eighteenth century, but the infusion of difference, the opportunity for "the gentler glow of woman's unobtrusive spirit [to] be fairly felt" (p. xi).

As part of this new emphasis on the domestic life of the writer, more attention is given to the social background of the author rather than to her formal scholastic attainments, the typical feature of early eighteenth-century commentary. As late as 1928, we find John Middleton Murry in his edition of the Countess of Winchilsea's poems (the edition quoted by Woolf in *A Room of One's Own*) lavishing as much praise on her conduct as her verse: "We find in her and her husband," he observes, "a very perfect example of a type which though it grows rarer, is assuredly not yet extinct in the English aristocracy: true ladies and true gentlemen who do not willingly provide paragraphs for the gossip columns."[58] Mothers, too, have a new, prominent place in the biographies, not so much as the guiding lights in the female authors' formal studies, but as models for womanly attainments. In general, the emphasis changes from judging the Renaissance and Restoration woman author as writer to judging her as a representative of her class and her sex. Without success as a "woman," a female writer can expect little credit to be given to her writings.

Bethune, for example, feels it necessary to devote a section of his preface to an analysis of women writers' domestic lives. "It is painful to observe how many of the writers . . . have been unhappy in their domestic lives," he announces gloomily (p. v). He refuses to believe that "Providence assigns to literary women worse husbands than to those of any other class," although unhappiness may cause a woman to write: "A happy wife and mother, cheerfully busy in her well ordered household, has little leisure and less inclination to solicit the notice of the world." The reason, therefore, he suggests, lies in the activity of authorship itself: "The restlessness of genius, its impatience of steady rules, its morbid sensitiveness, have unfitted many a literary woman in higher life for the every day and every hour exactions of home." Finally, he declares, sounding like twentieth-century critics of the Renaissance, "public exhibition of any kind rarely fails to impair the feminineness, which is the true *cestus* of woman's power over man's heart" (p. vii).

However, Bethune does note that "when literary women have been united to men of similar tastes . . . their intellectual pursuits only served to enhance the charms of their homes" (p. viii). He deduces, therefore, that "habits of authorship cannot in themselves be unfavourable to women's healthfulness of body or mind." He concludes happily that "the moral of the whole is, that genius is not necessarily incompatible with a woman's happiness, particularly if it be governed by common sense."

Jane Williams agrees with this vision of domestic authorship.

"The greater number of those literary Englishwomen were married, and many of them more than once," she notes, "from whence it would appear that their mental pursuits had not weakened their domestic affections" (p. 130). Speaking in general of women writers, Williams is resolute in defending them from charges of impropriety or mental peculiarity: "It may confidently be affirmed that the well-educated possessors of the finest natural abilities were, with few exceptions, exemplary in the discharge of practical duties, and lived in true piety to God."

Rowton and Robertson share a belief in the tie between domesticity and the quality of the verse as well: "We certainly have no female Shakespere [sic]," admits Rowton, prefiguring Woolf (p. xiii). Unlike Rowton, who calls for a more enlightened reception of the female voice to "soften" society, Robertson uses this emphasis on domesticity to explain the inferiority of women's verse to men's. Unlike the early eighteenth-century commentators on the rivalry of male and female poets, Robertson refuses to admit women even into the arena: "No woman has equalled man as a poet," he states bluntly, and "women have always been inferior to men as writers of poetry; and they always will be if [my] explanation . . . is the correct one." Her inferiority as a writer springs directly from the qualities that in his view make her so successful as a female.

Robertson sorts through what he calls a "psychological analysis" of the difference between men's and women's temperaments. The difference is that cited in the twentieth century by "essentialists," that biology is the determining factor in social and intellectual roles. "Faith is woman-like, doubt is man-like," he declares, "his is the uncreated, hers the created" (p. xiii). The ultimate form of creativity for woman is giving birth, since "the springs of maternal feeling within her bosom are the secret of her life": "All that the greatest poet has felt over his most perfect thought, the mother feels through her first-born." Although he recognizes that such views "that children are the best poems Providence meant women to produce" will be challenged by "latter day female prophets," Robertson nevertheless believes that "take away the lover, and husband, and child, from the poetry written by women, and what have you left?" (p. xiv).

Both Williams and Robertson state explicitly that the purpose of their volumes is didactic, to show role models for women. Robertson backs off slightly at the end of his introduction stating that "disparagement of women's verse, however, must not go too far" and that women have produced "beautiful poetry that is worthy of place in any rank but the very first" (p. xvi). The importance of his study, he maintains, is not therefore to resurrect or promote the reputations of early women writers.

> There is another beauty which it may be hoped that these pages will also reveal — the beauty of noble lives led by pure and able women. For with but one or two exceptions, the great Englishwomen of letters have left splendid examples of intellectual vigour in association with the most lovely qualities of personal character. (p. xvi)

It may produce bad poetry, but the feminine qualifications of the "unexpressed by unsuppressible poetry of motherhood" "sweetens" the world and supports the continued advance of human civilization.

Repeatedly in nineteenth-century accounts of sixteenth- and seventeenth-century women writers, such assessments of feminine domestic morality supersede any consideration of the merits of the writings, when they do not completely block the notion that women's writing could rival men's. By 1840, the criterion of excellence for women had changed, and the vocabulary of praise reflects the shift in the definition of "feminine" writings as well as in the ideology of the female role model. Male and female critics alike adopt a shared perception of the appropriate style of the female author. "Feminine" becomes equated with "Woman," a move that created a single, universal view of women's experiences: There is one true feminity, one true Woman.

Louisa Costello, for example, writing in 1844, is extremely critical of women she considers "eminent" if they lack "feminine qualifications." Queen Elizabeth "can never be popular with her sex," we are informed, because of her masculine nature. Vanity was the "only female trait" Queen Elizabeth possessed: "Tenderness, softness, pity, and forgiveness, were unknown to her mind, and, but for her vanity, she would have been scarcely woman or human."[59] Her accomplishments as a learned lady and a poet are silently dropped, and, as we shall see in the next chapter, her presentation in anthologies is severely qualified for these reasons.

The changing representation of Lady Mary Wortley Montagu is another interesting example. By 1824, Bryan Waller Procter ("Barry Cornwall"), the friend of Dickens, Hunt, and Lamb, records her not as Pope's sincere wit and "Heavenly Mind," but as Pope's "Sappho" in her greasy smock. His analysis of her portrait in *Effigies Poeticae:*

Or Portraits of the British Poets focuses on her exotic costume rather than her wit; he quotes Horace Walpole's assertion that "she was always a dirty little thing."[60] By 1843, Anne Elwood is able to offer an explanation not only for why Lady Mary's person was unkempt but also her writings.

> By the unfortunate loss of her mother, she had not the benefit of a kind and accomplished female to superintend her education, to soften her heart, and to polish her manners; hence probably the want of feminine qualifications in her, the absence of delicacy, and the coarseness of thought and expression, the want of conciliation and of attention to propriety and cleanliness.[61]

As to her verse, "it would have been far better for her fair fame had these [fugitive pieces] never been penned"; the spirit of her age, however, is partially to blame, for "such was the taste of the day" (1:37).

By 1883, in Eric Robertson's assessment of Lady Mary as a poet, he spends most of its space retelling biographical anecdotes about her and Pope. Of her writings, he comments that her poems have "not much about them to please," and her choice of subjects "does not accord with our notions of refinement"; "her satirical powers were little checked, and even toward a friend she could be rude for the sake of a jest" (pp. 47, 45). He does allow, however, that "we had best remember that both in life and utterance she was purer than much of the high society in which she lived" (p. 47).

Likewise, Margaret Cavendish's reputation changes from Giles Jacob's assessment of her as having "a great deal of wit and a more than ordinary propensity to dramatic poetry" to that featured in Ballard, the devoted wife and companion. Indeed, in Costello's eyes, Cavendish's literary activities mar her claim to female excellence.

> This singularly pedantic and self-sufficient lady . . . was one of those who, with some talent and no genius, contrive to bring themselves into notice by dint of resolute scribbling. . . . She belonged to that class of ladies of rank who are not content to understand and patronize the works of persons of merit, but indulge the ambition of imitating them, and fondly persuade themselves that they can compete with the best authors of the day.[62]

Fortunately, for Costello, Cavendish's reputation is saved somewhat by her domestic virtues: "This fantastic and singular person had many virtues, which might well counterbalance her absurd pretensions; for she was a most affectionate and devoted wife, following the fortunes of her exiled husband with persevering kindness, and soothing his lonely moments with her agreeable society; for she seems to have been a charming companion" (3:224).

By 1883, Eric Robertson can state with confidence about Cavendish that while "humour and wit are native in her . . . so woefully did she lack consistency of taste and that species of literary judgment which has been termed the power of selecting the significant, that her works are the oddest medleys ever hurried through a printing press" (p. 14). Her writings are like "a lady's over-turned work-basket" and would not be known in the nineteenth century except for the praise given her by Lamb for her biography of her husband. Robertson concludes his portrait of the female artist by asserting that "we have therefore to consider her, in our literature, as a kind of over-grown, spoilt girl, with a great deal of sweetness and purity and talent, and folly not seldom" (p. 15).

Thus, while Aphra Behn becomes repugnant because of her unwomanly wit and licentious content, presumptuous Margaret Cavendish, like Katherine Philips, is saved by her domestic virtues and sweet "girlishness." The writings of all three, however, are dismissed as lacking the qualities of even the least capable "modern," that is, nineteenth-century, female author, and their value dwindles to relics of a more primitive literary time. Certainly, they no longer occupy the position of muse for other female writers, because they do not represent the experience of Woman. Their only contribution to female literary progress is seen as damaging if not dangerous: "The disgrace of Aphra Behn and her pupils," notes Kavanagh, "is that, instead of raising man to woman's moral standard, they sank woman to the level of man's coarseness."[63] The terms of praise and blame given to these early women writers reflect the emphasis developed at length by Ballard's study on the middle-class virtues of domesticity and docility, virtues supposedly so lacking in Behn.

Women writers are no longer presented as potential rivals to males; instead they are excluded from the arena because of their sex. Jane Williams offers a remarkable statement of this shift from the perception of women's writings as potential rivals to those by men:

While intermingled with the productions of manly intellects, in the general growth of a nation's literature, women's writings and their elegant characteristics lie overshadowed and unremarked; mere speedwells and eyebright in a forest of stately trees, requiring separate consideration and comparison among themselves. This consideration and comparison is a principal object of the present work to afford; not under the fallacious impression that pretty herbs can rival giant oaks and lofty pines in fitness for shipbuilding, but simply taking them for what they are, and pointing out their real use and value. (p. 132)

In this scheme of literary history, women's voices have gone from being lead singers to a harmonizing chorus, the backup group dedicated to voicing sweet notes. In the seventeenth and eighteenth centuries, successful women writers were not presented as secondary singers. They were certainly accused of writing bad verse, but they were also considered capable of writing good. When they succeeded in transcending the limiting characteristics of either gender, they were called angels and empresses and their poetry was depicted as witty, strong, and vigorous, combining and transcending the characteristics of both sexes. By the end of the nineteenth century, the same women were unsexed, presumptuous, and sullied; their poetry was uninteresting, unfeminine, affected, and inferior.

We tend to smile both angrily and with dismissive pity at earlier critics' theories about the female character and women's texts. In the eighteenth- and nineteenth-century histories of women writers, however, terms central to feminist debates of our own time are actively engaged. The notion of the "androgynous" creative mind dominates commentary on women's writing in the seventeenth- and early eighteenth-century presentations, and a notion of difference and of a universal "Woman" marks the discourse of later collectors and annotators. Eighteenth-century critics and editors may have defined a view of androgyny which is much too male centered for our acceptance; nineteenth-century commentators offered a version of the feminine which we now find too passive and domestic for our tastes. The key point in surveying this history of histories, however, is that it reveals that our own linear, developmental account of the growth of women's literature and the female poetic is itself the product of a vision of women and their work with which we would consider ourselves now to have little in common.

Too often our own perceptions of the past have been formed by our acceptance of inherited models of history and literature. Eighteenth-century critics celebrating the growth of refined verse, nineteenth-century biographers and anthologists finding an advance toward a truly feminine character, and twentieth-century scholars tracing the evolution or rise of true female writing all share a progressivist vision of literary history which forces one to negate or condemn earlier periods' writing in order to praise that of the present. While we have kept their scheme of periodization and of evolutionary progress, we often have simply inverted their stated values: Earlier critics wanted a female role model who was domestic, passive, and modest, and we have assumed that the women obliged; therefore, we seek the outcast, the madwoman, the angry voice. In each case, the past is constructed as a primitive stage, so that the current era can be interpreted as an age of refinement, enlightenment, liberation.

In the construction of what is perhaps the pervasive modern theoretical model of the progress of women's literature, the inheritors of Ballard have played the key, though ironic, role. While we have rejected Victorian notions of what constitutes "Woman," we have assumed that Ballard and his later followers correctly voiced the ideal set for women in the sixteenth and seventeenth centuries. We have not heard the voices of earlier commentators such as Dryden or Cibber, who find a way to appreciate and applaud women writers as writers. Instead, we have followed the pattern set out in detail in the nineteenth century of focusing attention on women writers' domestic lives, with their texts being autobiographical revelations, and on the liabilities under which they wrote.

The nineteenth-century valorization of "the feminine" in its histories of women's writings, the increased attention lavished on women's verse as being "different" from men's, ironically led to the dismissal or the reduction of the reputation of most of the women writing before the Victorians. Little wonder, then, if Virginia Woolf did consult the most readily available reference texts that she would come away with such a bleak vision of Renaissance and Restoration literary ladies and turn her attention to explaining why they were either so bad or so silent.

Memorials of the Female Mind

Creating the Canon of Women's Literature
in the Eighteenth and Nineteenth Centuries

The editor has purposely omitted selections from several of the
older female writers of rhyme, . . . taking as he passed along, only
those of real merit or accidental distinction, to show the progress
of feminine talent; and reserving the bulk of the book for more
copious extracts from those whose writings are most highly
appreciated for moral and poetical excellence. – George
Washington Bethune,*The British Female Poets*

The public . . . has ceased to read coarse books and will no longer
tolerate them, and those tales of Mrs. Behn's which escape that
reproach are flat and uninteresting. – Julia Kavanagh, *English
Women of Letters*

Canons are created and shaped over time, by many different forces,
but the most noticeable factor in the creation of a canon of women's
literature is the scarcity of texts by Renaissance and seventeenth-
century women writers in print after 1860. By the end of the nineteenth century, only a small fraction of the works and authors celebrated by Dryden, Cibber, Phillips, and even Ballard would have been
available for Woolf's Girton protégés to read in order to form their
impressions of women's literary lives in the past. Not only were the
numbers of editions of early women writers minuscule by the end

of the century, but also the number and length of their entries in the anthologies were progressively eroded.

Until the 1850s, editions were still being printed of popular seventeenth- and eighteenth-century women writers, such as Elizabeth Singer Rowe and Lady Mary Wortley Montagu. After the 1860s, however, early women's writing was being printed only in the context of verse anthologies devoted to displaying the improvement of feminine talent during the Victorian era. As we shall see, this theory of the evolution of women's literature is reflected in both the different formats and aims of eighteenth- and nineteenth-century anthologies. It also resulted in a deliberate effort to create a canon with the writing of nineteenth-century women as the exemplars of feminine writing.

The process of separate editions of early women writers' works disappearing from the shelves can be traced in the publication history of Elizabeth Singer Rowe and Lady Mary Wortley Montagu. Rowe and Montagu were the two most published women writing in the early eighteenth century and were consistently anthologized. Particularly in the case of Rowe, we can track the path of the decaying descent of a once highly visible literary luminary into a minor flicker in the literary constellation. By the end of the nineteenth century, the status of the two women had been reduced from exemplars and muses to antiquarian curiosities; their works go from being the most reprinted to being reduced to short excerpts used to demonstrate earlier, primitive forms of feminine writing.

After the appearance of *Poems on Several Occasions . . . Written by Philomela* in 1696, Elizabeth Singer Rowe's writings in prose and verse were steadily reprinted until 1855. As we have seen, Dunton's "Pindarick Lady" enjoyed during her lifetime enormous repute for the quality of her devotional and secular verse, and her publication success continued after her death, peaking between 1790 and 1815. Her *Devout Exercises of the Heart* (1738), edited by Isaac Watts, had sixteen printings in the eighteenth century, with one a year between 1790 and 1796. There were twenty-two editions produced between 1800 and 1855. After this date, however, this once popular work disappeared completely. Rowe's prose composition, *Friendship in Death*, passed through thirty-four printings between 1728 and 1814 before it, too, vanished from the literary marketplace. During the eighteenth century and the first half of the nineteenth, one's bookseller could also stock Rowe's *History of Joseph* (thirteen editions,

1736–1815), *Letters Moral and Entertaining* (four editions, 1729–35), and *Miscellaneous Works*, edited by Theophilus Rowe (six editions, 1734–72). Her poems were collected and reprinted in 1804 and 1820. But by 1860, the Pindarick Lady was out of print. By 1897, she did not rate even a single line in the *Dictionary of English Authors.*

Lady Mary Wortley Montagu's publication history is more complex, but it follows a similar pattern of popularity and decline. The significant difference, which probably resulted in Woolf's being familiar with her name and not Rowe's, was the authoritative edition of her collected works published by her grandson, Lord Wharncliffe, in the nineteenth century. We find in general that women distinguished with nineteenth-century editions are edited by a family connection: Lady Mary by her grandson, Margaret Cavendish by a descendant of her husband, and Gertrude Aston Thimelby by the grandson of the fifth Lord Aston. This pattern suggests that the poems of the aristocracy, who had libraries and means of preserving manuscript volumes, would be more likely to survive and to be edited and subsequently anthologized in the nineteenth century. Obviously, this feature, too, affects the way in which the past is presented to us, the types of materials which are made available for our study. We like to believe that the literature we have received from the past has survived because of its enduring values—but for women's literature, having a well-born, well-educated grandchild with a taste for literature may indeed have been more of a factor in survival and inclusion in the canon of women's literature than typicality or literary merit.

Although her name was more commonly known by the end of the nineteenth century than Elizabeth Singer's, Lady Mary's writings would have been difficult to obtain. Her *Court Poems* was printed twice separately in the eighteenth century (1719 and 1726), and her letters underwent an astonishing thirty-one printings between 1763 and 1853. Perhaps even more significant, her works were collected and edited in substantial volumes with a critical apparatus, first by James Dallaway in 1803 (six editions by 1811), and then by Wharncliffe (1837, 1861, 1866, 1887, 1893). But without the Wharncliffe edition, Lady Mary, too, would have been out of print by 1855. By 1830, her poetry was sufficiently scarce that William Wordsworth queried Alexander Dyce whether she wrote much more apart from her letters.[1]

The publication patterns of early women writers are significant because nineteenth-century editors rarely used manuscript materials in compiling their editions and anthologies. Early publication success by women writers, however, was no guarantee of inclusion or even preservation in the newly forming canon of women's literature.

For those women who did receive editions of their writings in the nineteenth century, they could expect very different treatment at the hands of their editors than they had been accustomed to in the seventeenth or eighteenth century. Typically, seventeenth- and early eighteenth-century editions of poetry open with a dedication or preface explaining the author's intention and audience. There is a strong tradition of beginning with a section of commendatory verse by other writers, particularly in posthumous editions. Before one ever encountered a single line of Rowe's verse, for example, one would have had to pass through a eulogistic life of her by Theophilus Rowe and thirty pages of verse extolling her abilities as a poet and lamenting the loss of "the consummate mistress of the tuneful art." The reader is repeatedly informed that the poems that follow will combine "*Sapphic* sweetness, and *Pindaric* fire," display "piercing wit" and "elegance of thought," and in general "wake the nobler passions of the soul."[2] Aphra Behn likewise used copious amounts of laudatory verse to preface her miscellaneous verse collections. In short, one is instructed what to expect and what to seek in both the quality and the characteristics of the verse. The writer and her works are simultaneously complimented and validated.

Readers of Anne Killigrew's poems would have had a similar experience. Opening with a publisher's declaration ("Reader, dost ask, What work we here display? / What fair and Novel Piece salutes the Day? / Know, that a Virgin bright this POEM writ, / A Grace for Beauty, and a Muse for Wit!"), the volume starts with Dryden's ode. Likewise, readers of Jane Barker's *Poetical Recreations* (1688) would have had twelve pages of endorsement for the wit and judgment contained in her verses, with periodic reminders scattered through the rest of the volume. Mary Barber used Jonathan Swift's letter to Lord Orrery praising her poetry to open her *Poems on Several Occasions* (1734), which is then quoted in *Poems by Eminent Ladies;* she reinforces the presentation of her poetic credentials with a verse tribute to her by Constantia Grierson.

In seventeenth- and eighteenth-century editions of women's writings, the format of the editions themselves creates a specific environment for reading the verse. After having read about the verse and its author, the reader then encounters it with certain expectations, predisposed to like, admire, and perhaps even emulate the contents. It is irrelevant, actually, whether the praise in the commendatory verses and prefaces was sincere (or even accurate); what is significant is the context created for the reader, the expectation of pleasure and profit. The editorial presentation was designed to present the author and her works in the most favorable light to assist in the most favorable reception.

By the nineteenth century, however, editions of the same women writers had adopted a much different tone. When Sir Samuel Egerton Brydges (a descendant of the Duke of Newcastle) produced an edition of Margaret Cavendish's poems in 1813, he felt it necessary both to explain his choice and to warn his readers about what they would read. He opens by defending her from Walpole's ridicule, asserting as justification that her compositions were produced only as "innocent" amusements, "under the pressure of undeserved and patriotic misfortune."[3] In his own editorial role, he finds her "imagination was quick, copious, and sometimes even beautiful." But, he immediately adds, "her taste appears to have been not only uncultivated, but perhaps originally defective . . . we are too frequently shocked by expressions and images of extraordinary coarseness; and more extraordinary as flowing from a female of high rank, brought up in courts." While he does end the introduction on a positive note about her domestic life—she was "possessed of every attraction of person and every moral quality" including being the "pattern of conjugal affection"—the reader approaches her poetry with a mingled sense of resignation and voyeurism.

Nineteenth-century editors in general, when dealing with Renaissance and seventeenth-century texts, adopt a critical stance toward their materials. Instead of offering endorsements for the works that follow, their introductions offer disclaimers. As part of the theory of the evolutionary progress of literature and of female literature in particular, the presentation of earlier materials focuses on the ways in which they lack critical points. Thus, ironically, even in the process of preservation, we see in action critical erosion of the texts, leading to the eventual disappearance of the writer herself from the narrative of literary history.

The first disclaimer offered covers the general quality of the literature. In these editors' opinions, Renaissance and seventeenth-century women simply did not write works of genius. Brydges stresses that Cavendish "wanted the primary qualities of genius. She was neither sublime nor pathetic."[4] He concludes his analysis of Cavendish's poetic weaknesses by negating the importance not only of her writings, but also of those of her predecessors and contemporaries.

> But we must not compare these compositions with the more refined exactness of later times. In those days what female writer was there, who could endure the critical acumen of the present period? Who now reads Mrs. Katharine Phillips [sic] . . . . And Mrs. Behn, who lived somewhat later, is more remarkable for her licentiousness than for any better quality. Even of Mrs. Killigrew, the encomium bestowed by Dr. Johnson is generally thought to be undeserved. The Countess of Pembroke, Lady Carew, lady Wrothe, and a few others succeeded; but their productions are now unnoticed, except by a few black-letter literati.[5]

Even though Brydges records the names of several early women writers, few readers would be induced by reading this account to track down the out-of-print poets. Instead of becoming muses for other women writers, they have been neatly reduced to antiquarian artifacts in difficult type.

Although outside the nineteenth century, John Middleton Murry's edition of Anne Finch, Countess of Winchilsea's poems continues this tradition of reductive preservation. Murry opens by defending his decision to present only a selection rather than a complete edition: "Her gift, though exquisite and memorable, was intermittent: sometimes it failed her badly."[6] As we shall see later, Murry does credit Finch with writing "the *nec plus ultra* of feminine poetry," but his concluding observation is that "great poetry was not being written" in the countess's day (p. 20).

In addition to disclaimers about the level of poetic genius, editors frequently issue warnings about the nature of the subject matter or the type of language for which the reader should be braced. In a refreshing change, James Dallaway, Lady Mary Wortley Montagu's first editor, describes her as "one of the most accomplished of her sex in any age or country," but he also qualifies this by warning that her language will startle the refined reader.[7] He attempts to defuse the issue by noting that even acceptable standards of literature such as the *Spectator* contain language and topics offensive to cultivated readers. Dallaway also seems to soften the blow by editing her letters heavily, combining and rewriting them. In his edition, Wharncliffe descries Dallaway's manipulation of the text, but he, too, is careful to alert his readers about its contents. "With regard to that correspondence," Wharncliffe notes, "it cannot be denied that parts are written with a freedom of expression which would not be tolerated in the present day; and those parts may perhaps be deemed sometimes to trespass beyond the bounds of strict delicacy."[8] However, unlike Aphra Behn (who "loved grossness for its own sake, because it was congenial to her" in Kavanagh's analysis), the blemish is as much in Lady Mary's times as in her temperament. The letters, explains Wharncliffe, were written "at a period when the feeling upon such subjects was by no means so nice as it now is." Wharncliffe assures us that "expressions, with which we now find great fault, might then be used by persons of the greatest propriety of conduct" in satirizing vice, and were not merely a matter of "indulging in grossness of language."

Indeed, the editions and the anthologies are much more detailed in their criticisms than the general literary histories discussed in the previous chapter, especially in the central area of concern—coarseness. As we find in the commentary, coarseness need not necessarily refer to matters of sexual conduct. Instead, it involves a level of diction, most frequently tied to social class rather than gender. Dallaway reminds readers of Lady Mary Wortley Montagu's letters that they will encounter a crudity of language, but that such language was then acceptable even in aristocratic circles. Likewise, Brydges has a series of footnotes to Cavendish's poem "Mirth and Melancholy" illustrating the difference between crudity and delicacy: He declares that "in these days it seems a little wonderful that a lady of rank so high, and mind so cultivated, could use language so coarse and disgusting as is here seen."[9]

The modern reader may think it is a little wonderful such lines as he identifies should have caused such distress. "Melancholy" describes the person of "Mirth" in the following terms:

Her face with laughter crumples on a heap
Which makes great wrinkles and ploughs furrows deep;
Her eyes do water, and her skin turns red,
Her mouth doth gape, teeth bare, like one that's dead;
Her sides do stretch, as set upon a last,
Her stomach's heaving up, as if she'd cast;
Her veins do swell, her joints seem as unset,

Her pores are open, whence streams out a sweat;
She fulsome is, and gluts the senses all.

Fortunately for Brydges's and his readers' sensibilities, Melancholy then turns to describing her own situation:

I dwell in groves, that gilt are with the sun,
Sit on the banks by which clear waters run.

At this point in the text, the editor exclaims, "Here again the authoress breaks out into true poetry." This passage is also one marked by Leigh Hunt in his copy of Dyce's anthology, presumably for its poetic merit.[10] The point here is not whether one passage is any more "true" in its poetic vision than the other, but, as discussed later in this chapter, that other editors used Dallaway's tactic and tended to extract such "gross" passages entirely, leaving only those considered "delicate."

Although both Brydges and Wharncliffe have the same positive motive in their editorial disclaimers — to protect Cavendish and Lady Mary from charges of indulgence in coarse, unfeminine language — their defenses have the same negative impact on our perception of the women's writings. We turn to the pieces after these introductions assuming that we will be reading poems in which the standard of taste and the refinement of feeling and perception will not be very high. Such introductions do not create a context for reading which would lead to the appreciation of early women's writings. On the one hand, such editions preserve the names and works of early women writers; on the other, they offer more than ample excuses for readers to dismiss them as mere literary curiosities, unimportant in the scheme of literary history except as primitive forerunners. Given the lack of enthusiasm for the material displayed even by its editors, the decreasing number of editions of individual early women writers in the nineteenth century comes as little surprise.

The general reader, therefore, would most likely have relied on excerpts and individual poems published in literary magazines and anthologies for a knowledge of Renaissance and seventeenth-century women's literature. In the latter part of the eighteenth century, the *Ladies Magazine* occasionally used Restoration and early eighteenth-century women's writings as filler material. However, since the magazine did not date the poems, the reader would have already had to be familiar with Catherine Cockburn, Mary, Lady Chudleigh, Mrs.

Lennox, and "Ardelia" in order to appreciate such pieces as early specimens of women's writing.

The anthologies, therefore, were the key repositories for early women's literature and the shaping texts in creating a canon of women's writings. The three anthologies and their numerous editions were all that preserved the works of some early women writers from complete oblivion. The changes in the authors and pieces included, the critical framework surrounding each piece, all signal the changing definition of "feminine" writing which had been expressed in the critical theory.

Although *The Nine Muses* had united in 1700 to mourn the passing of John Dryden, the first general anthology devoted to women's writing was Colman and Thornton's *Poems by Eminent Ladies* (1755). Featuring only women publishing in the Restoration through the midcentury, this text makes no direct attempt to survey the history of women's writing in English or to offer a narrative linking the authors' lives or works in a coherent critical statement. However, the changes that this anthology underwent in its five editions suggest the beginning of the formation of a more sharply defined notion of "feminine" writing and its relationship to the male literary world.

This popular text was enlarged and retitled *Poems by the Most Eminent Ladies of Great Britain and Ireland* in 1773. The first edition offered selections by eighteen women writers with short biographical introductions. By the fourth edition in 1780, the number of authors had been increased to thirty-three, but in order to accommodate the women writing after 1755, extensive cuts were made in the sections for the original eighteen.

The contents of the first edition show a wide range of literary styles, genres, and topics. By the fourth edition in 1780, one detects a slight narrowing of focus, a change in the overall impression left by the contents of the volume. Using the specific examples of Mary Barber and Aphra Behn, one can trace in their treatments a shift toward a greater homogeneity in the concept of "female" literature, both in the pieces included and in the critical presentation. Both writers occupy large blocks of pages in the 1755 edition which are drastically eroded by 1780. Mary Barber starts with 28 poems on 50 pages and ends up with 6 poems on 14 by 1780. Behn drops from 49 poems commanding 117 pages to 4 poems needing only 6 pages. What got cut and why? What is the overall effect of these changes on one's perception of these authors as "feminine" writers?

As we have seen in the previous chapter, the Irish poet Mary Barber's verse was admired by contemporaries for its good strong sense and lack of artificial sentiment. The first edition of *Poems by Eminent Ladies* drew its materials from her volume *Poems on Several Occasions* published in 1734. The 1755 anthology presents Barber's good-humored views on education, child rearing, and women's poetry in a variety of styles and genres. She can be chatty and colloquial, as in her verse letters in which she announces baldly to a friend:

> 'Tis well I can write; for I scarcely can speak,
> I'm so plagu'd with my teeth, which eternally ake.

She can carry on running verse conversations with her young son on topics as diverse as the lamentable neglect of John Gay's *Fables* and the boy's schoolmaster threatening his students with a birch cane. Barber's son announces in the last instance that he prefers Locke's approach to education, a view not perhaps shared by his ironic mother:

> That sage was surely more discerning,
> Who taught to play us into learning,
> By graving letters on the dice:
> May heav'n reward the kind device,
> And crown him with immortal fame,
> Who taught at once to read and game![11]

Barber is also capable of much more formal diction and modes. The Irish visitor to Tunbridge does not write her name on the stones, as do the English tourists, but her thoughts.

> Hither the Britons, void of care
> A happy, free-born race, repair:
> Whilst I, who feel a diff'rent fate,
> Lament my country's wretched state;
> The pitying rocks return my lays,
> Just emblem of the barren bays. (1:38)

Barber is at her best in this anthology, however, when casting an ironic eye on Irish society. To a lady who prides herself on her plain speaking, which she calls "sincerity," Barber observes epigrammatically:

To be *sincere*, then, give *me* leave
And I will frankly own,
Since you but this *one* virtue have,
'Were better you had *none*. (1:45)

She is particularly on form in discussing attitudes toward women's writing by other women. In response to a request by a female friend to write a verse letter detailing how she succeeded in gaining subscriptions for her book, Barber depicts a gallery of polished ladies and gentlemen, lovers of the arts one and all, who find every possible excuse not to contribute.

Servilla cries, *I hate a Wit!*
Women should to their fate submit,
Should in the needle take delight;
'Tis out of character to write:
She may succeed among the men;
They tell me, *Swift* subscribes for ten.

. . . .

Thus *Silvia*, of the haughty tribe;
She never ask'd me to subscribe,
Nor ever wrote a line on me,
I was no theme for poetry!
She rightly judg'd; I have no Taste —
For Womens Poetry, at least.

. . . .

Then *Fulvia* made this sage reply;
(And look'd with self-sufficient eye;)
I oft have said, and say again,
Verses are only writ by men:
I know a woman cannot write;
I do not say this out of spite;
Nor shall be thought, by those who know me
To envy one so much below me. (1:46–47)

In short, the entries in the 1755 edition amply illustrate Mary Jones's praise of Barber's clear good sense and her control over diction. We still find that voice in the small section allotted to her in the 1780 edition, which does include her satire on the nonsubscribers. But the limited selection in the later editions concentrates our attention on her verse letters, her most informal and domestic pieces, and ones that focus on her relationships with men. In them, she invites the Earl of Orrery to dine, sends her son off to London, congratulates Swift on his birthday, and advises her son how to choose a wife. The tone is still sharp and clear, but the scope has narrowed considerably.

Aphra Behn undergoes even more extensive reshaping and refocusing. Unlike the selection of Barber (noted for her freedom from indelicate expressions), Aphra Behn's entry in the 1755 edition includes extensive sections of *A Voyage to the Isle of Love* from *Poems upon Several Occasions*, which depicts Lisander's sexual frustration at not being able to bed Aminta. The Gate to the Isle sets the tone of the piece. It is guarded by "the Graces with a wanton pride," armed with "darts" from the God of Love:

> None e'er escap'd the welcom'd blow,
>   Which ne'er is sent in vain;
> They kiss the shaft, and bless the foe,
>   That gives the pleasing pain.[12]

Poor Lisander faces a series of tantalizing opportunities that are snatched away. Just when he thinks he has Aminta "on the fragrant beds of roses laid," "An awful woman did to us repair; / Goddess of Prudence." He ignores her advice, and is once again in the process of advancing on the sleeping, semi-naked maid when "Respect, the eldest son of love," appears out of the bushes and "slack'd my courage." Not surprisingly, this sequence also includes a lengthy poem against Honor: Honor was created by

> Some woman sure, ill-natur'd, old, and proud,
> Too ugly ever to have been deceiv'd;
> Unskill'd in love, in virtue, or in truth,
> Preach'd thy false notions first, and so debauch'd our youth. (1:126–27)

By 1780, none of the Isle of Love poems are included. Instead, Behn is represented by her imitation of Horace and three innocuous pastoral lyrics: "Scots Song," "Sylvio's Complaint," and "Song." Behn's male speaker has gone from erotic dreams of possessing his ivory nymph to the edifying lament by Sylvio over his ambition for power:

Ye noble youths beware,
Shun ambitious powerful tales:

. . . .

See how my youth and glories lie,
Like blasted flowers in spring:
My fame, renown, and all die,
For wishing to be king.

The 1780 edition erases Behn's eroticism; her fondness for verse narrative sequences and longer poems is likewise obscured by the emphasis on her short lyrics. As with Barber, one receives a different impression of the skills and interests of Behn in the 1780 edition than in the 1755 edition.

In neither instance did the 1780 edition substitute poems not already present in the first edition, or leave out an author altogether. In that sense, both editions of Colman and Thornton offer us our broadest sweep of eighteenth-century women writers. However, the reduction of the pieces by each woman gives a stronger sense of the principles of selection; it also can alter our sense of the interests and scope of the individual writer. The poets added also contribute to one's sense that a deliberate effort was made to shape the later editions into a more unified expression of "feminine" writing.

The pages previously occupied by the adventures on the Isle of Love offer us in the 1780 edition Anna Letitia Barbauld's "Hymn to Content" and "The Mouse's Petition" and Mrs. Brooke's "Two Pastorals." While Barber, Behn, Killigrew, Cavendish, Philips, Mary Leapor, and Rowe have their entries cut by fifty percent or more, some authors hold their page numbers or even increase their entries in the 1780 edition. Eliza Carter—"famous for her refined taste, and excellent talent in poetry"—adds "Ode to Melancholy," "Written at Midnight in a Thunderstorm," and "A Night Piece." The serious-minded Catherine Cockburn holds her six poems uncut, as does Mrs. Madan. Lady Mary Wortley Montagu only loses two poems, but they are from her satiric "Town Eclogues." Elizabeth Singer Rowe, oddly, ends up being represented by "Despair" and "On the Death of Mr. Thomas Rowe," with none of her devotional poems included. The gardener's daughter, Mary Leapor, on the other hand—described by the *Ladies Magazine* in 1779 as "one of the most extraordinary women that ever appeared in the poetic world," whose "virtuous principles and . . . goodness of heart and temper" commanded as much respect as her poetry—manages to preserve twenty-five poems in the 1780 edition.[13]

Thus, while Colman and Thornton offer an invaluable stockpile of women's writing from the eighteenth century, they also include in the reshaping of the early eighteenth-century materials in the later editions a subtle suggestion concerning the nature of women's writings. Viewing the two different versions together, one senses a shift away from the eclectic collection in the first edition to a greater uniformity in subject and style. There are still satires included in the later editions, but the pastorals, odes, and verses of consolation far outnumber them. As with Ballard's memoirs of eminent ladies discussed in the previous chapter, we see again the ironic result of a celebration of female achievement which preserves texts and names for future generations, but at the same time narrows the focus with which the materials are viewed and blocks entirely those texts and authors who do not fit within the parameters. Colman and Thornton's volumes prepare the way for the later nineteenth-century critics' and anthologists' demarcation of a "feminine" literary sphere, characterized by decorous delicacy.

Three nineteenth-century editors follow Colman and Thornton's footsteps, producing between them nine editions of anthologies devoted to women's verse. Alexander Dyce, the editor of Shakespeare, offers the first and most scholarly in 1825; the American minister George Washington Bethune presents by far the most handsome volume in 1848, and the literary editor Frederic Rowton wins the honor of the most reprinted anthology. The changes seen in the presentation of early women's writings from Colman and Thornton's edition through Dyce's in 1825 to Rowton's final edition in 1874 display graphically how the ideology of the feminine ideal found in the literary theory of the times affected the reputation of Renaissance and seventeenth-century women writers. It is also significant to note the change in the literary and social backgrounds of the editors of women's verse themselves. Colman and Thornton were involved in the most commercial and popular aspect of literature, the theater. Of the three nineteenth-century editors, however, two were clergymen, and only one, Rowton, appeared to survive mainly on his literary labors.

Alexander Dyce (1798–1869) was closely involved with those we now consider to be the leading literary figures of his day and very much in tune with the poetic sensibilities of the early romantics.

In addition to editing Shakespeare and women poets, he edited Collins and Samuel Rogers. Dyce maintained long literary friendships with Wordsworth, Thomas Campbell, Mary Russell Mitford, and the novelist William Harrison Ainsworth. Through them he met Coleridge, Byron, the Lambs, Thackery, Dickens, and Disraeli.[14] Leigh Hunt owned and annotated an edition of *Specimens of British Poetesses* now in the Huntington Library, offering invaluable insight into the reception of the work. Assembled by an experienced and respected editor, Dyce's volume carried authority, and it remains one of the best anthologies of early women's writings.

His friendship with Hunt and Wordsworth is particularly noteworthy, given their response to the anthology. Wordsworth wrote in 1829 that he himself had wished to attempt such a project; he suggests that if Dyce wished to bring out another edition, "I should be pleased with the honour of being consulted by you about it."[15] Wordsworth was intrigued by Margaret Cavendish's verse (as was Hunt) and wanted to know the literary fate of Lady Mary Wortley Montagu. It was the Countess of Winchilsea, however, who most interested him, and his observations on Colman's and Dyce's presentations of her work illustrate the shift in critical and aesthetic criteria.

Writing in 1830, Wordsworth commends Dyce's performance as far superior to Colman and Thornton's. "British Poetesses make but a poor figure in 'Poems by Eminent Ladies,'" he declares, "but observing how injudicious that Selection is in the case of Lady Winchilsea, and in Mrs. Aphra Behn, from whose attempts they are miserably copious, I have thought something better might have been chosen by more competent persons."[16] He goes on in this letter to give minute directions for cuts to be made in order to improve the countess's verse — omitting specific passages he feels to be repetitious or unharmonious. By 1830, a second edition of the anthology had already been issued, and Dyce himself, as far as we know, never acted on Wordsworth's suggested revisions. But, as we shall see, Wordsworth's unhesitating policy of pruning others' verse to bring it in line with his sense of the appropriate poetic is the key to the editorial practices in Bethune's and Rowton's anthologies.

George Washington Bethune (1805–62) was an American minister in the Dutch Reformed Church. Active in the abolitionist movement, he took his clerical duties much more seriously than did Dyce. Nevertheless, he still found time to write a volume of his own poetry, lecture university groups on the role of the literary man in society, and compose a eulogistic memoir of his mother. Bethune had apparently planned to complete a companion volume of American female poets along with the British anthology, but passed that task along to Caroline May, "in whose judgment and taste he had great confidence."[17]

In a lecture foreshadowing his position in the anthology, he describes "genius" in literature as a combination of powers which must be focused on a greater social good: "It is not to be wasted on the mere personal enjoyment of its possessor. . . . God has exalted him above the common herd, to instruct, to enlighten, and to bless them."[18] His biographer states that "Dr. Bethune did not give himself to making poetry, it was merely an incident to his more severe labors which occupied his leisure hours."[19] This severity and emphasis on self-control and public responsibility is at the heart of his final literary exercise, his reverential memoir of his mother. Its editor assures us that "Christian ladies will read these pages, and be stimulated and guided in noble self-denying labors for the world around them; and aged women will here find a beautiful example of holy living and dying."[20] Not too surprisingly given Bethune's editorial practices, ladies reading Bethune's anthology of female verse would likewise be animated by similar feelings.

Of Frederic Rowton (1818–54) little is known except by negatives. He was not a cleric; nor did he matriculate from Oxford or Cambridge. He first appears on the literary scene as the editor of *The City of London Magazine*, which ran only for ten months in 1842–43. His only other publication apart from his very successful anthology was *The Debator: A New Theory of the Art of Speaking* (1846), frequently revised and updated throughout the nineteenth century. His interest in elocution and rhetoric is felt in his anthology; the most copious of all three editors in his notes, Rowton frequently bases his response on the grounds of style and harmony of the lines as they fit a feminine mold.

By the end of the nineteenth century, the selection of early women writers to be included in standard anthologies had become fairly uniform. In contrast with Colman and Thornton, who do not include Renaissance women writers, Dyce, Bethune, and Rowton have ten early women writers in common: Anne Boleyn; Queen Elizabeth; Lady Elizabeth Carew; Mary Sidney, Countess of Pembroke; Anne Howard, Countess of Arundell; Katherine Philips; Margaret Cavendish, Duchess of Newcastle; Anne Killigrew; Anne Wharton; and

Lady Mary Wortley Montagu. As we shall see, not only the names but also the selections for each remain constant over the nineteenth century.

Women included on this central list share several characteristics as they are presented in the anthologies. As a group, they are aristocratic or upper middle class. They are adamantly genteel. Missing are the eccentric hack writers such as Elizabeth Thomas or Delarivier Manley or Mary Fage and such commercial playwrights as Mary Pix. The Irish woolen merchant's wife, Mary Barber, imprisoned for carrying Swift's scandalous verses to London, has vanished. Some of these women are found in either Dyce or Rowton, but obviously they were not viewed as essential figures in women's literary history or even characteristic of feminine writing. The overwhelming impression left by the content of these volumes is that in the Renaissance and seventeenth century, literature was the province of genteel ladies, who did not write commercially, or need to derive an income from writing. Matching closely with Ballard's ideal, these women all are presented as sharing a sense of domestic decorum and as writing the poems anthologized with high moral seriousness.

Proportionally, these Victorian editions prefigure twentieth-century ones in assigning the bulk of their pages to women's writing after the Restoration. Dyce is by far the most generous to earlier women poets, but the balance in his volume signals the trend followed more radically by Rowton and Bethune. Dyce devotes approximately 200 pages to works written between 1460 and 1760, and about the same to works published between 1760 and 1820. By Bethune's time, the room allotted has shrunk considerably; he gives less than 50 pages out of nearly 500 to the Middle Ages, the Renaissance, and the Restoration/Augustan periods combined. Felicia Heman's verse, however, the exemplar of feminine writing for Rowton and others, is allotted almost twice the pages as the three periods together. In Rowton's anthology, there seems at first to be a more equal distribution of space with 121 pages out of 500 for pre-1760 writers; Rowton, however, gives nearly as much space to his biographical and editorial remarks as to the verse, leaving room only for snippets.

The nineteenth-century argument for such distribution of space probably mirrors that used in the twentieth century: Readers find early poetry too difficult and prefer verse written by contemporaries. All three nineteenth-century editors make conscious efforts to accommodate their readers, with modernized spelling and punctuation and explanatory notes. However, the dwindling space given to Renaissance and seventeenth-century women writers (not to mention medieval women writers, represented only by Juliana Berners) also offers a clear message concerning the relative value of the different periods in the chronicle of women's literary history. Like anthologists today, the nineteenth-century editors saw their century as the golden age of women's writing.

The commentary and the selection reinforce the diminution of earlier periods in this evolutionary scheme. As we have seen, there was a distinct shift toward consolidating an image of the woman author and of feminine poetry at the end of the eighteenth century. The nineteenth century continues this movement with its criterion of "delicacy" as the recurrent critical term associated with women's writing. Although it is not formally defined in the anthologies, their contents and apparatus illustrate how the term shaped perceptions of earlier women and their writings.

For example, the attitudes toward Queen Elizabeth and her verse are strongly marked in nineteenth-century anthologies by a tension between the desire to record the work of a monarch and a distaste for her as a female role model. In 1630, no such problem seemed to be present: Diana Primrose eulogized Elizabeth's virtues in *A Chaine of Pearle*, depicting her as not only the ideal monarch, but also the exemplary woman, "Thou English Goddess, Empresse of our Sex, / O Thou whose Name still raignes in all our hearts."[21] By 1848, in Bethune's eyes, Elizabeth is a "vain, pedantic but really accomplished woman."[22] All three nineteenth-century editors acknowledge Elizabeth's intelligence, but generally combine reference to it with qualifiers such as "pedantic" or "vain" and declare that in her poetry we see such traits most clearly. "Her vanity," Dyce informs us, "made her regard as tributes justly paid, the extravagant praises, which the courtiers . . . lavished on her royal ditties" (p. 15). Bethune likewise dismisses Elizabeth's efforts at verse as a display of vanity, but it is Rowton who most plainly states why her verses come in for such harsh criticism. "Among the vanities of this royal lady," he opens, "the most innocent, perhaps, was her desire of shining as a Poet" (p. 34).

Coyly, he states that *he* will not be the one to say her verse is bad, but he *will* say that when Puttenham praises "In Doubt of Future Foes," "it is to be feared that Mr. Puttenham's loyalty sent to sleep his taste" (p. 35). Of "I Grieve and Dare Not Show My Discontent" Rowton observes, " 'The beauty of queens' whines somewhat" (p. 36). But his most scathing criticism is coupled with his perception of Elizabeth as an unfeminine queen:

> whatever may have been Queen Elizabeth's poetical powers, she at least had not the faculty of self-portraiture. For when she says of herself—
> That she is soft, and made of melting snow,
> one cannot, with all the charity in the world, coincide with her. Had the royal Limner compared herself to ice instead of snow, she might have won our assent. (p. 37)

The extent to which Elizabeth is perceived and presented as lacking the "feminine qualifications" discussed in the previous chapter determines her spot in the history of women's literature. Although her poems are preserved, they are relegated to the scrap heap of female vanities rather than displayed as expressions of feminine poetry.

By contrast, the poems of both Anne Boleyn (included in all three anthologies) and Mary, Queen of Scots (who appears in two) are presented in much more favorable settings. Although the editors admit that attribution is a problem for both women's poems, the "womanly" qualities of the verses ensure them a place in the literary history. Dyce directly compares Elizabeth's and Mary's verses: "The Farewell to France," which he attributes to Mary, "written by that lovely, unfortunate, but surely not guiltless woman, will shew how much her poetical powers were superior to those of Elizabeth" (p. 18). Bethune also sees the two as contrasting types of female voices but focuses on the implication in Dyce's introduction, that they were very different types of women.

> This beautiful and highly accomplished woman [Mary], whose feminine character ill fitted her for the throne of a rude nation in the most agitated period of its history . . . none dared defend her against a haughty, powerful rival [Elizabeth], that united to a woman's jealousy of her superior charms, the sternest policy of unscrupulous ambition. (p. 20)

Like Mary, Queen of Scots, Anne Boleyn, too, is depicted as a womanly victim. The piece anthologized, "Defiled is my Name," supposedly was written by her in prison. Bethune describes her as "this accomplished as unfortunate lady whose beauty attracted the fatal notice, but could not fix the brutal passion of the king" (p. 16). In Rowton, she is elevated to "this ill-fated lady" who writes "pathetic and womanly verses" (p. 28). In both instances, Mary, Queen of Scots and Anne Boleyn are perceived as passive victims, victims whose womanly characters shine forth in their verse, while the verse of the victorious Elizabeth displays only her lack of true delicacy. The two victims' perceived femininity ensures their preservation in the chronicle of women's literary history, even though the attribution is questionable.

In these examples, we see in microcosm the mechanisms by which our perceptions of the past are shaped. One is exclusion: By simply leaving early women's writings out, or by relegating these women to a single poem, their voices are silenced or so muted as to be nearly inaudible. A second mechanism is to reshape the women and their writings that are included to conform to a preconceived notion of the period and to support the ideal of feminine writing as exemplified by nineteenth-century women. This is accomplished either by the hostile, dismissive introductions and explanatory notes or by the editing and even rewriting of the verse itself.

Anyone reading these anthologies as a group for the first time might well be struck by the surprising degree of uniformity in tone and subject found in early women's writings. Anne Wharton, one of the central list figures, is epitomized by two poems: "Verses on the Snuff of a Candle, made in Sickness" and "How hardly I conceal'd my Tears." Dyce notes the scarcity of her writings and calls them "by no means despicable" (p. 105). The other two editors both praise "a fine sweetness of sentiment" with "graceful" and "delicate expression" (Bethune, 38; Rowton, 89).

> See there the taper's dim and doleful light,
>   In gloomy waves silently rolls about,
> And represents to my dim weary sight,
>   My light of life almost as near burnt out.

Wharton closes this piece with a plea to her "Dear, melancholy Muse," a feature often found in other poems chosen for the anthologies. After perusing enough of this verse, one might be excused for concluding that women writers in the seventeenth century were remarkably gloomy and often ill.

All three editors include Mary Sidney, Countess of Pembroke's choruses from *The Tragedy of Antonie*. Their choices reveal similar concerns. Dyce and Rowton select: "But still as long as we / In this low world remain, / Mishaps, our daily mates, / Our lives do entertain." Bethune prefers: "Lament we our mishaps, / Drown we with tears our woe; / For lamentable happes / Lamented easy grow; / And much less torment bring / Than when they first did spring." Simultaneous with the desire to present specimens of British female verse is the desire to instruct and edify the reader, presumably the female reader; the lesson most frequently taught, as typified in Mary Sidney, is fortitude and resignation.

All three also include a section from the chorus of Lady Elizabeth Carew's *Mariam*. Rowton describes the piece as "a play abounding in fine womanly touches of feeling and sentiment" (p. 47). The passages selected by all three support this interpretation, although they do not reflect the concluding events of the play itself:

> In fairest action of our human life,
> > As scorning to revenge an injury:
> For who forgives without a further strife,
> > His adversary's heart doth to him tie.
> And 'tis a firmer conquest, truly said,
> > To win the heart, than overthrow the head. (Act 4)

Along with this exemplary statement of resignation, the anthologists all selected Anne Howard, Countess of Arundell's "In sad and ashie weeds I sigh." They rely on Lodge, who finds in the lament "the best style of the time and . . . a strain of unaffected piety and tenderness."[23] Given the expressed views on the subjects and nature of women's verse discussed in the previous chapter, it is not surprising that all three editors attribute the lady's grief to the death of her husband: "My watery eyes, like winter's skies, / My furrow'd cheeks o'er flow: / All heavens know why, men mourn as I / And who can blame my woe?" From contemporary manuscript copies, however, it appears that it was not a domestic lament, but was written on the death of Prince Henry to mark a public political tragedy rather than a private one.

Like the pieces attributed to Mary, Queen of Scots and Anne Boleyn, early women's writings are presented as uniformly edifying, domestic, and generally melancholy. In these narratives of women's literary history, they occasionally spring forth in the pastoral, but this genre, too, leaves the impression of the woman poet as escaping into a fantasy, an ideal world, rather than engaging in the real one. In general, the emphasis in the pieces selected for inclusion is on the pathos of the individual's situation, not satiric commentary on the state of society. Compared with earlier anthology selections, personal engagement with the topic has overshadowed critical detachment. Sentiment is more in evidence in their selections than wit, although the women writers of the Renaissance and seventeenth century did not lack it.

This controlling design of feminine writing can be seen in the specific examples of Margaret Cavendish and Anne Finch. Margaret Cavendish has, as we have seen, a rather checkered history in the anthologies, progressing from seven poems in Colman and Thornton's first edition to excerpts from one in the 1780 edition. The same specimens of her verse, usually drawn from the same long poem, are featured repeatedly in nineteenth-century anthologies to illustrate the "wildness" of her imagination and her apparent inability to prune or revise. The later editors seem to hold her writings in contempt, and yet still suggest that they are delightful.

The two long pieces that generally serve as the source of excerpts for Cavendish are "The Dialogue between Mirth and Melancholy," often shortened to "Mirth and Melancholy," and "The Pastime and Recreation of the Queen of Fairies in Fairyland," variously retitled as "The Elfin Queen" or "Queen Mab." The "Queen Mab" passages chosen depict the fairy queen in her fanciful landscape:

> She on a dewy leaf doth bathe,
> And as she sits the leaf doth wave;
> There, like a new fall'n flake of snow
> Doth her white limbs in beauty show.
> Her garments fair her maids put on,
> Made of the pure light from the sun.

In his copy of Dyce, Leigh Hunt marked these lines, as well as Melancholy's description of gilded streams. The images Hunt and the anthologists prefer are delicate, amusing, and imaginative: The Queen uses a mushroom covered with a spider's web as her table and lace cloth, and her cup is an acorn crown. Dyce, however, is the only one of the anthologists to include the entire section uncut. Bethune stops short of what the Queen actually eats, and Rowton cuts heavily when Cavendish begins describing the Queen's diet of "Flies of all sorts, both fat and good":

> Partridges, snipes, quails, and poult, her food,
> Pheasants, larks, cocks, or any kind,
> Both wild and tame, you there may find.

Amelets made of ant-eggs new,
Of these high meats she eats but few.
Her milk comes from the dormouse udder,
Making fresh cheese, cream, and butter;
This milk doth make many a fine knack,
When they fresh ant's-eggs therein crack.[24]

Likewise, Dyce is the only one of the three to include the description of Mirth, which Brydges found so disgustingly coarse. The other two settle on the preferred depiction of Melancholy.

Reading only the selections included in these anthologies, one would be quite surprised to find the tone and type of poem Margaret Cavendish featured in her volume *Poems and Fancies* (1653). A large part of that volume is taken up with the duchess's verses on scientific matters, particularly "atomic" theory. The contents include "A World made by Atomes," "The Foure Principal Figur'd Atomes make the Foure Elements," "Of Aiery Atomes," "What Atomes make Heate and Cold," "What Atomes cause Sicknesse," and "What Atomes make the Wind Collick." Read in context, her poems on the world of Queen Mab are less an indication of a dreamy, escapist reverie as implied by her nineteenth-century presenters than an extension of her passionate curiosity about the "new science" and what it could reveal about the composition of the natural world. She returns repeatedly to the possibility of "Many worlds in this World."

Just like unto a *Nest* of *Boxes* round,
Degrees of *sizes* within each *Boxe* are found.
So in this *World*, may many *Worlds* more be,
Thinner, and lesse, and lesse still by degree;
Although they are not subject to our *Sense*,
A *World* may be no bigger then *two-pence*.
Nature is curious, and such *worke* may make
That our dull *Sense* can never finde, but scape.
For *Creatures*, small as *Atomes*, may be there,
If every *Atome* a *Creatures Figure* beare.
If foure *Atomes* A *World* can make, then see,
What several *Worlds* might in an *Eare-ring* bee.
For *Millions* of these *Atomes* may bee in
The *Head* of one *small*, little, *single Pin*.
And if thus *small*, then *Ladies* well may weare
A World or *Worlds*, as *Pendents* in each *Eare*.[25]

Ironically, Cavendish says of her own verse: "I rather chose to leave the *Elegance* of *words,* then to obstruct the *sense* of the *matter.* For my desire was to make my *conceit* easie to the *understanding* though my *words* were not so fluent to the *ears.*"[26] Nineteenth-century editors, however, resolutely chose passages that rely almost entirely on their ability to please the ear rather than tantalize the intellect. Their selections have shaped our perceptions of both her interests and her skills.

Anne Finch undergoes a similar domestication in the subjects and tone of her poetry. She, unlike Cavendish, had the advantage of being canonized by Wordsworth, whose comment on "Nocturnal Reverie" as containing one of the few new images of nature written between *Paradise Lost* and *The Seasons* is used as a preface to her verse in all three anthologies. While "Nocturnal Reverie" does represent her in Dyce and Rowton, Bethune finds it "tame." He prefers instead "Life's Progress," a poem included in all three nineteenth-century anthologies but not the eighteenth-century ones, which featured her verse fables. "Life's Progress" displays in its tone and subject the characteristics demanded by the nineteenth-century theorists of the female poetic:

> How gaily is at first begun
> Our life's uncertain race!
> Whilst yet that sprightly morning sun,
> With which we just set out to run,
> Enlightens all the place.
>
> . .   .   .
>
> But oh! too soon, alas! we climb,
> Scarce feeling, we ascend
> The gently rising hill of Time,
> From whence with grief we see that prime.
> And all its sweetness end.

The passages taken from "The Spleen" likewise highlight a melancholic temper in the poet and the burdens in human life:

> By thee [Spleen] Religion, all we know
> That should enlighten here below,
> Is veiled in darkness, and perplext
> With anxious doubts, with endless scruples vext.

Given the nature of the selections, one can see how Wordsworth would assess Finch's style as "often admirable, chaste, tender, and vigorous; and entirely free from sparkle, antithesis, and . . . over-culture." Of her topics as displayed in the anthology selections, one would agree with Wordsworth's summary: "Of Love as a passion she is afraid, no doubt from a conscious inability to soften it down into friendship."[27]

Although his anthology lies outside the nineteenth-century framework of this chapter, John Middleton Murry's depiction of Anne Finch and her poetry in his 1928 edition is worth considering as the final statement of this earlier presentation of early women's writings — as well as because it is Woolf's stated source. Murry explicitly sets forth a critical theory of feminine writing which is implied in the earlier anthologies' selections for both Finch and Cavendish. Although Murry resolutely maintains that Finch was a minor poet, he nevertheless finds in her lines "an exquisite sense of nuance, and a simple felicity in expressing it." Unlike the nineteenth-century editors, Murry does not include "Life's Progress"; his interest is focused less on the edifying sentiment than on the countess's melancholic nature and what he calls "the music" of her lines.

Murry cites the lines from "The Bird" to demonstrate Finch's talents. "Softer than love, softer than light / When just escaping from the night" are in his eyes a "woman's phrases . . . they have a peculiar perfection of femininity."[28] Likewise, a passage from "The Spleen" stands in Murry's estimation as "the *nec plus ultra* of feminine poetry: a perfect specimen of the Countess of Winchilsea's lovely gift": "Nor will in fading silks compose / Faintly the inimitable rose." Delicate, evocative, the passages indeed show no sparkle or satiric wit, but instead highlight the sensibility of the poet and a pervasive sadness.

Murry does not include in his edition any of the countess's verse epistles — to her husband, to Swift, the Countess of Hertford, Lady Tufton, Mrs. Randolph, Dr. Waldron, Edward Jenkinson, Matthew Prior, Lady Worsley, the Thynne family, and the family of Lord Thannet — which were reprinted in Reynolds's 1903 edition. But Murry does include "The Introduction," "The Apology," and "The Miser and the Poet" — all pieces dealing with the difficulties of being a poet, and a female one at that — with no commentary in his introduction concerning the countess's real celebrity in her own time for her poetry. The impression left by both Murry and Woolf — which descends directly from the reshaping of the countess's canon in the nineteenth century—is of a sad and isolated aristocrat, unread and bitter over her lack of appreciation and encouragement.

Woolf perpetuates this image of the pensive countess by quoting Murry; she goes one step further by assigning the cause of Finch's melancholy to her thwarted literary ambitions. However, if one returns to the 1713 edition of her writings, a very different image of the countess emerges. In addition to the literary support group suggested by the extensive selection of verse epistles to friends published, the countess was a proficient satirist, showing a great deal of wit and sparkle. She was also capable of descending from high moral seriousness to describe the plot of a wife to dress herself up like a fury to cure her husband from coming home drunk.

> A Female, to a Drunkard marry'd,
> When all her other Arts miscarry'd,
> Had yet one Stratagem to prove him,
> And from good Fellowship remove him;
> Finding him overcome with Tipple,
> And weak, as Infant at the Nipple,
> She to a Vault transports the Lumber,
> And there expects his breaking slumber.[29]

Her view of the natural world also is not quite as expected from Wordsworth's praise of "Nocturnal Reverie." In "The Man Bitten by Fleas," nature is red in pincher and jaw:

> A Peevish Fellow laid his Head
> On Pillows, stuff'd with Down;
> But no sooner warm in Bed,
> With hopes to rest his Crown,
> But Animals of slender size,
> That feast on humane Gore,
> From secret Ambushes arise,
> Nor suffer him to snore. (223–24)

Finch was indeed a sensitive, evocative poet, fully sensible of her posture as a female writer, but she was not as limited in her response to either life or poetry as suggested in the image created for her.

The anthologists of the eighteenth and nineteenth centuries were deeply concerned with the questions raised by "feminine" writing and the connections between gender and creativity. We owe them a debt for preserving the names and writings of their chosen canonical women writers—Katherine Philips, Lady Mary Wortley Montagu, and the rest would be less familiar to us now if they had not been selected for attention by the nineteenth-century popular anthologists. However, in the very act of creating "memorials to the female mind" to preserve them from oblivion, these same editors erased and silenced many other early women writers. In order to produce a coherent linear account, an evolutionary narrative, of women's literature, they reshaped the lives and writings of Renaissance and seventeenth-century women poets. By privileging certain types of literary forms in a hierarchical presentation of periods in the past, the previous generations of editors have given us selections that negate the impact early women's writing had on the literary environment in general. By seeking to preserve and to present to their readers only the "best," that is, most womanly, poets, the early anthologies did give us a chorus of women's voices, but one that could sing only a single song.

We began our investigation of women's literary historiography in the twentieth century, and with our own efforts to enable the serious study of women's texts through the definition of a female tradition, the search for continuity. As we have seen, in this process, when we come to view women's texts written before 1700, we have inherited two centuries of commentary, editing, and rewriting of women's texts and lives. Working back through our own perceptions of women's writings before 1700, we can recognize that, indeed, often we have viewed the Renaissance and Restoration through nineteenth-century spectacles, seeing what those editors and anthologists believed was suitable as examples of feminine writing, given their definitions of the natures of each period. In one sense, in clinging to the vision of Judith Shakespeare as the model for early women writers, we have not challenged this nineteenth-century assessment of the literature of previous generations so much as simply inverted its terms: Whereas nineteenth-century editors sought to define the female tradition by delicate domesticity, we have celebrated angry social rebellion. What both these visions of the past have not been able to see or to bring into the general discussion are those early women writers whose lives and works lie outside traditional definitions or categories, both social—women's "proper sphere"—and literary—what constitutes our definition of "literature" itself. With these preconceptions and assumptions in mind, we turn in the next chapter to consider an example of what has been overlooked, what could be found, and of what questions could be asked of early women's texts, should our model of history and definition of the past be expanded.

Breaking the Seventh Seal

Writings by Early Quaker Women

It is by taking words seriously, a life and death game in the body
of language, that the secret of what they give is torn from them.
. . . One more thing, perhaps, is mystical: the establishment of a
space where change serves as a foundation and saying loss is
another beginning. — Michel de Certeau, "Mystic Speech"

And when he had opened the seventh seal, there was silence in
heaven. . . . And I behelde, & heard one Angel flying through the
middes of heaven, saying with a loud voice, Wo, wo, wo to the
inhabitants of the earth. — Revelation 8:1–13

This final chapter is intended to explore the possibilities that are
uncovered when we cease to accept without question previous generations' constructions of either the literary past or the feminine
ideal. As I indicated in the Introduction, this chapter offers an example of one kind of application which might be done as part of a
"re-visioning" of feminist literary practices. Throughout this study,
I have maintained that the existing models of women's literary history, structured as a linear, evolutionary narrative, which originally
enabled us to see and to pursue women's writing as a serious study,
now block our perception of those modes of literary activity which

do not fit within the traditional terms. This chapter investigates one such "lost" group of women writers.

This chapter is not an attempt, however, to formulate an alternative aesthetic criterion for a canon of women's writings. Instead, the emphasis is on the attempt to use Cixous's reading strategy of *"démoïsation,"* to hear a group of silenced women writers, to hear "their desires," to apply to texts what Jane Marcus refers to as "still practice," trying not to intrude or inflict one's own critical preconceptions on a text. If there is any aesthetic promoted in this study, it is that of diversity, multiplicity. We do not need a controlling, delimiting reconstruction of the past to fit it within existing knowledge. What we do need is an archeology of an early body of writings which strips away layers of assumptions between us and these past texts without seeking to impose immediately a preconceived hierarchy of literary values and the progress of feminist thought on what we find. The goal is to open ourselves to new voices, to let them, in Cixous's words, speak out of their own desires, not ours.

The largest single body of early women's printed texts in the Restoration was created by Quakers; ironically, this material almost without exception is excluded from our literary histories of women's writings. The mechanisms of exclusion have been the subjects of the previous chapters (although the more particular history of the exclusion of early women writers from the Quaker canon will be touched on here). At this stage, the question changes from "can we uncover our assumptions about the past" to "what can be discovered about these texts and early women's authorship if we change the questions we ask of the literary past?" How can it help us to re-vision our image of the early woman writer, to think of new questions to ask about even familiar texts? It is not merely a matter of finding, cataloging, or even reproducing these texts. It involves re-visioning our image of the early woman writer.

In his discussion of the creation of a Romantic ideology, Jerome McGann argues for the importance of works from the past "because they are time and place specific, because they are—from our point of view—*different.*" He goes on to observe, "We do not contribute to the improvement of social conditions or even to the advancement of learning . . . by seeking to erase the difference, but rather by seeking to clarify and promote it."[1] An absolute sense of difference from the past, on the other hand, is probably neither achievable nor desirable. In my reading of Quaker women's texts which follows — which draws on certain aspects of French feminist thought — there is a clear tie made between the present and the past: No one can be free of critical and political ideologies in reading, but we can attempt in the process of analysis to become more aware of them and the effects they have on our processes of interpretation and presentation. Perhaps at that point, we can begin to "re-vision" both the literary past and our critical practice.

Social historians have long recognized that women played an important part in the early days of seventeenth-century Quakerism; more recent studies by Phyllis Mack underline the importance of women's contributions to the development of the movement both in its organization and its spiritual essence.[2] Literary historians, however, have made little use of Quaker women's writings; with the exception of Margaret Fell, the handmaidens of the Lord have slipped into oblivion, even where feminist literary history is concerned. As David Latt pointed out, "If [women's] participation were judged on the basis of some modern accounts of early Quaker history and editions of their writings, the conclusion would certainly be that women played a peripheral role in the development of Quaker theology."[3] The writings and fate of this group form a case study of how women's writing in general is lost in the institutions that seek in part to preserve it. I begin this investigation of works published by Quaker women between 1653 and 1672 (when censorship by the Second Morning Meeting was established) with a survey of how these works have been received, categorized, and defined and consider what factors might have contributed to shaping the literary historiography of this group of writers as Quakers and as women.

In her account of literary activity by women during the seventeenth century, Angeline Goreau asserts, "Many women answered from the pulpit, but Margaret Fell was one of the few who had the leisure to construct an argument in writing."[4] In fact, as Patricia Crawford's preliminary checklist indicates, of the nearly two hundred first editions by women published between 1651 and 1670, ninety-three of them were by Quaker women; between 1651 and 1660, twenty-eight Quaker women published more than four works each.[5] Quaker women dominated the publication patterns of women writers through 1700; their writings form a large body of literature which is highly conscious of gender issues. And yet their existence and writings have all but vanished from accounts of women's literary history. Why?

Part of the answer may lie in our perceptions of this group's historical identity as women of a certain social background. Before discussing the specific content of these women's writings, therefore, let us first consider how they have been studied by social historians as Quakers. In his frequently cited article on women in the English civil war sects, Keith Thomas points out that "women were numerically extremely prominent among the separatists" in general; in particular, "the female sex played so large a part among the Quakers that it was rumoured at first that the sect was confined to them alone."[6] Elizabeth Hooten, "a very tender woman," is often cited as Fox's first convert. Barry Reay estimates that by 1662, women made up between forty and fifty percent of the Norwich, Norfolk, and Buckinghamshire Quakers.[7] Historians are still in disagreement over the exact number of Quakers practicing in the seventeenth century, but they uniformly agree that of the nearly forty thousand Quakers in the 1660s, a significant number were women.

These early Quakers are generally believed to have come from the "middle" sort of people, artisans, wholesalers and retail traders, yeomen and husbandmen.[8] In general, membership in the seventeenth century was not drawn from the laboring poor or the higher classes. Unfortunately, less work has been done specifically on the social origins of the women members. Richard Vann cites Margaret Fell and Elizabeth Fletcher as examples of "gentlewomen" among the original "Valiant Sixty," but Hugh Barbour asserts that "of Quaker women who became preachers, a surprising number had been domestic servants, and the prominence of such women among the early Quakers shows their indifference to social standing and convention."[9]

While studies of the education of early Quaker men show them to have been surprisingly well educated, the women are usually characterized as semi- or completely illiterate.[10] Our notion of seventeenth-century female education is that opportunities were extremely limited, even among upper classes. How, then, do we explain women such as Anne Travers, a gifted polemicist who began a boarding school, or Anna Trapnel, the daughter of a shipwright who declared, "I was trained up to my book and writing"?[11] The tobacconist's widow Rebecca Travers (no relation to Anne) wrote prefaces to James Nayler's pamphlets, and Anne Audland Camm was sent at age thirteen to London specifically for her education; Sarah Cheevers and Katherine Evans were merely two housewives and mothers from the west country, but they set off to Alexandria to preach and wrote a hundred-page account of their travels and persecution in Malta.

In accounts of conversions, one sees a close association of maids and their mistresses which may account in part for how the women of the servant classes learned to read and write. Jane Waugh, a servant of the early leader John Camm, is depicted in modern accounts as "quite illiterate but on fire with the Quaker message," although her sister Dorothy wrote an account of her persecution in Carlile.[12] Margaret Fell's daughters all were tutored by William Caton, and it appears from her correspondence that her female servants were literate as well.[13] The large number of Quaker women writers, supposedly drawn mostly from the lower middle classes, suggests that there is still work to be done on the extent and nature of women's literacy in the seventeenth century. In this group, at least, it does not appear that one can simply take for granted that the women were illiterate because of their social status.[14] Our assumptions about women's literacy, however, may well be one reason that this body of writings has been overlooked, with only the "gentlewoman" Margaret Fell used to represent them: Given our notions of their educational possibilities, we have simply assumed they did not write or publish.

It is also important to remember that women were not confined to supporting roles in the earliest days of the Quaker movement. Quakerism is described by historians such as Mack, Reay, and Thomas as offering women a spiritual equality unequaled in any of the other sects or the established church.[15] Women participated in aspects of religion usually considered strictly masculine, but as George Fox put it, "*Moses* and *Aaron,* and the *Seventy Elders,* did not say to those *Assemblies* of Women, We can do our Work our selves, and you are fitter to be at home to wash Dishes."[16] Forty-five percent of the ministers sent to America between 1656 and 1663 were women.[17] Their sex did not invoke mercy from the magistrates or pity from the mobs: Elizabeth Fletcher and Elizabeth Leavens were ordered whipped out of Oxford after angry scholars had "violently pushed Elizabeth Fletcher against a grave-stone, and then threw her into the grave. . . . they threw them into a miry ditch, through which they dragged [her] . . . and so cruelly abused her, that she was in a painful condition till her death, which fell out not long after."[18]

In addition to their activities in public preaching and missionary work, of particular importance to this study is the prominence of women in the early history of the Quaker press. Arnold Lloyd answers the question of how the Quakers could succeed in publishing more than twenty-five hundred pieces by 1700 under strict government censorship by pointing to the fact that "during the early years of the Restoration, Quaker books and pamphlets were printed surreptitiously, often by women, one at least of whom worked a private press."[19] Mary Westwood, Tace Sowle, and "Mrs. Dover" assisted in publishing these titles in open defiance of the law. Quakerism offered women an important position in the literary life of the movement which far exceeded the range of activities of women publishing in other areas. Quaker women do not fit our pattern of socially controlled and intimidated women writing for "private" readership; instead, we have a sizable group of women, signing their names, using the printed word to reach as large an audience as possible.

Literary endeavors were encouraged by several features of early Quakerism. Chief among its tenets is the belief in the "Inner Light" as the sole teacher and guide to a spiritual life. The early Quakers believed that the Light of Christ dwells in every person; obeying it can lead one out of sin by forcing one, as Fell explained it, to "deal plainly with [yourself]; it will rip you open and lay you open . . . naked and bear [sic] before the Lord God."[20] This spirit is infallible, and the Quakers believed that one could become truly regenerate, to return to the state of Adam and Eve before the Fall.

The belief in the Inner Light did away with the need for external authorities. In one of his earliest revelations in 1646, Fox stated: "The Lord opened unto me that being bred at Oxford or Cambridge was not enough to fit and qualify men to be ministers of Christ; and I stranged at it because it was the common belief of the people."[21] This must have had enormous appeal for women, who, literate or not, would never have had the slightest opportunity for university theological training. Instead of being subordinate to the external, masculine institutions of academia and the church, the woman sought knowledge residing in her; she, and she alone, became the "authority" through the Light.[22]

Therefore, a specific appeal of the doctrine of the Inner Light for women was the autonomy it offered, freedom from external controlling structures of thinking, speaking, and writing. As Sarah Blackborrow, among many, pointed out, "Christ the Power was one in the Male and in the Female, one Spirit, one Light, one Life, one Power, which brings forth the same Witness and Minsters forth it self, in the Males as in the Female."[23] Men and women were equally capable of spiritual perfectibility. Specific defenses of this position to audiences that in some cases, according to Fox, did not believe that women even had souls were written by both male and female Quakers; Fell, Blackborrow, and Dorothy White stand out among the women polemicists on this issue. Given this general social climate and the violent response to women's preaching, the doctrine of the Inner Light guaranteed these early women writers both the freedom to write and an acute sensitivity to issues concerning gender and the hostility it could provoke.

Fox used the issue of women preaching as a distinguishing element of the teachings of the Inner Light as opposed to false academic interpretations of the Scriptures. He recounts how in 1648 he attended a debate among different groups, including Presbyterians, Baptists, and Independents.

> At last one woman asked a question out of Peter . . . and the priest said to her, "I permit not a woman to speak in the church." Whereupon I was rapt, as in a rapture, in the Lord's power; and I stepped up in a place and asked the priest, "Dost thou call this place a church? Or doest thou call this mixed multitude a church?" For the woman asking the question he should have answered it. . . . and it broke them all to pieces and confused them, and they all turned against me into jangling.[24]

Seventeenth-century Quakerism did not overturn all notions concerning the roles of women in the family and in society, but it openly challenged many of them. Certainly it offered its female members the widest possible scope for activities, and it provided organized financial as well as moral support for women's writings.

And print occupied an important and defining role in the early history of Quakerism. The press was used by Fox to shape public opinion, to refute antagonists, and to define and to cohere a scattered and often persecuted membership. Authorship by women, therefore, was not a marginalized activity: "It is quite impossible," declared Lloyd, "to estimate the influence of books in moulding the character, in setting the standards, and it may be said, in enhancing the self-esteem of the Quakers during the formative period of growth in their society."[25] The seventeenth-century Quakers as a body set up presses, financed printing, and oversaw distribution; they also established a library of their writings, collected documents relating to the early period, and assembled an archive, the Swarthmore papers, from which their history could be written. After 1672, they controlled both the content and style of every piece of writing which wished to be identified as Quaker.

In their writings as well as their speech, Quakers used language to distinguish themselves from the unregenerate masses. As Richard Bauman noted, Quakers frequently referred to themselves as speakers of "plain" language, meaning that they were the "remnant of Israel singled out by the Lord as the people of the 'pure language,' as foretold by the prophet Zephaniah."[26] In addition to refusing to rely on external authorities to shape their spiritual experiences, Quakers' use of language reflects their refusal to value the external signifier over the internal signified. Maurice Creasey refers to this tension between the "Outward" and the "Innerward" as typical of Quaker prose. When Ann Gargill criticizes the Catholic faith, it is on the grounds that it relies on the external symbols rather than the experience of true faith; it is characterized in her words by "making of Images, and painting of likenesses of things without substance . . . [Christ] you never knew to be the light of the world, who leads to plainness, and honesty."[27] The danger of relying on external forms is that they are products of man, even the Scriptures, and are thus reflections of his fallen nature and limitations. "Images and Likenesses is your religion," Gargill charges; "you worship the works of your own hands . . . [and] exault one another, and . . . make up a God like yourselves" (pp. 5, 12).

This concept of "form" versus experience has direct consequences for reading and for authorship. "Imagination" is condemned in these writings because it is a manipulation of reality, projected by the individual self. Unfortunately, the unregenerate reader may mistake it for inspiration, particularly if he or she is misled by false teachers. Ministers and scholars may think they know the Scriptures, but, warns Fell, "they have read a Chapter, and then turn and pervert it, and mix it with their own dark Imaginations of their evil Hearts."[28] "Fill not your head," admonishes Rebecca Travers, "but feel the life."[29] As we shall see, a key problem faced by these women as writers was to discover a discourse that was not merely a repetition of Scripture or a recitation of theology, but instead a direct and immediate rendition of the experience of being filled with the Light.

The "plain" style of the Quakers has been defined in two distinct ways. T. Edmund Harvey and Luella Wright describe it as "austere" in its refusal to use honorific titles or the pagan names of the days and months and its "diffidence over positive statement."[30] Wright uses Penn to establish her three principles of Quaker literary style: (1) no display of learning, (2) no ornament to call attention to the act of writing, and (3) an appeal not just to the intellect alone.[31] Jackson Cope, on the other hand, uses Fox as his example and arrives at a very different notion of "plain" style. Cope sees the obliteration of the distinction between the metaphorical and the literal, often at the expense of grammatical structure, as the key feature of Quaker prose.[32] This "incantatory" style is marked by repetition, a combining of clusters of words and phrases from Scripture, producing an almost hypnotic effect. Certainly, as N. H. Keeble pointed out, contemporary opponents of Quakerism tended to view their prose as "distinguished by an abuse of language . . . [a style] neither civil nor sensible, but vulgar, indulgent, and idiosyncratic."[33]

Where do early Quaker women's writings fit in these contrasting definitions of "plain" style? None of these studies use women's writings. As Catherine Blecki pointed out in her essay on two later seventeenth-century Quaker women, critics have consistently "neglected or undervalued" Quaker women's literary achievements.[34] Fell's letters to Fox are occasionally cited in the general histories as examples of "extravagance of statement," the "excesses of language into which ardent devotees might be led," and "perilous rhapsody."[35] Sarah Blackborrow's *Just and Equall Balance Discovered* is applauded by Elisabeth Brockbank and Mabel Brailsford as a "touching little autobiography alive with poetic feeling," although it is neither short by Quaker standards nor an autobiography.[36] Most recently, Mary Anne Schofield has done an innovative study of the autobiographical narratives as precursors of the novel, focusing on the "romance" elements of the self-presentation. However, in the process, she maintains the model of women's literary history as a hierarchical progression to a more sophisticated "novel" narrative at the end of the eighteenth century: While lauding the late Quaker women writers for their supposed "greater awareness of a larger, more educated community . . . more acknowledgement of feminine convention, and . . . more attention paid to the larger female audiences," Schofield continues the presentation of the early Quaker women writers as semiliterate, primitive feminists.[37] Otherwise, the ninety-three plus first editions by Quaker women remain untouched by critical analysis.

We might expect, given the depiction of these first female Quakers as mostly lower class and semiliterate, that their writings would be crude, stylistically unsophisticated, and/or hysterical. What we do find is a great range of rhetorical strategies and modes of discourse. Before Quaker censorship was imposed, we find women producing texts for six essential purposes: inspirational epistles to Friends, prefaces to Friends' books, appeals to the unconverted, prophetic warnings to authority, rebuttals to attackers, and personal testimonies of persecution and of faith. Depending on the perceived audience, the women's use of language in these forms is strikingly different.

The epistle is perhaps one of the oldest and most practiced of all literary forms; Paul Schubert calls it "the most universal form of linguistic expression."[38] However, unlike our modern concept of domestic correspondence which assumes that a single writer is communicating personally and spontaneously to a single reader, even a "familiar" epistle is designed for wide, "public" readership. There are certain formulaic features in the epistle, certain recurring forms of salutation, structure, and closure, which mark the form as a document intended for multiple readership. The writer's rhetorical dexterity, therefore, may be as important as the content if his or her intention is to persuade or refute in a public forum. It can thus be a powerful form, one associated with making policy, and traditionally seen as a masculine one. The ancient Greeks and Romans, notably Cicero, brought the epistle to a high art as a mode of polished political communication; likewise, political as well as social epistolary techniques were taught through books of model letters throughout the Renaissance and Restoration periods.

But it was probably the epistles of Saint Paul that these lower- and middle-class women used as their model of epistolary style and purpose. While the women in these classes were rarely trained in the classics during this period, all had access to the Bible; of the twenty-seven books of the New Testament, twenty-one of them are in letter form. In the epistles of Paul, moreover, these early women writers found a literary model through which to express their anger at the wrongs suffered at the hands of contemporary society, their loyalty to the beleaguered and persecuted flock, and their passionate faith that the dawning of the new age was coming for the Children of Light.

Like Paul, these women wrote their epistles during a time when their faith was considered not only perverse, but also dangerous to the very fabric of society. Therefore, it is not surprising that, like his epistles, many of theirs also deal with immediate crises or challenges that needed the attention of the group at large. In 1659, a group of Quakers living in London led by Anne Gould published *An Epistle to All the Christian Magistrates* lamenting the laws, passed in an effort to control subversive activities, which permitted magistrates to fine people for traveling on Sundays and to forbid assemblies on Mondays, the Quakers' "First Day Meetings." Gould argues that magistrates who consider themselves Christians should honor, not harass, those attempting to worship. After her salutation, she offers a plea for tolerance and understanding. "Why do ye fine your Brethren about dayes?" she wonders; "Why do you Judge them, and set them at nought? Let us not Judge therefore one another, but rather judge that we put not a stumbling block before our brethren."[39] But she also points out the contradiction in the latitude shown to others as compared with the treatment of the Quakers: "Now do not you sell victuals on the Sabbath day, open your shops on the Sabbath day, and set open your shops of all sorts?" she queries. Even more telling is the behavior of the magistrates themselves:

> Many of ye will hardly go to your worship (on that day) without horses drawing of you in your Coaches. And your Cooks labour that day, and dresseth the meat for money on that day . . . now what confusion is this? Is not the Cook working for money, and the other working for money all one? (pp. 10–11)

The crowning irony for Gould is that although the magistrates claim to be simply upholding the biblical injunction not to labor or make profit on the Sabbath, "how many hundreds of pounds hath been taken from the people called Quakers for travelling to their meetings on the day, and how many 100 l. doth your Priests get on that day?" (p. 11).

Although it is addressed to "All Christian Magistrates," clearly there is a more general audience intended in this epistle. Gould appeals not only to the magistrates—a readership unlikely to be sympathetic, as their aggressive implementation of the laws had proved—but also perhaps more to the general reader, the potential convert who might not have decided whether this strange group posed a threat or not. Its balanced, reasonable tone with its telling ironic examples and its simple plea that true justice be carried out makes it an effective recruiting text by showing the supposedly Christian magistrates acting more like the Pharisees in their intolerance.

One finds this calm defense of the Quakers and their beliefs in numerous women's epistles. The title page of Margaret Fell's *True Testimony from the People of God* (1660) sets forth the purpose of the open epistle: "Published for this End, (viz) That all Sober-minded People may see the Unity and Agreement of our Doctrine and Testimony, with the Testimony of Jesus, and all the Holy Men of God. With the Difference between Us, and Them that have the Form of Words, but not the Power thereof." Like Paul's epistles to the Galatians, these open epistles to different groups, including the Jews as well as the established Anglican church and the other radical sects such as the Ranters, are primarily designed to refute the errors in popular beliefs about Quakers.

This did not mean, however, that these same women were not capable of righteous anger against their oppressors. "Feare the living God" is the ringing opening of Margaret Killin's blast to the ministers and magistrates in Plymouth; "Howle ye Rich men," she announces dramatically, "for the misery which is coming upon you, for the rust of your Silver and Gold shall eat you thorow as a Canker, and shall rise up in judgement against you."[40] Using verses from prophets Micah, Ezekiel, and Jeremiah, Killin establishes a continuity between the sinners of the biblical past and England's present powers:

> Howle ye proud Priests, for the misery that is coming upon you, for ye shall run to and fro, as drunken men, and none shall be to pitie you. Wo to you that have fed yourselves with the fat, and cloathed your selves with the wool, and the people perish for want of knowledge. . . . If ye had stood in my counsel [saith the Lord], ye should have turned many awaie from the evill of his doings, but because ye have departed out of my counsel, I wil spread dung upon your faces, yea I have cast dung on your faces alreadie; and now the false prophet rides on the beast, but they both shall be cast into the Lake, which is prepared for the devill and his angels. (p. 2)

Killin offers a catalog of the oppressors of the Quakers, rebuking not only their persecution of the Quakers but also their misleading of the general public; she includes "covetous Lawyers, Drunkards, Swearers, Whoremongers, Adulturers, and all that telleth and maketh a lie . . . all you proud and lustfull ones, who feeds on dainty dishes, and spends the creation upon their lusts" (p. 3). After flattening the opposition through establishing their connection with those reviled by the prophets, she signs herself, "From one who is a lover of your faults, and should rejoyce to hear that any of you is turned from the evill of his doings."

But it was not only to correct the ignorant or rebuke the oppressor that Quaker women wrote their epistles. While the epistle did serve an important function as a type of recruiting document, it also was extremely important in helping the group to stay together and to develop a sense of joint identity during the times of persecution. The seventeenth-century editor of Margaret Fell's epistles points out to the "Friendly Reader": "The following Epistles were written at the first Appearance of Truth among us, when we were young in it," yet they are worth reading in later days. The epistles display Fell's first steps toward understanding the principle that the Quakers call the "Inner Light" that should guide all actions, and as such they chronicle not only her individual spiritual development but also the process in general by which the Quakers came together.

> And so we came to discern betwixt the Precious and the Vile, and betwixt the Holy and the unclean, and betwixt the Chaff and the Wheat; and between those that served God, and those that served him not. And when we came to this Sight, and Knowledge, and Discerning, then we became very zealous for God, and for his Truth, and for the Preservation of this People in the Truth: And our Hearts became tender, and we had a pity for all People's Souls, that remained in Darkness. And we were moved of the Lord to write often to Friends, and our Testimony was very much to the Light of Christ in the Conscious.[41]

The editor concludes, "So, here is a few Epistles preserved . . . in Love to all People, we bring these that we have to open view; that, if the Lord gives a Blessing to them, they may be serviceable hereafter, as they have been to many heretofore" (p. 47). Like Paul's epistles to Romans, and George Fox's to the congregations, Fell's are intended to educate the fledgling flock and to support their infant faith as it develops under harsh circumstances.

And there is little question but that Quaker women's epistles such as Fell's did have a major impact in helping to cohere the early Quaker movement. Anne Audland wrote to Fell from prison in 1655, "My sufferings hath been great since I saw thee. Dear heart, pray for me that I may be kept in the eternal wisdom of God. . . . My dear and near and eternal mother, by thee I am nourished. I see and feel thy care over all the lambs of my Father."[42] She writes to Fell that she "hast been strength unto me when I was weak, and pure refreshment have I found in thy presence"; through Fell, even this prison "is a place of joy indeed."

The range of the women's epistles helps to counterbalance our image of the early women writers as semiliterate "rhapsodic" writers. These women are also capable of shaping different modes of discourse not only in separate pieces, but also within a single work. Margaret Fell's pamphlet writings are often based on a three-part structure, in which different voices are employed for different goals. Her appeals to the Jews are characterized by a persuasive call to recognize common ground, with no invective or "excessive" language. She even closes with a part of a prayer for true faith in Hebrew to demonstrate her ability to place herself in her reader's frame of reference.

This same tone of quiet rationality, emphasized by controlled use of parallel structures and repetition, is likewise found in the middle section addressed to the unconverted Puritans in *A Testimonie of the Touchstone* (1656). The reader is urged to take the Scriptures and to apply them to the teachings and lives of his or her minister: "Now all you people see where you are, and try your teachers what they lead you into."[43] She shows none of the excesses of diction attributed to her in the letters to Fox; she speaks the language of the world to the as yet unregenerate. And yet, in the same pamphlet, when Fell addresses the "False Prophets" who are responsible for misleading the people, the gentleness vanishes: "Your profession without you will not serve you, it strikes in the Lords nostrils, and all your righteousness shall be spread as dung upon your faces, it is as filthy rags, and as the early dew it shall pass a way, and never be mentioned" (p. 3). In her condemnation, the literal preachers have merged with the seducers of the people in Mal. 2:3, who will suffer a similar fate.

In the final section of the pamphlet, Fell handles attacks made on the Quakers by the Ranters. It was extremely important for the

Quakers to establish themselves as different from this group, with whom they were often lumped in their early period. Rather than issuing a straightforward denunciation or a reasonable plea to reconsider, Fell adopts a dialogue format, in which she, of course, gets the last word. It is a presentation style designed to appeal to the reader who is a potential convert from the middle section rather than to any Ranter, proving by logical demonstration the difference between the two groups. Fell sets the Ranter up so that his final question reveals an internal contradiction of his professed beliefs.

> Here thou serpent hast made thy self manifest to be the tempting into sin and transgression all thy paper through, and pleaded for lust, filthinesse, and uncleannesse and liberty of flesh, which lusteth against the spirit; and now at last thou hast uttered forth blasphemy and confusion, and laid thy self open to all. (p. 34)

In this one piece by Fell, we find three rhetorical voices: the tone of quiet reasonable persuasion which invites the reader rather than coerces; the tone of righteous invective which strips away false trappings of spiritual authority to reveal the essence of its evil; and the tone of triumphant disputation, whereby the opponent is defeated by having his own words turned back on him.

We find this use of multiple voices in many of the early female Quaker polemicists. Ann Gargill, Mary Howgill, Margaret Killin, Barbara Pattison, and Dorothy White all make use of shifts in voice and argumentative strategy within single works. Their tones within these pieces range from emotional pleas to repent to cold denunciations of mercenary motives behind keeping congregations in ignorance. They are capable of both love and rage within a few pages, passing from simple austere statements of personal faith to lurid insults and nearly overwhelming accusations.

The same control over diction and tone for desired effect is also revealed in early Quaker persecution narratives, some of which are cast in epistolary form. The closest to the "plain" austere style described by Harvey is found in the accounts of the trials and persecution and in the appeals to the unconverted, many of which were presented in epistolary form. Both of these genres presuppose an audience of the potentially regenerate. The language is designed, therefore, to be accessible and acceptable, to persuade and also to gain sympathy for the Quakers.

In persecution narratives, the aim is often to shock. Rebecca Trav-

---

ers's description of Nayler's brutal beating is stark, and its very lack of emotional excess makes it even more chilling.

> To my best discerning there was not a space bigger than the breadth of a mans nail free from stripes and blood, from his shoulders near his waste [*sic*]. And his right Arm was sorely striped. His hands were also sorely hurt with the Cords, that they bled, and were swell'd. The blood and wounds on his back did very little appear at first sight, by reason of the abundance of Dirt that covered them, till it was washed off.[44]

Travers concludes her account by noting that Nayler had been left in this condition untreated for several hours prior to her arrival, underlining the lack of humanity shown by the supposedly "civil" authorities.

One finds this same calm detailing of horrific situations in Dorothy Waugh's account of being "bridled" in Carlile. In addition to describing the instrument of her punishment, a great weighted iron helmet with a thick plate forced in her mouth, Waugh establishes the violence of the "keepers of the peace" as well as the illegality of the proceedings. The mayor was "so violent & full of passion" that he refused to listen to her answers or to specify the charges against her.[45] In the process of "bridling" her, the guards tore her clothes and hair, and "the people to see me so violently abused were broken into teares, but [the mayor] cryed out on them and said, for foolish pitty, one may spoil a whole Citty. And the man that kept the prison doore demanded two pence of every one that came to see me while their bridle remained on me." Unable to shake her composure, the mayor completely lost his: "[He] gave me very vile and unsavory words, which were not fit to proceed out of any man's mouth, and charged the Officer to whip me out of the Towne, from Constable to Constable to send me, till I came to my owne home, when as they had not any thing to lay to my charge." In the persecution narratives, there is no question who the villains are. But there are no conventions of female "romance" narrative, as Schofield suggested, either—for example, no male intervenes to save the day in these early women's accounts of persecution. The self-controlled teller of these bloody tales remains in possession of her faith and her words, while those who persecute her display in their blustering excuses and barbarous actions violations of not only English law, but also human decency.

As seen in this last example, the persecution narratives are designed to have two functions: To sway public opinion to the unjustly persecuted Quakers and to testify to Friends that faith triumphs over the rage of the wicked. The lengthy account of the imprisonment of Katherine Evans and Sarah Cheevers displays both of these functions and provides an example of the range of literary modes used by the women to achieve them. It also introduces us to another mode of discourse, that of ecstatic prophecy.

This is a Short Revelation of some of the Cruel Sufferings (For the Truths sake) of Katherine Evans and Sarah Cheevers, In the Inquisition in the Isle of Malta (1662) delivers everything promised in the title except brevity. The two women left their families in the west country and were on their way to Alexandria when they were seized by the Inquisition in Malta in 1659; they were not released until the end of 1662. The treatise consists of their collected writings smuggled out by Daniel Baker, supplemented with letters written to refute the Inquisitor, to convert the unbeliever, and to reassure their families and fellow Quakers.

Katherine Evans wrote the first section, which describes their arrest and initial questioning. The women were kept in "an inner Room in the Inquisition which had but two little holes in it for light or air; but the glory of the Lord did shine round us."[46] Her depiction of their lives there is plainly and simply written and enormously powerful.

> The Room was so hot and so close, that we were fain to rise often out of our bed, and lie down at a chink of their door for air to fetch breath; and with the fire within, and the heat without, our skin was like sheeps Leather, and the hair did fall off our heads, and we did fail often; our afflictions and burthens were so great, that when it was day we wished for night; and when it was night we wished for day; we sought death, but could not find it; We desired to die, but death fled from us. (p. 13)

The cadences are biblical; the careful balancing of antithetical clauses and the repetitious structure of the sentences impose control and order on an unbearable existence, demonstrating in the process how suffering can be endured with resolution.

Conditions became so bad that Evans wrote to the Inquisitor to tell him that if he desired their deaths, there were more efficient means available to kill them. It was not their blood that the Inquisition wanted, of course, but their conversion. Both women record in lively detail conversations with the Inquisitor and the friars. "He said I should be whipt, and quartered, and burnt that night in Malta, and my Mate too; wherefore did we come to teach them?" Evans recounts; "I told him I did not fear, that the Lord was on our side . . . and they were all smitten as dead men, and went away" (p. 10). Every conversation is a triumph for the women: "The fryar then came to me, and askt me, why I did not work? I said unto him, What Work dost thou do? He said he did write. I told him I would write too, if he would bring me a Pen, Ink, and Paper; and I would write truth" (p. 41). Attempts to get Sarah Cheevers to admire paintings of the Madonna and Child prove equally unsuccessful: "I stampt my foot and said Cursed be all Images and Imagemakers, and all that fall down to worship them" (p. 39). The two women even managed to preach in prison. "The Lord did work wonderfully for us and his Truth," Evans explains, because there were many workers about repairing the palace; "we were carried forth with great power to declare in the Name of the Lord Jesus, not fearing the face of man" (p. 15).

In addition to narratives of the events and conversations during their imprisonment and of their bouts with the Inquisitor, the women also include transcendent visions and celebratory verse. These elements, omitted in Schofield's discussion, lift the narrative out of any resemblance to temporal, secular romance. In her fevered state, Evans experienced a vision of the woman clothed in the sun, wearing the crown of twelve stars, which is found in Revelation 12, which deals with the persecution of the church by the Antichrist. She declares, however, "Whatsoever I have written, it is not because it is recorded in the Scripture, or that I have heard such things; but in obedience to the Lord I have written the things which I did hear, see, tasted, and handled of the good Word of God" (p. 12). In her words, we see a manifestation of the doctrine of the Inner Light. The words of the Scriptures are no longer merely external signs defined by a human authority. Evans, in her vision, has lived them. The passage ceases to be a symbol to be solved by the intellect, but has become a moment to be experienced, involving her whole sensory being—she doesn't read and comprehend the Scriptures, she hears, sees, tastes, and holds the Word.

The language used to retell this experience is not that of the theological discourses of the false ministers, the discourse of Babel.

The same Katherine Evans who could so bluntly and pithily put the Inquisition in its place turns to a very different style to celebrate the power of the Lord to her fellow sharers in the Light.

> [God] hath carryed us through, and ever as great affliction as most of our Brethren and sufferers for his Name, both in mockings, scoffings, scornings, reproaches, stripes, contradictions, perils at Land, and perils at Sea, fiery tryals, cruel threatenings, fears within, and frightenings without, terrible temptations and persecutions, and dreadful imprisonments and buffeting of Satan. . . . O the sorrows, the mournings, the tears! but those that sow in tears, shall reap in joy. A true sorrow begets a true joy; and a true Crosse, a true Crowne: For when our sorrows did abound, the Love of God did abound much more; the deeper the sorrows, the greater the joys; the greater the Crosse, the weightier the Crowne. (pp. 30–31)

This is much closer to Cope's description of incantatory prose, yet it appears as part of a much longer "plain" chronological narrative. The sentences in this section run for paragraphs; the writer allows the feelings to overflow grammatical banks. The short cadenced phrases of the conclusion act as a dam to check the rising tide and to delineate the significance of the experience being re-created.

The intent of this use of language is not to persuade, but to sweep the reader into a different frame of reference, the inner rather than the outward, literal circumstance. While the outward world proceeds narratively, in a chronological progression, the experience of the Inner Word transcends physical location and time, and biblical past and spiritual present become one. When Evans receives a command from the Lord to rise up, she leaves her sickbed: "We stood at the door in the power of the Lord[,] I did scarce know whether I was in the body, or out of the body" (p. 9). When a mob comes to lynch them, it is the Lord who "smote them with blindness, they could not find the way." When the mob returns the next night: "They came up to the Gate to devour us in a moment. But the Lord lifted up his Standard with his own Spirit (of Might) and made them to retreat, and they fled as dust before the Wind" (p. 10). The spiritual and literal have merged. The confusion of those in the crowd is both a physical and spiritual inability to see their way, and their retreat is not only from the prison gate in Malta, but also from David, in chapter 18 of the Psalms. In her retelling, Evans does not simply fill the head with events, but also "feels the life" of the Scriptures, inviting the believing reader to do so, too.

The fullest expression of early Quaker women's command of both the Bible and colloquial English is displayed in the prophetic writings such as these. As Michel de Certeau characterized sixteenth- and seventeenth-century "mystic speech" in general, it stems in part from a desire to reinterpret the "tradition" "by a set of procedures allowing a new treatment of language – of all contemporary language, not only the area delimited by theological knowledge of the corpus of patristic and scriptural works."[47] Mystic speech is an attempt, thus, to articulate a re-vision of received tradition.

In these works, one of the most important goals is to separate clearly the state of the writer from that of the spiritually degenerate, to establish the "otherness" of the Quaker experience as opposed to the orthodox Protestantism the early Quakers condemn. In this way, early Quaker women's writings function in a very similar fashion to the *l'écriture feminine* envisioned by Cixous: "A feminine text cannot fail to be more than subversive. It is volcanic; as it is written it brings about an upheaval of the old property crust, carrier of masculine investments; there's no other way." For Cixous, the woman in the act of writing as a woman escapes defining boundaries, both linguistic and institutional.

> This doesn't mean that she's an undifferentiated magma, but that she doesn't lord it over her body or her desire. . . . Her libido is cosmic, just as her unconscious is worldwide. Her writing can only keep going, without ever inscribing or discerning contours, daring to make these vertiginous crossings of the other(s) ephemeral and passionate sojourns in him, her, them, whom she inhabits long enough to look at from the point closest to their unconscious from the moment they awaken. . . . She alone dares and wishes to know from within, where she, the outcast, has never ceased to hear the resonance of forelanguages. She lets the other language speak – the language of 1,000 tongues which knows neither enclosure nor death. To life she refuses nothing. Her language does not contain, it carries; it does not hold back, it makes possible.[48]

Acceptance by conventional authorities using conventional standards is not the goal in either type of writing. In the case of the first Quaker women, not only were they erupting through the prescribed, masculine institutional framework of spiritual experience, but also, through the creation of a heteroglossia of Quaker prophecy, the language and structure of these pieces bound together the understanders, while repelling nonbelievers.

Revelation is the source of much of the vocabulary of these women's visions. Mary Howgill retells her experiences with the loosing of the chained beasts: "And now is the time of the Lord, wherein he hath required me to write what he shewed me by Vision, much of whereof is already come on this Land."[49] She does not say she read and understood the Scriptures; she was made to feel, see, and smell terrible things, and she recognizes her England in Revelation. "Blessed, Blessed are all who wait upon the living God, and hear what he saith unto them," she declares, and in particular, "blessed are they that in the Lord's time either speak or write by Revelation, by Prophecy, or Vision."[50]

The writings of Dorothy White and Sarah Blackborrow offer extended contrasting examples of Quaker women's use of prophetic discourse and of this merging of the concrete and the spiritual, the transformation of the landscape of England into that of Revelation. Little is known about these women; all that remains of Dorothy White is the record of her imprisonment in Southwark in 1663 and the titles of nineteen pamphlets. Unlike Hester Biddle, another prolific writer of prophecy who was primarily interested in announcing impending punishment, White shows a greater desire to celebrate the coming of Zion. She wrote mostly during the early years of the Restoration when Quakers were imprisoned by the thousands under the 1661 Proclamation. Her writings repeatedly emphasize that the day is near when God will gather his flock, and that the present trials are merely a means of refining the gold.

While she is quite capable of issuing "alarums" of considerable force ("O LONDON! hasten, hasten, prepare; prepare, to meet the Lord God, who is riding swiftly to the Battel; whose day of Vengeance is coming"), she identifies herself as primarily an instrument to announce the glories of salvation: "Yea, the Lord God hath spoken, and therefore I will prophesie."[51] In the midst of persecution, "Now is the Glory of all Nations come, and the Bridegroom's Voice is in the Land of the Redeemed." White often reverses curses on the damned to show the felicity of the saved. While the voice of "our beloved is terrible unto the unrighteous part," she offers reassurance to those who are ready, like the ten virgins in the parables:

> God is now bringing forth his own Likeness, and his own image, in his Sons and Daughters; and he is creating a New in Christ Jesus, all that do believe.

And so that which was before the world began, God is bringing forth and this must indure for ever, when the world shall be no more.[52]

White's visions transform reality into a process of refinement, of plucking the lilies from admist the thorns; Friends should endure and rejoice, because the persecution itself is actually a sign of the near arrival of the Judgment Day.

As a writer, White depicts herself as an instrument of God, specifically directed by him to write and to publish. "And the Lord God hath spoken, and therefore I will speak, for God hath unloosed my tongue, to speak the praise of his Name."[53] Like Evans, she is adamant that she is not merely repeating what she has read or heard from man; "this mine eye hath seen, in the invisible and eternal power."[54] Like the prophet in Revelation, she is "ravished" by the Word. Her transmittal attempts to re-create the overflowing, overwhelming nature of the experience:

for the *ravishing* Glory of God did overshadow me, often saying, Publish the day of the Lord God, lift up thy voice like a Trumpet, as a mighty shout; and this is to go through this Nation, as it was given into me, for this very end, to send it with speed, as the everlasting Message of Life, as greetings of Peace, by the Word of Salvation.[55]

White also indentifies herself with David, the singer of the Lord's praises. "The Lord hath lighted my Candle, and it must not be hid," she declares. The persecuted Friends, too, shall "sing the new Songs" as they "follow the Lamb through Tribulation . . . [and] play the Harp of David."[56] Several of her pamphlets mix prose and verse; given the nature of her celebratory prose, which uses short repeated phrases rather than logical progression of cause and effect, there is little difference in content or presentation apart from the imposition of a rhyme pattern. "Arise O Seed of *Sion*, arise in thy Beauty, in Glory, in the Brightness, in the Majesty of the most High," she calls; "Oh! Rejoyce for ever, and sing *Hallalujahs* and Praises unto the God of Power."[57] Her visions call for a similar response from the reader, an uplifting of the spirit, a singing of praises let freely forth to transcend the limitations of prison and persecution, the recovery of the thousand voices.

Sarah Blackborrow, too, wrote out of her experiences of persecution. The wife of William Blackborrow of London, she was active in the movement from its start, setting up a meeting at Hammersmith in 1655, and starting up the "box meetings" to provide relief for Quaker families.[58] "Dreamer and poet though she was," Brailsford noted, "she proved herself perhaps the most practical in good works of all the London women."[59] She was a friend of both Nayler and Richard Hubberthorne, writing prefaces to their pamphlets; she nursed Hubberthorne through his last days in Newgate Prison and recorded his dying words.

Her literary career spans from 1657 to 1663 and consists of seven pieces of which we know. She shares with White the discourse of prophecy, but her vision of the future is apocalyptic; rather than the shining Everlasting, she sees the presence of evil in the present, and her prophecy generally takes the form of warnings or admonitions. Blackborrow's treatment as a writer by scholars typifies the problems of working with this type of material: Her spiritual awakening described in *The Just and Equall Balance Discovered* (1660) has been labeled by Brockbank and Brailsford as "poetic" with no explanation, and the rest of that treatise and all her polemical works remain unexamined.

Her *Visit to the Spirit in Prison* (1658) demonstrates her abilities as a polemicist and her literary skills. Like many of Fell's pieces, it has a three-part structure: an address to the false ministers, a personal testimony, and a plea to those still seeking Christ. She shows her awareness of rhetorical convention not only by her ability to change style and structure depending on her audience, but also in her manipulation of the appearance of the printed text itself. She changes into italics for her personal testimony, a visual sign of the experience and the flow of the prose, and back into roman letter for the final plea to the unregenerate. In her presentation, she shows more than a semiliterate understanding of the ways in which print can be manipulated to affect perception of content.[60]

The core of her argument is the discrepancy between the ministers' professions of faith and their actions. It would have been better for them, she declares, if "[they] had laboured with [their] hands, doing the things which is [are] honest, then to have coveted the wages of the unrighteous."[61] They are guided not by the Inner Light, but by "one spirit, and 'tis [their] own." Their words and their actions do not correspond because they are using a fallen language to explain what should be a divine revelation, and their persecution of the Quakers hardly fits with their professed Christianity. In the "poor despised people, who suffer whippings, stockings, imprisonments, scoffings," warns Blackborrow, God "hath appeared in power and great glory," but not in the ministers who have only "[their] brains . . . to boast of."

In her later pieces, one can see Blackborrow's growing anger with those she views as comfortable commercial ministers, living off the blood of their congregations. She lets fly a magnificent warning in 1659 to the "hireling" ministers. "You Priests who preach for money, and prepare for war if you have it not, the blood of the innocent ones who have dyed in stinking holes and dungeons (thrown there by you because they could not deny Gods Witness in them, to pay you your money) that blood cryeth loud, *Vengeance, Vengeance.*"[62] By 1660, her vocabulary has become closer to that in Revelation, condemning still those ministers who embrace "another spirit, which is proud, impatient, wrathfull, covetuous, persecuting, and rejoycing to strengthen the same in others."[63] Again, she makes use of external, visual cues to signal a shift in her mode of discourse; when she moves into her apocalyptic denunciation of the ministers, which runs for a full page linked only by commas, the type changes to italics.

The persecution, of course, did not stop, and her friend Richard Hubberthorne was one of its victims. Her account of his death is a striking contrast in style from her prophetic discourse; she is creating a memorial to a close friend as well as the hagiography of an important early Friend. "His mind was redeemed out of visible things," as he lay dying in Newgate, "his mind was kept feeding on the retyredness within, so that one might feel his strength in the still spirit which kept him."[64] She includes his dying words so that all Friends will be able to share this strength of spirit. He sent for her to tell her that he would die within the next day:

> he put his Arme about me, and said Do not seek to hold me, for it is too strait for me; and out of this straitness I must go, for I am wound into largeness, and am to be lifted up on high, far above all; so in the Evening being the first day of the weeke, and the 17th of the 6th month he left the Body. (a)3r

This is the strength that makes a saint, and Blackborrow relates it with great simplicity and restraint, in a prose precise yet tender, completely different from her denunciation of those responsible for his being there.

When she is celebrating the blessings of being in the Inner Light,

Blackborrow—like Fell, Evans, and White—must overcome a stylistic difficulty in retelling her spiritual experiences. She cannot fall into the patterns of authorized, institutional spiritual discourse created by the academic preachers and theologians (who have only their brains to boast of), which she has so roundly denounced. "You have been long wording of it," she charges the ministers; "Oh that there were an heart in you to answer the Lords love . . . [you] know nothing, nor answer the Call of the Lord, though you may profess it in words."[65] How does one so suspicious of language as an empty external shell write about a profound spiritual moment to share it with fellow believers?

This tension between experience and language is most clearly seen in the autobiographical sections of *A Visit to the Spirit in Prison* and *The Just and Equall Balance Discovered.* As a child of eight or nine, Blackborrow had felt the power of the Inner Light but did not understand what it was; "notwithstanding all my profession, I never witnessed a separation between the light and the darkness, nor never so much as heard that such a thing was to be."[66] It was the words of the false ministers which in part blocked her realization. Their language was beautiful but deceitful: "Notwithstanding all your high words, you are out of the power, in the alienation, out from the life of God," she charges, "you are lyeing down at ease in a habitation which is not eternal, but are Vagrants, having no habitation in God" (p. 9).

Therefore, when she comes to her own spiritual turmoil and revelation, the power of the account cannot arise from "high words" or conventional theological formulations of the experience. The language must not be alienated from the spirit, issuing only out of the fallen intellect. The process again recalls Cixous's depiction of *l'écriture feminine:* Writing must be rediscovered within, not learned in forms and patterns from the visible world.

> I could never find out the beginning nor the ending of it with all my falling wisedome, and then I said in my heart, but where is Sion the Citty of God, which is at unity in it selfe, in one eternall spirit, and I went forth and was very active to enquire both of Priests and others, but could never find that which could satisfie me, whilst mine eye and eare were abroad, then I said in my heart all men are liars, and then a resolution was begotten in me, to find Christ in me, as neare and as willing to deliver me as the Devill was to destroy me, I should never be saved, so

I returned into the silence out of all babling talke, and daily felt that spirit to lead and teach me which was a convincer in my conscience, and then some friends who were called Quakers, came to visit me, and I confess I was very loath to see them, for I was afraid of being deceived, or going forth any more; for I began to feele a Teacher in me.[67]

The movement in this passage is from the external — seeking in books and from preachers, using "fallen" wisdom, "very active to enquire," "going forth" — regressing to the internal — "I returned into silence," "I began to feel." The external is characterized by action and frustration, and its language is a lie. The internal is still, silent, and satisfying; it does not "babble" its message, but instead one discovers it through "feel." [68]

Blackborrow's choice to use parataxis rather than the simple declarative sentences in her other pieces works in two ways. It mirrors the lack of closure in her pursuit through logic of "the beginning and the end" where one question simply leads to the next. It also suggests the synchronic nature of the experience of discovering the inner Teacher, in whom the beginning is also the end, the alpha and the omega. Once retired into silence, she finds the seamless unity that the fragmented, alienated speech of the preachers denied her.

It is ecstatic prose such as Blackborrow's which most dramatically characterizes the writings of the early Quaker women, whether it is of the "incantatory" style described by Cope most typically found in women's denunciations of the false prophets, or the fluid parataxis of their visions of Zion. As we have seen, these women had a much more sophisticated command of language and of the conventions of print than our assumptions about their level of literacy have led us to believe. The same woman who writes with passionate lyricism about seeking the Inner Light is equally capable of pithy put-downs of unregenerate magistrates. Ironically, as powerful as the ecstatic prose is, it may also be the principle reason that these women as writers have received so little attention.

The ecstatic writings put barriers in the path of appreciation. They do not fit our conventional definitions of "literature," being in several ways closer in format to what we term journalism and in printing to "popular" literature: They are typically one to twenty pages, often coauthored, and often directed at specific individuals, usually antagonists. Most important, however, is that the ecstatic writings are extremely difficult to read. The form ignores or, in my view, deliberately subverts orthodox grammatical structures; its appeal is to the emotions rather than the analytic mind—once one begins a sentence, one must continue in the flow, or get hopelessly lost three-quarters of the way down the page, for meaning is not available in the middle. It is a prose style for believers, not for cool, detached, unregenerate critics.

In addition, these writings rarely figure in the Quaker canon. As we have seen, the seventeenth- and early eighteenth-century Quakers were at some pains to establish and to preserve through reprinting a body of early Quaker literature. With the exception of "the nursing Mother of Quakerism," Margaret Fell, these women have been left out of the Quaker canon. As Wright pointed out, many "second-generation" Quakers disapproved of the early founders' writings "because they believed these laments to emanate from fanatically inclined representatives . . . [and] they strove to check them through the Morning Meeting."[69] Cope describes Penn's generation as "anti-evangelical" and cites its censorship efforts as the cause of the "disappearance of the vivid stylistic traits" of early Quaker writers such as Fox.[70]

The second-generation Quakers were consciously shaping their public image and creating a history to strengthen the development of their movement by defining more closely what was "Quaker." They ruled on style and content "in their fuller consciousness that they had become the makers of Quaker literature."[71] They rejected a paper by Fox himself and a book by Fell; they wrote to Abigail Fisher of her writings that "as to what's in verse, they rather advise to have it in prose."[72] Given such close control, it is easy to see how and why the writings of women such as Dorothy White, Margaret Killin, Mary Howgill, Martha Simmonds, and Sarah Blackborrow were allowed to sink out of sight, while their charitable works and heroic actions in the early days were carefully recorded and celebrated in Quaker history. Apart from Fell, the pieces by women which were reprinted tended to be the historical accounts of persecution, such as that by Evans and Cheevers, in which the ecstatic visions are presented within a controlled narrative.

Twentieth-century literary historians, especially those interested in women's writings, need to recognize the extent to which our perceptions of this group of women have been shaped by the policies of Penn and the second-generation Quakers, in much the same fashion as the nineteenth-century editors remade the Renaissance in their attempt to define "womanly" writing. This chapter merely suggests possible ways in which a very large and mostly untouched body of literature by women could be read in the context of women's writings. It also suggests the range and nature of their work: Margaret Fell, as important as she is, is not the epitome of the corpus of these women's writings.

These women writers are significant to the study of women's literary history for several reasons. As a group, the early Quaker women writers confound our notions about women's education, involvement in publication, and attitudes toward authorship and audience. Their writings are designed for print, conceived as public utterances, and consciously used to create and to cohere a growing social movement. They display a mastery of different discursive styles, from blunt colloquial English to soaring visionary "pure" language that consciously attempts to transcend the boundaries of fallen speech. By leaving them out of our canon of women's literature, we deny them their mastery of their chosen forms and impoverish our understanding of the abilities and influence of early women writers in general.

Their fate also demonstrates how the processes of categorization and hierarchical ranking can effectively block our perception of women's literary lives in the past. The early Quaker women writers do not fit in the traditional literary categories—therefore, as far as existing accounts of literary history are concerned, they have no voice. When they are mentioned, they are marginalized because of the genres in which they wrote. Because we privilege certain genres, the questions we bring to their texts hide their sophistication. In our current theoretical model of women's literary history, our critical vocabulary cannot discuss these texts except to dismiss them as mad. Our existing modes of literary historical analysis, searching for literary role models, grouping in patterns of literary development, cannot help us to hear these women's voices, cannot help us to read these women's texts as part of any female literary experience.

However, if we change the patterns of our inquiry, this group of women reveals almost luxuriant literary talents. In their persuasive epistles, their polemical texts, they confront and confound their enemies with seventeenth-century wit and spirit. In their prophetic discourses, we hear the mystic speech re-vision the traditional and declare a new beginning, a new world. If we become conscious of our patterns of inquiry, if we consider what other types of questions can be asked of the literary past, in the writings of the early Quaker women we have the first step of a re-visioning of women's literary history, demonstrating what it *could* involve and reveal. If we will only ask the questions, instead of silence, there are a thousand voices that may answer.

Conclusion

Revelations and Re-visioning

[Women] from the moment they venture to speak what they have to say, will of necessity bring about a shift in metalanguage. And I think we're completely crushed, expecially [*sic*] in places like universities, by the highly repressive operations of metalanguage, the operations, that is, of the commentary on commentary, the code, the operation that sees to it that the moment women open their mouths . . . they are immediately asked in whose name and from what theoretical standpoint they are speaking, who is their master and where they are coming from: they have, in short, to salute . . . and show their identity papers. There's work to be done against *class*, against categorization, against classification . . . against the pervasive masculine urge to judge, diagnose, digest, name. — Hélène Cixous, "Castration or Decapitation?"

In her introduction to Kristeva's "Women's Time," Alice Jardine discusses Kristeva's concept of "future perfect." In Jardine's reading, Kristeva invokes it "to characterize a new social formation now in the process of rediscovering what part of it has forgotten."[1] Women's studies as a whole, French and Anglo-American, have always had this as a goal—to rediscover the part of human experience which had been forgotten. Recent trends in interpretive reading, French feminism and new historicism, invite feminist critics to continue the process by discovering what the field of women's studies itself may have forgotten about women's past literary life in its quest to preserve a woman's literary tradition. These critical points of view invite us to try to understand why we have come to the conclusions about the past which we have and to ask ourselves if the resulting model does justice to the experience it attempts to structure.

As we have seen, scholars and editors interested in women's literature from the late eighteenth century on have viewed the central issue as defining through illustration what is "female" writing. Initially it might seem that no two works could be further apart than a nineteenth-century anthology of women's verse such as Bethune's *British Female Poets* with its celebration of the delicate middle-class muse and the twentieth century's *Norton Anthology of Literature by Women* with its denunciation of passive, docile female writers. While the anthologies of the eighteenth and nineteenth centuries sought to show how different the writing of their periods was from that of the early barbaric versifiers, we openly seek continuity with the past, hoping, even, for lives and writings with which to identify. While the eighteenth- and nineteenth-century critics praised women writers who did not permit their art to interrupt their domestic duties, the twentieth century has focused its attention on the outlaw figure, treating with sympathy those women whose own times rejected their life-styles or literary creations.

Despite these striking differences, however, the historiography of women's literature has always operated with the same approach. Anthologies are created by acts of choice; they are not simply a gathering together of all available materials, as some introductions would lead one to believe. Their contents reflect the ideology of the editors and their time; their structures reveal how those editors approached the past in the first place. Viewed in these terms, the choices made by the nineteenth-century editors have much in common with the choices of more recent ones.

Both the nineteenth- and twentieth-century commentators on women's verse tackled the problem of defining women's writing in a historical context by putting women's writings in a hierarchical, evolutionary framework. The definition of "female" has been created through exclusion. In the nineteenth century, the defining characteristic of feminine writing was "delicacy," and that which did not, in the editors' view, demonstrate this characteristic in sufficient degree was not worthy of the title of "feminine" verse. In the twentieth century, the defining characteristic for feminist writing has been "anger," and though recent anthologies may include specimens that do not meet the requirement, the critical apparatus ensures that the reader is aware of their failings. The critical criteria thus tend to create a homogeneous presentation of women's writings.

Women's literature has traditionally, then, been analyzed through a process of categorization and ranking. However, as we have seen, this process was performed long before the extent of women's literary activities in earlier times was fully realized. The establishment of a "tradition" using this method gives the impression that we have a much better grasp of the materials than we actually do — it imposes order on an admittedly confused picture.

But what have we sacrificed to obtain this order? In our search for continuity, a family of female authors, what have we left out? Ironically, those very ground-breaking feminist texts that established women's studies as a viable, significant area of scholarly investigation, which enabled works such as this one to come about, may now stand in the way of the very re-visioning task they initially performed. As we have seen, there were many women's voices in the sixteenth and seventeenth centuries which were silenced by later editors and commentators rather than by their contemporaries. In the act of preserving some, we have inadvertently exiled many.

The simple solution, of course, is to declare that women's literary history simply will have no "canon" at all. As Cixous argues in the quotation that begins this section, and as I would extend this assault on patriarchal metalanguage to include some of the metalanguage created by women, "there's work to be done against *class*, against categorization, against classification."[2] Cixous's rejection of controlling, coercive structures and forms speaks to all of us working on subjects marginalized in the traditional academic scheme, and it is not so far from Rich's call for a "new critical direction." Both demand that feminist literary criticism not be simply one more decorative flourish in the existing pattern. There is that desire to break out of molds and patterns, to break the seventh seal and usher in that new day beyond old institutions.

The problem is that literature, once taken into the academy, will never regain that imagined innocence before canon formation. We carry ideological prejudices that only become apparent when we explore our own histories and examine our own efforts theoretically. Many have argued, and I agree, that canons are a feature of modern education structures. Unless we somehow ban all textbooks, burn all anthologies, and forbid teaching standard syllabi, a canon of the most frequently taught works will remain with us. To say we will have no canon is to ignore what actually happens in the classroom and examination hall.

This does not mean, however, that we must try to create a canon that mimics the traditional one, whether it be the nineteenth-century standardized curriculum, Watt's "rise" of the novel, or Leavis's "great tradition." We can instead be conscious of the criteria used and actively seek to challenge and expand the range of possibilities. Instead of trying to create a single, monolithic scheme of women's literature, in which every piece neatly fits the predetermined design or is excluded and devalued, we can recognize that the literary past is much more chaotic and diverse than we have previously implied in our literary histories.

Nor do we have to content ourselves with accepting standard practices of anthologizing, which, as we have seen, have changed little from a nineteenth-century format. Instead, if we wish to become speculative about the course of literary studies in the next century, let us consider how the new modes of literary production enabled by advanced computer technology could expand—even explode—the traditional notion of the monolithic text for women's studies. An electronic data base could contain *all* known early women's writings (as has been done for classical Greek texts), instead of being a single, fixed collection of pieces preselected by an editor. Such a full-text data base and the electronic texts it generates could enable the individual student, scholar, and teacher to have access to the whole range of early women's texts. Instead of defining the canon for its users, an electronic data base permits the user to select texts and to bring together different combinations of texts for different purposes. It offers a multiplicity of female expression, not a single vision.

It also offers the possibility to re-vision literary history outside traditional limiting definitions, which, while they do serve to organize and control materials, also may stop us from perceiving what questions could be asked of the literary past. I have, in many ways, offered in this book a very conventional historical narrative—an analysis of the historiography of women's writings and the construction of the feminine upon which it has rested. My goal, however, as I warned in the Introduction, was not to replicate and transmit this same historiography, but to make it—and the literary past it seeks to configure—unfamiliar, strange, different. My history of histories seeks to free women's literary studies from traditional literary history, not by substituting my own preconceptions for those of previous generations, but by exploring the assumptions we *can* uncover and understand, perhaps to glimpse the full complexity of the past, Kristeva's "multiplicity of female expressions and preoccupations," which will always escape confinement and complete definition, feminist or otherwise. To cite Kristeva here is not to say that the ultimate goal of a feminist historicism will be to capture and isolate that essential female, the universal woman. What feminist theory and new historicism have offered us, after all, is the possibility that there is more than one story in history: A feminist historicism using the strategies of both reveals that the past is not just the theater of male dramas narrated by male voices. We may not be comfortable with all the roles women played in the historical past, but we cannot accept that they played no significant part, or that they had only one voice, or even that the experience of women writing in earlier times can be contained within one tidy narrative, whether they are cast as victim or queen. While we should recognize and applaud the real political accomplishment of establishing the field of women's studies and creating a canon of women's literature, we should recognize as well that institutions that initially enabled us to re-vision a patriarchal, hegemonic history may now act to shut off our experience of another very different story if we do not perceive the assumptions in which we are grounded.

Breaking the seventh seal in Revelation signals the end of the old institution and the unleashing of powerful and destructive chaotic forces. For the early Quaker women writers, however, it also signaled the beginning of the new order, the new heavens and the new earth. It signals a radical reconfiguration of existence. On a much less cosmic level, perhaps it is time for a re-visioning of women's literary history, down to the very methods used when searching for, evaluating, and presenting early women's writings. Perhaps then we will be able to write women's literary histories that do insist on the value of these early women writers' experiences and texts but are not built on restrictive categories and competitive hierarchies—ones that allow the thousand voices from the past to be heard for themselves.

Notes

Introduction. Patterns of Inquiry

1. Elaine Showalter, ed., *The New Feminist Criticism: Essays on Women, Literature, and Theory* (New York: Pantheon, 1985), 6.

2. As Teresa de Lauretis commented of feminist studies in general, "An all-purpose feminist frame of reference does not exist, nor should it ever come prepackaged and ready-made. We need to keep building one, absolutely flexible and readjustable, from women's own experience of difference, or our difference from Woman and of the difference among women." Teresa de Lauretis, "Feminist Studies/Critical Studies: Issues, Terms, and Contexts," in *Feminist Studies/Critical Studies*, ed. de Lauretis (Bloomington: Indiana Univ. Press, 1986), 14).

3. Felicity A. Nussbaum and Laura Brown, eds., *The New Eighteenth Century: Theory, Politics, English Literature* (London: Methuen, 1987), 4.

4. Elaine Hobby, *Virtue of Necessity: English Women's Writing 1649–88* (Ann Arbor: Univ. of Michigan Press, 1989), 204.

5. This same concern with the ways in which scholarship often tends merely to replicate past ideologies rather than replacing or re-visioning them is also a key element in the work of several of the earliest exponents of new historicism. See, for example, Jerome J. McGann's *Romantic Ideology: A Critical Investigation* (Chicago: Univ. of Chicago Press, 1983).

6. Sandra M. Gilbert, "What Do Feminist Critics Want?" in *The New Feminist Criticism*, 44.

7. Examples of recent work concerned with these issues, although focusing on different historical moments, include the collections of essays edited by Margaret W. Ferguson, Maureen Quilligan, and Nancy J. Vickers, *Rewriting the Renaissance: The Discourses of Sexual Difference in Early Modern Europe* (Chicago: Univ. of Chicago Press, 1986); Mary Beth Rose, ed., *Women in the Middle Ages and the Renaissance: Literary and Historical Perspectives* (Syracuse, N.Y.: Syracuse Univ. Press, 1986); Constance Jordan, *Renaissance Feminism: Literary Texts and Political Models* (Ithaca, N.Y.: Cornell Univ. Press, 1990); Mary Poovey, *Uneven Developments: The Ideological Work of Gender in Mid-Victorian England* (Chicago: Univ. of Chicago Press, 1988); Donna Landry, *The Muses of Resistance: Laboring-Class Women's Poetry in Britain, 1739–1796* (Cambridge: Cambridge Univ.

Press, 1990); and Felicity A. Nussbaum, *The Autobiographical Subject: Gender and Ideology in Eighteenth-Century England* (Baltimore: Johns Hopkins Univ. Press, 1989).

8. de Lauretis, "Feminist Studies/Critical Studies: Issues, Terms, and Contexts," 14.

9. Jane Marcus, "Still Practice, A/Wrested Alphabet: Toward a Feminist Aesthetic," in *Art and Anger: Reading like a Woman* (Columbus: Ohio State Univ. Press, 1988), 215–49.

Chapter One. A Tradition of Our Own

1. Judith Lowder Newton, "Feminism and the 'New Historicism,'" in *The New Historicism,* ed. H. Aram Veeser (New York: Routledge, 1989), 152–67.

2. Janet Todd, *Feminist Literary History: A Defense* (Oxford: Polity Press, 1988), 138.

3. Hélène Cixous, "Castration or Decapitation?" trans. Annette Kuhn, *Signs* 7 (1981): 53.

4. Hélène Cixous, "From the Scene of the Unconscious to the Scene of History," in *The Future of Literary Theory,* ed. Ralph Cohen (New York: Routledge, 1989), 13.

5. Numerous feminist literary critics have already voiced concern over what many view as the drive to conceptualize women's literary history before essential archival and bibliographical studies have even been truly begun. Germaine Greer warned in 1982 that it was too soon to make generalizations about women's writings when so little was known about the individual cases; likewise, Jane Marcus noted that "it is an ironic turn of events when one declares that a socialist feminist criticism should defend its old enemies, the very bibliographers, editors, textual scholars, biographers, and literary historians who wrote women out of history to begin with. But without the survival of these skills and the appropriation of them, women will again lose the history of their own culture" (*Art and Anger,* 225–26). Counter to this practice of theory before text are the most recent studies of individual Renaissance women writers. Studies by Elaine Hobby, Betty Travitsky, Josephine Roberts, Marilyn Williamson, and Elaine Beilin and the essays in collections edited by Mary Beth Rose (*Women in the Middle Ages and the Renaissance*) and Katharina M. Wilson (*Women Writers of the Renaissance and Reformation,* Athens: Univ. of Georgia Press, 1987), by Mary Ellen Lamb, Leah Marcus, Elizabeth McCutheon, Coburn Freer, Frances Teague, Margaret Hannay, and Elizabeth Hageman foreground in their analyses the necessity of continuing the search for early texts.

6. Germaine Greer, "The Tulsa Center for the Study of Women's Literature: What We Are Doing and Why We Are Doing It," *Tulsa Studies in Women's Literature* 1 (1982): 5.

7. Alice Walker, *In Search of Our Mothers' Gardens: Womanist Prose* (New York: Harcourt Brace Jovanovich, 1983), 13.

8. Ellen Moers, *Literary Women: The Great Writers* (Garden City, N.Y.: Doubleday, 1976), 44.

9. Todd, *Feminist Literary History*, 48. (Hereafter, page numbers of works already cited may be given parenthetically in the text.)

10. Elaine V. Beilin, *Redeeming Eve: Women Writers of the English Renaissance* (Princeton: Princeton Univ. Press, 1987), 116–17.

11. Linda Gordon, "What's New in Women's History," in *Feminist Studies/ Critical Studies*, 26. Gordon's views are interestingly modified by Nancy Armstrong's assertion of the "rise" of the woman novelist at the end of the eighteenth century, a "rise" she believes was based in a cultural "domestication" of the female occurring over the course of the later eighteenth century, which parallels Gordon's reading of the later period. See Nancy Armstrong, *Desire and Domestic Fiction: A Political History of the Novel* (Oxford: Oxford Univ. Press, 1987), especially chap. 1.

12. Ann Snitow, "Pages from a Gender Diary: Basic Divisions in Feminism," *Dissent* (Spring 1989): 205.

13. Alice Jardine, "Prelude: The Future of Difference," in *The Future of Difference*, ed. Hester Eisenstein and Alice Jardine (New Brunswick, N.J.: Rutgers Univ. Press, 1985), xxv–xxvi.

14. Moers, *Literary Women*, 14.

15. Toril Moi, *Sexual/Textual Politics: Feminist Literary Theory* (London: Methuen, 1985), 62.

16. Sandra M. Gilbert and Susan Gubar, *The Madwoman in the Attic: The Woman Writer and the Nineteenth-Century Literary Imagination* (New Haven: Yale Univ. Press, 1979), 78.

17. Sandra M. Gilbert, "Patriarchal Poetics and the Woman Reader: Reflections on Milton's Bogey," *PMLA* 93 (1978): 376.

18. Catharine R. Stimpson, "Ad/d Feminam: Women, Literature, and Society," in *Literature and Society*, ed. Edward Said (Baltimore: Johns Hopkins Univ. Press, 1986), 175.

19. Mary Poovey, *The Proper Lady and the Woman Writer: Ideology as Style in the Works of Mary Wollstonecraft, Mary Shelley, and Jane Austen* (Chicago: Univ. of Chicago Press, 1984), 246.

20. *The Norton Anthology of Literature by Women: The Tradition in English* (hereafter *NALW*), ed. Sandra M. Gilbert and Susan Gubar (New York: W. W. Norton, 1985), 14.

21. Ruth Perry, *The Celebrated Mary Astell: An Early English Feminist* (Chicago: Univ. of Chicago Press, 1986), 13.

22. Jacqueline Pearson, *The Prostituted Muse: Images of Women and Women Dramatists 1642–1737* (New York: St. Martin's Press, 1988), 8.

23. Moira Ferguson, ed. *First Feminists: British Women Writers 1578–1799* (Bloomington: Indiana Univ. Press, 1985), 84.

24. Sara Heller Mendelson, *The Mental World of Stuart Women: Three Studies* (Amherst: Univ. of Massachusetts Press, 1987), 55.

25. Showalter, *The New Feminist Criticism*, 6.

26. *NALW*, 15.

27. Armstrong, *Desire and Domestic Fiction,* 7.

28. Pearson, *The Prostituted Muse,* 1.

29. Mary R. Mahl and Helene Koons, eds., *The Female Spectator: English Women Writers before 1800* (Bloomington: Indiana Univ. Press, 1977), 8.

30. Rosalind Miles, *The Female Form: Women Writers and the Conquest of the Novel* (New York: Routledge and Kegan Paul, 1987), 36.

31. Jane Spencer, *The Rise of the Woman Novelist from Aphra Behn to Jane Austen* (Oxford: Basil Blackwell, 1986), 22.

32. Moira Ferguson, *First Feminists,* 2.

33. Poovey, *The Proper Lady,* 35.

34. Miles, *The Female Form,* 2.

35. Dale Spender, *Mothers of the Novel: 100 Good Writers before Jane Austen* (London: Pandora, 1986), 4.

36. Virginia Woolf, *A Room of One's Own* (1929; reprint, New York: Harcourt Brace Jovanovich, 1957), 80.

37. Elaine Showalter, *A Literature of Their Own: British Women Novelists from Brontë to Lessing* (Princeton: Princeton Univ. Press, 1977), 4.

38. Bridget Hill, ed., *The First English Feminist: Reflections on Marriage and Other Writings by Mary Astell* (New York: St. Martin's Press, 1986), 23.

39. Margaret J. M. Ezell, *The Patriarch's Wife: Literary Evidence and the History of the Family* (Chapel Hill: Univ. of North Carolina Press, 1987), chap. 3; Harold Love, "Scribal Publication in Seventeenth-Century England," *Transactions of the Cambridge Bibliographical Society* 9 (1987): 130–54, and "Scribal Texts and Literary Communities: The Rochester Circle and Osborn b.105," *Studies in Bibliography* 17 (1989): 219–35. For more general studies of men's participation in coterie activities during the Renaissance and Restoration, see Arthur F. Marotti, *John Donne, Coterie Poet* (Madison: Univ. of Wisconsin Press, 1986). For studies of the preparation of such manuscript texts, helpful articles are W. J. Cameron, "A Late Seventeenth-Century Scriptorium," *Renaissance and Modern Studies* 6 (1963): 24–52, and Brice Harris, "Captain Robert Julian, Secretary to the Muses," *ELH* 10 (1943): 294–309.

40. Spender, *Man-Made Language* (London: Routledge and Kegan Paul, 1980), 192.

41. Showalter, *A Literature of Their Own,* 19.

42. Stimpson, "Ad/d Feminam," 176.

43. Poovey, *The Proper Lady,* 36–37.

44. Pearson, *The Prostituted Muse,* 197; Spender, *Man-Made Language,* 196–97.

45. Louise Bernikow, ed., *The World Split Open: Women Poets 1552–1950* (London: Women's Press, 1979), 20.

46. Poovey, *The Proper Lady,* 38.

47. Cora Kaplan, ed. *Salt and Bitter and Good: Three Centuries of English and American Women Poets* (New York: Paddington Press, 1975), 14.

48. *NALW,* 39.

Chapter Two. The Myth of Judith Shakespeare

1. Katherine M. Rogers, *Before Their Time: Six Women Writers of the Eighteenth Century* (New York: Frederick Ungar, 1979); Joan Goulianos, *By a Woman Writt: Literature from Six Centuries by and about Women* (Baltimore: Penguin, 1973); Bernikow, *The World Split Open*; Angeline Goreau, ed., *The Whole Duty of a Woman: Female Writers in Seventeenth-Century England* (New York: Dial Press, 1985); Fidelis Morgan, ed., *The Female Wits: Women Playwrights of the Restoration* (London: Virago Press, 1981); Gilbert and Gubar, *NALW*; Germaine Greer et al. eds., *Kissing the Rod: An Anthology of Seventeenth-Century Women's Verse* (London: Virago Press, 1988). There are also fine collections of medieval and Renaissance women writers, such as that edited by Betty Travitsky (*The Paradise of Women: Writings by Englishwomen of the Renaissance*, New York: Columbia Univ. Press, 1989) and two other volumes that are not specifically focused on English women's writings edited by Katharina M. Wilson, *Medieval Women Writers* (Athens: Univ. of Georgia Press, 1984) and *Women Writers of the Renaissance and Reformation*. Even though they do include British women such as Lady Mary Wroth, Queen Elizabeth, and Katherine Philips who figure in my argument, because these particular anthologies are not focused on English women writers only and thus do not attempt to formulate a narrative of Anglo-American women's literary history, they fall outside the discussion of this study.

2. Rogers, *Before Their Time*, vii.

3. Bernikow, *The World Split Open*, 24.

4. Angeline Goreau, *Reconstructing Aphra: A Social Biography of Aphra Behn* (London: Oxford Univ. Press, 1980), 8.

5. Goreau, *The Whole Duty*, 17; Greer et al., *Kissing the Rod*, 1,6.

6. Todd, *Feminist Literary History*.

7. Goulianos, *By a Woman Writt*, xiii.

8. *NALW*, xxvii.

9. Marcus, *Art and Anger*, 83.

10. *NALW*, 3.

11. Virginia Woolf, *A Room of One's Own*, 43.

12. Patricia Crawford, "Women's Published Writings 1600–1700," in *Women in English Society 1500–1800*, ed. Mary Prior (London: Methuen, 1985), 211–82.

13. Mary Eagleton, ed., *Feminist Literary Theory* (Oxford: Basil Blackwell, 1986); Marcus, *Art and Anger*, 70, 216.

14. Morgan, *The Female Wits*, 23.

15. Goulianos, *By a Woman Writt*, xiv, xvi.

16. Peter Laslett, *The World We Have Lost—Further Explored*, 3d ed. rev. (London: Methuen, 1983); E. A. Wrigley with Roger Schofield, *The Population History of England 1541–1871* (London: Edward Arnold, 1981); Lawrence Stone, *The Family, Sex and Marriage in England 1500–1800* (London: Weidenfeld and Nicolson, 1977); Peter Clark, ed., *The Transformation of*

the *English Provincial Town 1600–1800* (London: Hutchinson, 1984); Valerie Elliott, "Single Women in the London Marriage Market: Age, Status and Mobility, 1598–1619," in *Marriage and Society: Studies in the Social History of Marriage*, ed. R. B. Outhwaite (London: Europa Press, 1981), 81–100; David Souden, "Migrants and the Population Structures of Seventeenth-Century Provincial Cities and Market Towns," in *The Transformation of the English Provincial Town*, ed. Clark, 133–68.

17. Ann Kassmaul, *Servants in Husbandry in Early Modern England* (Cambridge: Cambridge Univ. Press, 1985); Margaret Spufford, *Contrasting Communities: English Villages in the Sixteenth and Seventeenth Century* (Cambridge: Cambridge Univ. Press, 1974) and *Small Books and Pleasant Histories: Popular Fiction and Its Readership in Seventeenth-Century England* (Athens: Univ. of Georgia Press, 1981); Sandra Clark, *The Elizabethan Pamphleteers: Popular Moralistic Pamphlets 1580–1640* (Rutherford, N.J.: Fairleigh Dickinson Univ. Press, 1985).

18. Rogers, *Before Their Time*, vii–viii; Bernikow, *The World Split Open*, 19.

19. Hobby, *Virtue of Necessity*, 129, 206.

20. Carolyn Ruth Swift, "Feminine Identity in Lady Mary Wroth's *Urania*," *English Literary Renaissance* 14 (1984): 328–46; Margaret Patterson Hannay, "Lady Wroth: Mary Sidney," in *Women Writers of the Renaissance and Reformation*, ed. Wilson, 548–565; Josephine Roberts, ed., *The Poems of Lady Mary Wroth* (Baton Rouge: Louisiana State Univ. Press, 1983), introduction; Roberts, "Lady Mary Wroth's Sonnets: A Labyrinth of the Mind," *Journal of Women's Studies in Literature* 1 (1979): 319–29.

21. See Perry, *The Celebrated Mary Astell*, Appendix D.

22. See Margaret J. M. Ezell, "To Be Your Daughter in Your Pen: The Social Functions of Literature in the Writings of Lady Elizabeth Brackley and Lady Jane Cavendish," *Huntington Library Quarterly* 51 (1988): 281–96.

23. Ezell, *Patriarch's Wife*, 125–26.

24. Goreau, *Reconstructing Aphra*, 153–54.

25. Rogers, *Before Their Time*, vii.

26. Greer, "The Tulsa Center for the Study of Women's Literature," 23.

27. Marilyn L. Williamson, "Toward a Feminist Literary History," *Signs* 10 (1984): 138.

28. Lillian S. Robinson, "NALW: Is There a Class in This Text?" *Tulsa Studies in Women's Literature* 5 (1986): 300.

29. Barbara Herrnstein Smith, "Contingencies of Value," in *Canons*, ed. Robert von Hallberg (Chicago: Univ. of Chicago Press, 1983), 29.

Chapter Three. The Tedious Chase

1. Stuart Curran offers an interesting analysis of the fate of women writers during the romantic period and why they were silently dropped from the canon, but no comparable study yet has been done concerning the early eighteenth-century popular female writers. See Curran, "Romantic Poetry:

The I Altered," in *Romanticism and Feminism*, ed. Anne K. Mellor (Bloomington: Indiana Univ. Press, 1988), 185–207.

2. Mary Hays, *Female Biography: Or Memoirs of Illustrious and Celebrated Women, of All Ages and Countries*, 6 vols. (London, 1803), vol. 1, p. iii (hereafter, 1:iii).

3. Anne Elwood, *Memoirs of the Literary Ladies of England, from the Commencement of the Last Century*, 2 vols. (London, 1843), 1:v–vi.

4. Edward Phillips, *Theatrum Poetarum, Or a Compleat Collection of the Poets, Especially the Most Eminent of All Ages* (London, 1675), 157.

5. Phillips, *Theatrum Poetarum*, preface.

6. Giles Jacob, *An Historical Account of the Lives and Writings of Our Most Considerable English Poets* (London, 1720), xiv.

7. *The Letters of John Dryden*, ed. Charles E. Ward (Durham, N.C.: Duke Univ. Press, 1942), 126. Cibber quotes this letter extensively in his account of Thomas in *The Lives of the Poets* (1753).

8. Ibid., 125.

9. Ibid., 127.

10. Cixous, "Castration or Decapitation?" 52.

11. Quoted in George Colman and Bonnell Thornton, eds., *Poems by Eminent Ladies*, 2 vols. (London, 1755), 1:4.

12. Theophilus Cibber, *The Lives of the Poets of Great Britain and Ireland, to the Time of Dean Swift*, 5 vols. (London, 1753), 3:25.

13. Jane Spencer in her account of the "rise" of the woman novelist comments briefly on this pattern of praising Katherine Philips and Aphra Behn in "heroic" terms, using battle imagery to establish their role in the literary community. See *The Rise of the Woman Novelist*, 25–27.

14. Abraham Cowley, "On the Death of Mrs. Katherine Philips," in *The Complete Works in Verse and Prose* (n.d.; reprint, New York: AMS Press, 1967), 165.

15. Alexander Pope, *Minor Poems*, ed. Norman Ault (London, Methuen, 1954), 211–12.

16. Jacob, *An Historical Account*, 310.

17. *The Nine Muses or Poems Written by Nine Several Ladies upon the Death of the Late Famous John Dryden* (London, 1700), preface.

18. In Colman and Thornton, *Poems by Eminent Ladies*, 1:255.

19. Elizabeth Carter, quoted in Elizabeth Singer Rowe, *The Miscellaneous Works in Prose and Verse of Mrs. Elizabeth Rowe*, ed. Theophilus Rowe, 2 vols. (London, 1739), vol. 1, preface.

20. Ephelia, "To Madam Bhen," in *Female Poems on Several Occasions* (London, 1679), 72.

21. "A Pindarick Ode," in Greer et al., *Kissing the Rod*, 261.

22. Philo-Philippa, quoted in Katherine Philips, *Poems by the Most Deservedly Admired Mrs. Katherine Philips, the Matchless Orinda* (London, 1710), preface.

23. Catherine Trotter Cockburn, "Calliope's Directions How to Deserve and Distinguish the Muses Inspiration," in Colman and Thornton, *Poems by Eminent Ladies*, 1:229.

24. Cowley, "On the Death of Mrs. Katherine Philips," 165.

25. Cowley, "On Orinda's Poems," 154.

26. George Ballard, *Memoirs of Several Ladies of Great Britain: who have been celebrated for their writings or skill in the learned languages, arts and sciences*, 1752, ed. Ruth Perry (Detroit: Wayne State Univ. Press, 1985), 13.

27. Perry, *The Celebrated Mary Astell*, 46.

28. Ballard, *Memoirs*, 382.

29. *Biographium Faemineum: The Female Worthies*, 2 vols. (London, 1766), 1:20–21.

30. Hays, *Female Biography*, 1:213.

31. Matilda Betham, *A Biographical Dictionary of Celebrated Women of Every Age and Country* (London, 1804), 84.

32. Sarah Josepha Hale, *Woman's Record; Or Sketches of All Distinguished Women, from Creation to AD 1854*, 2d ed. rev. (Philadelphia, 1860), 182.

33. *DNB*, 10:673.

34. Horace Walpole, ed., *Vertue's Antecedents of the Painters*, 4 vols. (London, 1786), 1:134.

35. Ballard, *Memoirs*, 27.

36. Ruth Perry, "George Ballard's Biographies of Learned Ladies," in J. D. Browning, ed., *Biography in the Eighteenth Century* (New York: Garland Publishing, 1980), 88.

37. Quoted in Ballard, *Memoirs*, 37.

38. Ballard MS. 43, fol. 89r, Bodleian Library, Oxford.

39. Ballard MS. 64, Bodleian Library, Oxford.

40. Ballard MS. 43, fol. 155r, Bodleian Library, Oxford.

41. Ballard, *Memoirs*, 27–28.

42. Quoted in Morgan, *The Female Wits*, 59.

43. Ballard MS. 43, fol. 155r, Bodleian Library, Oxford.

44. Jane Williams, *The Literary Women of England* (London, 1861), 130.

45. Cibber, *The Lives of the Poets*, 2:162.

46. Ibid., 3:26.

47. Colman and Thornton, *Poems by Eminent Ladies*, 1:iii.

48. Williams, *Literary Women*, 142.

49. Ibid., 140.

50. Eric S. Robertson, *English Poetesses: A Series of Critical Biographies, with Illustrative Extracts* (London, 1883), 9.

51. Julia Kavanagh, *English Women of Letters: Biographical Sketches*, 2 vols. (London, 1863), 1:6.

52. Louisa Costello, *Memoirs of Eminent Englishwomen*, 4 vols. (London, 1844), 3:257.

53. George Washington Bethune, *The British Female Poets* (Philadelphia, 1848), v.

54. Alexander Dyce, ed., *Specimens of British Poetesses* (London, 1827), iii, v.

55. Robert Folkstone Williams, "Felicia Hemans," *Ladies Magazine and Museum* (1832), 12.

56. Rufus Wilmot Griswold, *The Female Poets of America* (New York, 1874), 4.

57. Frederic Rowton, ed., *Cyclopedia of Female Poets* (Philadelphia, n.d.), xvii.

58. In Anne Finch, Countess of Winchilsea, *Poems by Anne, Countess of Winchilsea,* ed. John Middleton Murry, (London, Jonathan Cape, 1928), 11.

59. Costello, *Memoirs of Eminent Englishwomen,* 1:iv–v.

60. [Bryan Waller Procter], *Effigies Poeticae: Or Portraits of the British Poets,* 2 vols. (London, 1824), 1:73.

61. Elwood, *Memoirs of Literary Ladies,* 1:36.

62. Costello, *Memoirs of Eminent Englishwomen,* 3:211.

63. Kavanagh, *English Women of Letters,* 1:22.

Chapter Four. Memorials of the Female Mind

1. William Wordsworth, *The Letters of William and Dorothy Wordsworth. The Later Years,* ed. Ernest de Selincourt (Oxford: Clarendon Press, 1939), 473.

2. Elizabeth Carter, quoted in Elizabeth Singer Rowe, *The Miscellaneous Works,* vol. 1, preface.

3. Sir Samuel Egerton Brydges, ed., *Select Poems of Margaret Cavendish* (Lee Priory, Kent, 1813), advertisement.

4. Sir Samuel Egerton Brydges, ed., *A True Relation of the Birth, Breeding, and Life, of Margaret Cavendish, Duchess of Newcastle* (Lee Priory, Kent, 1814), 8.

5. Ibid., 9.

6. In Finch, *Poems by Anne, Countess of Winchilsea,* ed. Murry, 3.

7. James Dallaway, quoted in Lady Mary Wortley Montague, *The Works of the Right Honourable Lady Mary Wortley Montagu,* ed. Dallaway, 5 vols. (London, 1803), 1:iii–iv.

8. Lord Wharncliffe, quoted in Lady mary Wortley Montagu, *The Letters and Works of Lady Mary Wortley Montagu,* ed. Lord Wharncliffe, 3 vols. (London, 1837), 1:iii.

9. Brydges, *Select Poems,* 5.

10. Leigh Hunt's copy of Dyce's *Specimen,* Huntington Library Collection, #472120.

11. Colman and Thornton, *Poems by Eminent Ladies* (1755), 1:21.

12. Ibid., 1:65.

13. *Ladies Magazine* (1779): 1640.

14. See *The Reminiscences of Alexander Dyce,* ed. Richard J. Schrader (Athens: Ohio State Univ. Press, 1972).

15. Wordsworth, *Letters,* 422.

16. Ibid., 473.

17. A. R. Van Nest, *Memoirs of Rev. Geo. Bethune* (New York, 1867), 226.

18. George Washington Bethune, *Genius* (Philadelphia, 1837), 8–9.

19. Van Nest, *Memoirs*, 226.

20. George Washington Bethune, *Memoirs of Mrs. Joanna Bethune* (New York, 1863), iv.

21. Diana Primrose, *A Chaine of Pearle. Or a Memoriall of the Peerless Graces and Heroick Vertues of Queene Elizabeth, of Glorious Memory* (London, 1630), introduction.

22. Bethune, *The British Female Poets*, 22.

23. Edmund Lodge, *Illustrations of British history, biography, and manners* (1791), quoted in Bethune, *The British Female Poets*, 19. Interestingly, the most recent anthology of seventeenth-century women's verse, *Kissing the Rod*, omits Anne Howard, its editors not believing the verse in question to be written by a woman at all.

24. Dyce, *Specimens of British Poetesses*, 91.

25. Margaret Cavendish, Duchess of Newcastle, *Poems and Fancies* (London, 1653), 44.

26. Ibid., 212.

27. Wordsworth, *Letters*, 477.

28. In Finch, *Poems by Anne, Countess of Winchilsea*, ed. Murry, 14.

29. Anne Finch, Countess of Winchilsea, *Miscellany Poems, on Several Occasions* (London, 1713), 22–24.

Chapter Five. Breaking the Seventh Seal

1. McGann, *The Romantic Ideology*, 2.

2. Phyllis Mack, "Gender and Spirituality in Early English Quakerism, 1659–1665," in *Witnesses for Change: Quaker Women over Three Centuries*, ed. Elisabeth Potts Brown and Susan Mosher Stuard (New Brunswick, N.J.: Rutgers Univ. Press, 1989), 57.

3. David Latt, in his introduction to Margaret Fell, *Womens Speaking Justified* (1667; reprint, Augustan Reprint Society #194, Los Angeles: William Andrews Clark Memorial Library, 1979).

4. Goreau, *The Whole Duty*, 108.

5. Crawford, "Women's Published Writings," tables 7.3 and 7.4. Crawford's checklist is a preliminary one, and these figures actually underestimate the number of Quaker women writing between 1652 and 1672 and the number of first editions. In the process of reading for this essay, I came across seven women whose names were not included and six further titles by authors listed between 1652 and 1672. The additional authors are Prudence Harding, Martha Plats, Hannah Reckless (John Reckless), and Sarah Watson, "In the Unity and Life of God" (1663); Elizabeth Newton, "In the Movings of Pure Love," in William Smith's *A Real Demonstration of the True Order* (1663); Barbara Pattison (with Margaret Killin), *A Warning from the Lord* (1656); Dorothy Waugh, "A Relation concerning Dorothy Waughs cruell Usage by the Mayor of Carlile," in *The Lambs Defence Against Lyes* (1656). Additional titles by listed authors are Sarah Blackborrow, "To the Reader," in *A Collection of . . . Richard Hubberthorne* (1663), and "To the Reader," in James

Nayler's *How Sin is Strengthened* (1657); Margaret Fell, "Preface to Divers Epistles to Friends," "To All the Professors in the World" (1656); Rebecca Travers, "To the Reader," in Nayler's *A Message from the Spirit of Truth* (1658); and Mary Webb (with Anne Gould), *An Epistle to All the Christian Magistrates* (1659). The correct title of the work by Elizabeth Coleman and Anne Travers is *The Harlots Vail Rent* (1669) in Stephen Crisp's *A Backslider Reproved*. No doubt many more names and titles will be added to this list as interest grows in England and America in this particular form of early women's literature, spurred by studies such as those by Elaine Hobby and Phyllis Mack.

6. Keith Thomas, "Women in the Civil War Sects," in *Crisis in Europe 1560–1660*, ed. Trevor Aston. (London: Routledge and Kegan Paul, 1965), 44, 47.

7. Barry Reay, *The Quakers and the English Revolution* (London: Temple Smith, 1985), 26.

8. Both Richard Vann (*The Social Development of English Quakerism, 1655–1755*) and Reay offer extensive analyses of the social origins of the early Quakers by profession, but do not break down the categories by sex. For an analysis that considers class, genre, and gender in the context of eighteenth-century autobiographical narratives, see Felicity Nussbaum's account of Margaret Fell in *The Autobiographical Subject*; see also Bonnelyn Young Kunze's interesting article "Religious Authority and Social Status in Seventeenth-century England: The Friendship of Margaret Fell, George Fox, and William Penn" (*Church History* 57 [1988]), which focuses on the tension between "gentry" Quakers and those of humbler origins.

9. Richard T. Vann, *The Social Development of English Quakerism, 1655–1755* (Cambridge: Harvard Univ. Press, 1969), 56; Hugh Barbour, *The Quakers in Puritan England* (New Haven: Yale Univ. Press, 1964), 92.

10. Reay, *Quakers and the English Revolution*, 143; Luella Wright, *Literature and Education in Early Quakerism*, Univ. of Iowa Studies/Humanistic Studies Series, vol. 5, no. 2 (Iowa City: Univ. of Iowa, 1933).

11. Isabel Ross, *Margaret Fell, Mother of Quakerism* (London: Longmans, 1949), 342; Mabel Richmond Brailsford, *Quaker Women, 1650–1690* (London: Duckworth, 1915); Anna Trapnel, *The Cry of a Stone, Or a Relation of Something Spoken in Whitehall by Anna Traphel, Being in the Visions of God* (London, 1654), 3.

12. William C. Braithwaite, *The Beginnings of Quakerism*, 2d ed., rev. Henry J. Cadbury (Cambridge: Cambridge Univ. Press, 1955), 199.

13. Helen C. Crossfield, *Margaret Fox of Swarthmore Hall* (London, Headley Brothers, 1913), 27.

14. See Margaret Spufford's arguments on the extent of literacy among the lower classes in general during the seventeenth century in *Small Books and Pleasant Histories: Popular Fiction and Its Readership in Seventeenth-Century England* (Athens: Univ. of Georgia Press, 1981), chaps. 2 and 3, especially pp. 34–37.

15. Mack, "Gender and Spirituality," 39; Thomas, "Women in the Civil War Sects," 47; Reay, *Quakers and the English Revolution*, 26; Elaine C.

Huber, "'A Woman Must Not Speak': Quaker Women in the English Left Wing," in *Women of Spirit: Female Leadership in the Jewship and Christian Traditions,* ed. Rosemary Ruether and Eleanor McLaughlin (New York: Simon and Schuster, 1979), 154–81.

16. George Fox, "Epistle #320," in *A Collection of Many Select and Christian Epistles, Letters and Testimonies,* 2 vols. (London, 1698), 1:369.

17. Reay, *Quakers and the English Revolution,* 26.

18. William Sewel, *The History of the Rise, Increase, and Progress of the Christian People Called Quakers,* 2 vols. (Philadelphia, 1881), 1:126.

19. Arnold Lloyd, *Quaker Social History, 1669–1738* (London: Longmans, 1950), 150.

20. Quoted in Barbour, *Quakers in Puritan England,* 98; see also Huber, "'A Woman Must Not Speak,'" Reay, and Vann for more detailed analyses of the concept.

21. George Fox, *Journal,* rev. ed. John L. Nickalls (Cambridge: Cambridge Univ. Press, 1952), 7.

22. This process of turning away from external authority bears a striking resemblance to what contemporary sociologists and psychologists refer to as "subjectivism." "The shift into subjectivism is . . . a particularly significant shift for women. . . . that has repercussions [their] relationships, self-concept and self-esteem, morality, and behaviour. . . . Women become their own authorities." Mary Field Belenky et al., *Women's Ways of Knowing: The Development of Self, Voice, and Mind* (New York: Basic Books, 1986), 54. Certainly, one sees this air of self-possession and self-direction determining behavior in Quaker women's persecution narratives, where they must confront and defeat hostile, usually male, authorities and institutions.

23. Sarah Blackborrow, *The Just and Equall Balance Discovered* (London, 1660), 14.

24. Fox, *Journal,* 24.

25. Lloyd, *Quaker Social History,* 154.

26. Richard Bauman, *Let Your Words Be Few: Symbolic Speaking and Silence among Seventeenth-Century Quakers* (Cambridge: Cambridge Univ. Press, 1983), 7.

27. Anne Gargill, *A Brief Discovery of that Which is Called the Popish Religion with a Word to the Inquisition discovering their seat of Injustice and Cruelty* (London, 1656), 2.

28. Margaret Fell, *A True Testimonie from the People of God . . . ,* in *Collection* (London, 1710), 234.

29. Rebecca Travers, "To the Reader," in *A Message from the Spirit of Truth unto the Holy Seed* (London, 1658), preface.

30. T. Edmund Harvey, "Quaker Language," *Journal of the Friends' Historical Society* Supplement 15 (1928): 5–7.

31. Luella Wright, *The Literary Life of the Early Friends, 1650–1725* (New York: Columbia Univ. Press, 1932), 58–59.

32. Jackson I. Cope, "Seventeenth-Century Quaker Style," *PMLA* 71 (1956): 729.

33. N. H. Keeble, *The Literary Culture of Nonconformity in Later Sev-*

enteenth-Century England (Athens: Univ. of Georgia Press, 1987), 245.

34. Catherine La Courreye Blecki, "Alice Hayes and Mary Pennington: Personal Identity within the Tradition of Quaker Spiritual Autobiography," *Quaker History* 65 (1976): 19.

35. Braithwaite, *The Beginnings of Quakerism,* 104–5.

36. Elisabeth Brockbank, *Richard Hubberthorne of Yealand* (London, Friends' Book Center, 1929), 94–95; Brailsford, *Quaker Women,* 254.

37. Mary Anne Schofield, " 'Womens Speaking Justified': The Feminine Quaker Voice, 1662–1797," *Tulsa Studies in Women's Literature* 6 (1987): 68.

38. Paul Schubert, "Form and Function of the Pauline Letters," *Journal of Religion* 19 (1939): 365.

39. Anne Gould et al., *An Epistle to All the Christian Magistrates and Powers in the Whole Christendom* (London, 1659), 9.

40. Margaret Killin and Barbara Pattison, *A Warning from the Lord to the Teachers of the People of Plimouth* (London, 1656), 1.

41. Margaret Fell, *Collection,* 46.

42. Quoted in Ross, *Margaret Fell,* 48–49.

43. Fell, *A Testimonie of the Touchstone* (London, 1656), 16.

44. Rebecca Travers, in *A True Narrative of the Examination, Tryall, and Sufferings of James Nayler* (n.p., 1657), 53.

45. Dorothy Waugh, "A Relation concerning Dorothy Waughs cruell Usage by the Mayor of Carlile," in *The Lambs Defence Against Lyes* (London, 1656), 30.

46. Katherine Evans and Sarah Cheevers, *This is a Short Revelation of some of the Cruel Sufferings (For the Truths Sake)* . . . (London, 1662), 6.

47. Michel de Certeau, "Mystic Speech," in *Heterologies: Discourse on the Other,* trans. Brian Massumi (Minneapolis: Univ. of Minnesota Press, 1986), 81.

48. Hélène Cixous, "The Laugh of the Medusa," trans. Keith Cohen and Paula Cohen, in *The Signs Reader,* ed. Elizabeth Abel and Emily K. Abel (Chicago: Univ. of Chicago Press, 1983), 292–93. See also the interesting account of the eighteenth-century prophet Jane Lead by Catherine F. Smith, who also implies the value of a new perspective offered by French feminist reading of mystic texts. "Jane Lead: The Feminist Mind and Art of a Seventeenth-Century Protestant Mystic," in Ruether and McLaughlin, *Women of Spirit,* 183–204.

49. Mary Howgill, *The Vision of the Lord of Hosts* (London, 1662), 6.

50. Howgill, *The Vision,* 5. Those interested in prophetic writings by Quaker women should look in particular at the writings of Hester (Ester) Biddle, who produced a series of pamphlets including *Oh! Wo, wo from the Lord, Wo to the town of Cambridge, Wo to thee city of Oxford,* and *A Warning from the Lord God of Life,* along with two "Trumpets" from the Lord and a general admonition of Dartmouth. Margaret Braidley, Margaret Killin, and Barbara Pattison's writings are also interesting in their merging of the temporal with the spiritual, the conversion of the literal landscape into that of Revelation.

51. Dorothy White, *A Trumpet of the Lord of Hosts, Blown unto the City of London* (London, 1662), 3.

52. Dorothy White, *A Visitation of Heavenly Love unto the Seed of Jacob Yet in Captivity* (London, 1660), 2.

53. Dorothy White, *An Epistle of Love and of Consolation unto Israel* (London, 1661), 2.

54. Dorothy White, *An Alarm Sounded to Englands Inhabitants, But More Especially to Englands Rulers* (London, 1661), 8.

55. White, *Epistle of Love*, 6.

56. White, *Trumpet of the Lord*, 9.

57. Ibid., 7–8.

58. Braithwaite, *The Beginnings of Quakerism*, 341.

59. Brailsford, *Quaker Women*, 256.

60. Early Quaker writers were published by only a handful of printers; however, the use of italics and punctuation is highly individualized, not consistent in their use even in works published by the same printer. This suggests that it was not the printer who made the choice to change type for certain sections within a piece, but the author.

61. Sarah Blackborrow, *A Visit to the Spirit in Prison: and an Invitation to Come to Christ* (London, 1658), 4.

62. Sarah Blackborrow, *Herein is Held Forth the Gift and Good-Will of God to the World* (London, 1659), 8.

63. Blackborrow, *Just and Equall Balance*, 3.

64. Sarah Blackborrow, "To the Reader," in *A Collection of the Several Books and Writings of that Faithful Servant of God Richard Hubberthorne* (London, 1663), (a)3r.

65. Blackborrow, *Herein is Held Forth*, 3.

66. Blackborrow, *A Visit to the Spirit*, 5.

67. Blackborrow, *Just and Equall Balance*, 8.

68. Although Patricia Caldwell feels that seventeenth-century Quaker discourse is separate and distinct from Puritan, it is interesting to note the similar movement from action to stillness in her analysis of a conversion narrative by a seventeenth-century Puritan domestic servant, "Katherine," who also shifts from a self-willed "seeking" to an inner experiential "hearing," "seeing," and "finding." *The Puritan Conversion Narrative: The Beginnings of American Expression* (Cambridge: Cambridge Univ. Press, 1983), 21, 27–28.

69. Wright, *The Literary Life*, 128–29.

70. Cope, "Seventeenth-Century Quaker Style," 753.

71. Wright, *The Literary Life*, 31.

72. Quoted in Lloyd, *Quaker Social History*, 11, 51.

Conclusion. Revelations and Re-visioning

1. Alice Jardine, "Introduction to Julia Kristeva's 'Women's Time,'" *Signs* 7 (1981): 7.

2. Cixous, "Castration or Decapitation?" 51.

Bibliography

Pre-1900 Sources

Adams, H. G. *A Cyclopedia of Female Biography*. London, 1857.

Adams, W. H. Davenport. *Child-Life and Girlhood of Remarkable Women*. London, n.d.

Anderdon, Mary. *A Word to the World*. Exeter, 1662.

Audland, Anne. "A Warning from the Spirit of the Lord." In *The Saints Testimony Finishing Through Sufferings*, 10–12. London, 1655.

Ballard, George. Ballard MSS. 43, 64. Bodleian Library, Oxford.

———. *Memoirs of Several Ladies of Great Britain: who have been celebrated for their writings or skill in the learned language, arts and sciences*. 1752. Edited by Ruth Perry. Detroit: Wayne State Univ. Press, 1985.

Barber, Mary. *Poems on Several Occasions*. London, 1734.

Barker, Jane. *Poetical Recreations: Consisting of Original Poems, Songs, Odes, etc.* London, 1688.

Behn, Aphra. *The Land of Love. A Poem*. London, 1717.

Betham, Matilda. *A Biographical Dictionary of Celebrated Women of Every Age and Country*. London, 1804.

Bethune, George Washington. *The British Female Poets*. Philadelphia, 1848.

———. *The Claims of Our Country on Its Literary Men*. Cambridge, Mass.: 1849.

———. *Genius*. Philadelphia, 1837.

———. *Memoirs of Mrs. Joanna Bethune*. New York, 1863.

Biddle, Hester. "The Trial of Ester Biddle and Three Women More." In *A Brief Relation of the Persecutions and Cruelties that Have Been Acted upon the People Called Quakers*. London, 1662.

Biographium Faemineum: The Female Worthies. 2 vols. London, 1766.

Bishop, George. *New-England Judged by the Spirit of the Lord*. London, 1703.

Blackborrow, Sarah. *Herein is Held Forth the Gift and Good-Will of God to the World*. London, 1659.

———. *The Just and Equall Balance Discovered*. London, 1660.

———. "To the Reader." In *A Collection of the Several Books and Writings of that Faithful Servant of God Richard Hubberthorne*. London, 1663.

————. "To the Reader." In James Nayler, *How Sin is Strengthened*. N.p. 1657.

————. *A Visit to the Spirit in Prison: and an Invitation to Come to Christ*. London, 1658.

Booth, Mary. "Preface to the Reader." In James Nayler, *Milk for Babes: And Meat for Strong Men*. London, 1661.

Braidley, Margaret, with Christopher Taylor. *Certain Papers Which is the Word of God*. n.p. 1655.

A Brief Relation of the Persecutions and Cruelties that Have Been Acted upon the People Called Quakers. London, 1662.

Brooksop, Jone. *An Invitation of Love unto the Seed of God, Throughout the World. With a Word to the Wise in Heart and a Lamentation for New-England*. London, 1662.

Brydges, Sir Samuel Egerton, ed. *Select Poems of Margaret Cavendish*. Lee Priory, Kent, 1813.

————, ed. *A True Relation of the Birth, Breeding, and Life, of Margaret Cavendish, Duchess of Newcastle*. Lee Priory, Kent: 1814.

Cavendish, Margaret, Duchess of Newcastle. *Poems and Fancies*. London, 1653.

Chudleigh, Mary, Lady. *Essays upon Several Subjects in Prose and Verse*. London, 1710.

————. *Poems on Several Occasions. Together with the Song of the Three Children Paraphras'd*. London, 1703.

Cibber, Theophilus. *The Lives of the Poets of Great Britain and Ireland, to the Time of Dean Swift*. 5 vols. London, 1753.

Clifford, Arthur, ed. *Tixall Letters; Or the Correspondence of the Aston Family*. 2 vols. Edinburgh, 1815.

————, ed. *Tixall Poetry*. Edinburgh, 1813.

Colman, George, and Bonnell Thornton, eds. *Poems by Eminent Ladies*. 2 vols. London, 1755.

The Correspondence of Jonathan Swift. Edited by Harold Williams. 5 vols. Oxford: Clarendon Press, 1963–65.

Costello, Louisa. *Memoirs of Eminent Englishwomen*. 4 vols. London, 1844.

Cowley, Abraham. *The Complete Works in Verse and Prose*. n.d. Reprint. New York, AMS Press, 1967.

Crisp, Stephen. *A Blackslider Reproved*. London, 1669.

Dryden, John. *The Letters of John Dryden*. Edited by Charles E. Ward. Durham, N.C.: Duke Univ. Press, 1942.

Dyce, Alexander. *The Reminiscences of Alexander Dyce*. Edited by Richard J. Schrader. Athens: Ohio State Univ. Press, 1972.

————, ed. *Specimens of British Poetesses*. London, 1827.

Elwood, Anne. *Memoirs of the Literary Ladies of England, from the Commencement of the Last Century*. 2 vols. London, 1843.

Ephelia. *Female Poems on Several Occasions*. London, 1679.

Evans, Katherine, and Sarah Cheevers. *This is a Short Revelation of some of the Cruel Sufferings (For the Truths sake) of Katherine Evans and Sarah Cheevers, In the Inquisition in the Isle of Malta*. London, 1662.

Fell, Margaret. *A Brief Collection of Remarkable Passages and Occurences Relating to the Birth, Education, Life, Conversion, Travels, Services, and Deep Sufferings of that Ancient, Eminent, and Faithful Servant of the Lord, Margaret Fell.* London, 1710.

———. *Concerning Ministers Made by the Will of Man.* London, 1659.

———. *A Loving Salutation to the Seed of Abraham among the Jews.* London, 1657.

———. *A Testimonie of the Touchstone, for All Professions, and all Forms, and Gathered Churches (as they call them) . . . Also some of the Ranters Principles Answered.* London, 1656.

———. *A Touch-Stone, Or a Perfect Tryal by the Scriptures of all the Priests, Bishops, and Ministers. . . Unto which is annexed Womens Speaking Justified.* London, 1667.

———. *A Touch-Stone: Or, a tryal by the Scriptures of the Priests, Bishops, and Ministers.* 1667. In *Collection.*

———. *A True Testimony from the People of God (who by the World are called Quakers).* 1660. In *Collection.*

———. *Womens Speaking Justified.* 1667. Edited by David Latt. Reprint. Augustan Reprint Society #194. Los Angeles: William Andrews Clark Memorial Library, 1979.

Finch, Anne, Countess of Winchilsea. *Miscellany Poems, on Several Occasions.* London, 1713.

———. *Poems by Anne, Countess of Winchilsea.* Edited by John Middleton Murry. London, Jonathan Cape, 1928.

———. *The Poems by Anne, Countess of Winchilsea.* Edited by Myra Reynolds. Chicago: Univ. of Chicago Press, 1903.

Fletcher, Elizabeth. *A Few Words in Season to All the Inhabitants of the Earth.* London, 1660.

Forster, Mary. "To the Reader." In *These Several Papers was sent to the Parliament.* London, 1659.

Fox, George. *A Collection of Many Select and Christian Epistles, Letters and Testimonies.* 2 vols. London, 1698.

———. *Concerning Marriage.* London, 1661.

———. *Journal.* rev.ed. John L. Nickalls. Cambridge: Cambridge Univ. Press, 1952.

———. *The Womans Learning in Silence: Or, the Mystery of Womans Subjection to her Husband.* London, 1656.

Gargill, Ann. *A Brief Discovery of that Which is Called the Popish Religion with a Word to the Inquisition discovering their seat of Injustice and Cruelty.* London, 1656.

Gould, Anne, et al. *An Epistle to All the Christian Magistrates and Powers in the Whole Christendom.* London, 1659.

Griswold, Rufus Wilmot. *The Female Poets of America.* New York, 1874.

Hale, Sarah Josepha. *Woman's Record; Or Sketches of all Distinguished Women, from Creation to AD 1854.* 2d ed., rev. Philadelphia, 1860.

Hallifax, Charles. *Familiar Letters on Various Subjects of Business and Amusement.* 2d ed., rev. London, 1754.

Hays, Mary. *Female Biography: Or Memoirs of Illustrious and Celebrated Women, of All Ages and Countries*. 6 vols. London, 1803.

Haywood, Eliza. *The Female Spectator*. 4 vols. London, 1745.

Hendericks, Elizabeth. *A Epistle to Friends in England, to be Read in their Assemblies in the Fear of the Lord*. Amsterdam, 1672.

Hincks, Elizabeth. *The Poor Widows Mite, Cast unto the Lord's Treasury*. London, 1671.

Howgill, Mary. *A Remarkable Letter of Mary Howgill to Oliver Cromwell Called Protector*. London, 1657.

———. *The Vision of the Lord of Hosts*. London, 1662.

Jacob, Giles. *An Historical Account of the Lives and Writings of Our Most Considerable English Poets*. London, 1720.

———. *The Poetical Register: Or, the Lives and Characters of the English Dramatick Poets*. London, 1719.

Kavanagh, Julia. *English Women of Letters: Biographical Sketches*. 2 vols. London, 1863.

Killin, Margaret and Barbara Pattison. *A Warning from the Lord to the Teachers of the People of Plimouth*. London, 1656.

Knapp, Samuel L. *Female Biography: Containing Notices of Distinguished Women, In Different Nations and Ages*. Philadelphia, 1846.

The Ladies Magazine and Museum.

Lady's Magazine, or, entertaining companion for the fair sex.

Leapor, Mary. *Poems upon Several Occasions*. London, 1748–51.

Lee, Anna Maria. *Memoirs of Eminent Female Writers*. Philadelphia, 1827.

May, Caroline. *The American Female Poets*. Philadelphia, 1848.

Montagu, Lady Mary Wortley. *The Letters and Works of Lady Mary Wortley Montagu*. Edited by Lord Wharncliffe. 3 vols. London, 1837.

———. *The Works of the Right Honourable Lady Mary Wortley Montagu*. Edited by James Dallaway. 5 vols. London, 1803.

Newton, Elizabeth. "In the Movings of Pure Love." In *A Real Demonstration of the True Order in the Spirit of God*, edited by William Smith, 7–8. London, 1663.

The Nine Muses or Poems Written by Nine Several Ladies upon the Death of the Late Famous John Dryden. London, 1700.

Philips, Katherine. *Poems by the Most Deservedly Admired Mrs. Katherine Philips, the Matchless Orinda*. London, 1710.

Phillips, Edward. *Theatrum Poetarum, Or a Compleat Collection of the Poets, Especially the Most Eminent of All Ages*. London, 1675.

Pope, Alexander. *Minor Poems*. Edited by Norman Ault. London, Methuen, 1954.

Primrose, Diana. *A Chaine of Pearle. Or a Memoriall of the Peerless Graces and Heroick Vertues of Queene Elizabeth, of Glorious Memory*. London, 1630.

Prior, Matthew. *The Literary Works of Matthew Prior*. Edited by H. Bunker Wright and Monroe K. Spears. 2d ed. 2 vols. Oxford: Clarendon Press, 1971.

[Procter, Bryan Waller.] *Effigies Poeticae: Or Portraits of the British Poets.* 2 vols. London, 1824.

Read, Thomas Buchanan, ed. *The Female Poets of America.* Philadelphia, 1848.

Reckless, Hannah, et al. "In the Unity of the Love and Life of God." In *Real Demonstration of the True Order in the Spirit of God,* edited by William Smith. London, 1663.

Robertson, Eric S. *English Poetesses: A Series of Critical Biographies, with Illustrative Extracts.* London, 1883.

Rowe, Elizabeth Singer. *Devout Exercises of the Heart in Meditation and Prayer and Praise.* Edited by Isaac Watts. London, 1738.

————. *The Miscellaneous Works in Prose and Verse of Mrs. Elizabeth Rowe.* Edited by Theophilus Rowe. 2 vols. London, 1739.

Rowton, Frederic, ed. *Cyclopedia of Female Poets.* Philadelphia, n.d.

Sewel, William. *The History of the Rise, Increase, and Progress of the Christian People Called Quakers.* 2 vols. Philadelphia, 1881.

Sharp, R. Farquarson, ed. *A Dictionary of English Authors, Biographical and Bibliographical.* London, 1897.

Smith, Joseph. *A Descriptive Catalogue of Friends' Books.* 2 vols. London, 1867.

Smith, William, ed. *A Real Demonstration of the True Order in the Spirit of God, and of the Ground of all Formality and Idolatry.* London, 1663.

Stainforth, Francis. *Catalogue of the Extraordinary Library Unique of Its Kind, formed by the late Rev. F.J. Stainforth consisting entirely of works of British and American Poetesses, and Female Dramatic Writers.* London, 1867.

Thomas, Elizabeth. *Miscellany Poems on Several Subjects.* London, 1722.

Thomas, Elizabeth, and Richard Gwinnett. *Pylades and Corinna.* London, 1731.

Tomkins, John, and John Field. *Piety Promoted, Being a Collection of the Dying Sayings of Many of the People Called Quakers.* Dublin, 1721.

Trapnel, Anna. *The Cry of a Stone, Or a Relation of Something Spoken in Whitehall by Anna Trapnel, Being in the Visions of God.* London, 1654.

————. *Report and Plea. Or a Narrative of her Journey from London into Cornwall.* London, 1654.

Travers, Anne, and Elizabeth Coleman. *The Harlots Vail Rent, and Her Impudency Rebuked in a Short Answer to one Elizabeth Atkinson.* In Crisp's *A Blackslider Reproved.* London, 1669.

Travers, Rebecca. "To the Reader." In James Nayler, *A Message from the Spirit of Truth unto the Holy Seed.* London, 1658.

A True Narrative of the Examination, Tryall, and Sufferings of James Nayler. N.p. 1657.

Van Nest, A. R. *Memoirs of Rev. Geo. Bethune.* New York, 1867.

Walpole, Horace. *A Catalogue of the Royal and Noble Authors of England, Scotland, and Ireland.* 5 vols. London, 1806.

————, ed. *Vertue's Antecedents of the Painters.* 4 vols. London, 1786.

Waugh, Dorothy. "A Relation concerning Dorothy Waughs cruell Usage by the Mayor of Carlile." In *The Lambs Defence Against Lyes*, 29–30. London, 1656.

Webb, Maria. *The Fells of Swarthmore Hall and Their Friends*. London, 1865.

White, Dorothy. *An Alarm Sounded to Englands Inhabitants, But More Especially to Englands Rulers*. London, 1661.

———. *A Call from God out of EGYPT, by his Son Christ the Light of Life*. London, 1662.

———. *An Epistle of Love and of Consolation unto Israel*. London, 1661.

———. *A Trumpet of the Lord of Hosts, Blown unto the City of London*. London, 1662.

———. *Unto All Gods Host, in England*. London, 1660.

———. *A Visitation of Heavenly Love unto the Seed of Jacob Yet in Captivity*. London, 1660.

Williams, Jane. *The Literary Women of England*. London, 1861.

Williams, Robert Folkstone. "Felicia Hemans." *Ladies Magazine and Museum* (1832): 11–13.

Wordsworth, William. *The Letters of William and Dorothy Wordsworth. The Later Years*. Edited by Ernest de Selincourt. Oxford: Clarendon Press, 1939.

Twentieth-Century Sources

Adburgham, Alison. *Women in Print: Writing Women and Women's Magazines from the Restoration to the Accession of Victoria*. London: George Allen and Unwin, 1972.

Anderson, Howard, Philip B. Daghalian, and Irvin Ehrenpreis, eds. *The Familiar Letter in the Eighteenth Century*. Lawrence: Univ. of Kansas Press, 1966.

Armstrong, Nancy. *Desire and Domestic Fiction: A Political History of the Novel*. Oxford: Oxford Univ. Press, 1987.

Auerbach, Nina. *Romantic Imprisonment: Women and Other Glorious Outcasts*. New York: Columbia Univ. Pres, 1985.

———. *The Woman and the Demon: The Life of a Victorian Myth*. Cambridge Harvard Univ. Press, 1982.

Bacon, Margaret Hope. *Mothers of Feminism: The Story of Quaker Women in America*. New York: Harper and Row, 1986.

Barbour, Hugh. *The Quakers in Puritan England*. New Haven: Yale Univ. Press, 1964.

Bauman, Richard. *Let Your Words Be Few: Symbolic Speaking and Silence among Seventeenth-Century Quakers*. Cambridge: Cambridge Univ. Press, 1983.

Baym, Nina. "The Madwoman and Her Languages: Why I Don't Do Feminist Literary Theory." *Tulsa Studies in Women's Literature* 3 (1984): 45–59.

Beilin, Elaine V. *Redeeming Eve: Women Writers of the English Renaissance*. Princeton: Princeton Univ. Press, 1987.

Belenky, Mary Field, et al. *Women's Ways of Knowing: The Development of Self, Voice, and Mind.* New York: Basic Books, 1986.

Benstock, Shari, ed. *Feminist Issues in Literary Scholarship.* Bloomington: Indiana Univ. Press, 1987.

Bernikow, Louise, ed. *The World Split Open: Women Poets 1552–1950.* London: Women's Press, 1979.

Blecki, Catherine La Courreye. "Alice Hayes and Mary Pennington: Personal Identity within the Tradition of Quaker Spiritual Autobiography." *Quaker History* 65 (1976): 19–31.

Brailsford, Mabel Richmond. *A Quaker from Cromwell's Army: James Nayler.* London: Swarthmore Press, 1927.

———. *Quaker Women, 1650–1690.* London: Duckworth, 1915.

Braithwaite, William C. *The Beginnings of Quakerism.* 2d ed., rev. Henry J. Cadbury. Cambridge: Cambridge Univ. Press, 1955.

———. *The Second Period of Quakerism.* 2d ed., rev. Henry J. Cadbury. Cambridge: Cambridge Univ. Press, 1961.

Brockbank, Elisabeth. *Richard Hubberthorne of Yealand.* London: Friends' Book Center, 1929.

Browning, J. D., ed. *Biography in the Eighteenth Century.* New York: Garland Publishing, 1980.

Caldwell, Patricia. *The Puritan Conversion Narrative: The Beginnings of American Expression.* Cambridge: Cambridge Univ. Press, 1983.

Cameron, W. J. "A Late Seventeenth-Century Scriptorium." *Renaissance and Modern Studies* 6 (1963): 24–52.

Christianson, Paul. *Reformers and Babylon: English Apocalyptic Visions from the Reformation to the Eve of the Civil War.* Toronto: Univ. of Toronto Press, 1978.

Cixous, Hélène. "Castration or Decapitation?" Translated by Annette Kuhn. *Signs* 7 (1981): 41–55.

———. "From the Scene of the Unconscious to the Scene of History." In *The Future of Literary Theory,* edited by Ralph Cohen, 1–18. New York: Routledge, 1989.

———. "The Laugh of the Medusa." Translated by Keith Cohen and Paula Cohen. In *The Signs Reader,* edited by Elizabeth Abel and Emily K. Abel, 279–97. Chicago: Univ. of Chicago Press, 1983.

Clapp, Sarah L. C. "Subscription Publishers Prior to Jacob Tonson." *Library,* 4th ser. 13 (1932): 158–83.

Clark, Peter, ed. *The Transformation of the English Provincial Town 1600–1800.* London: Hutchinson, 1984.

Clark, Sandra. *The Elizabethan Pamphleteers: Popular Moralistic Pamphlets 1580–1640.* Rutherford, N.J.: Fairleigh Dickinson Univ. Press, 1985.

Cohen, Ralph, ed. *The Future of Literary Theory.* New York: Routledge, 1989.

Cope, Jackson I. "Seventeenth-Century Quaker Style." *PMLA* 71 (1956): 725–54.

Crawford, Patricia. "Women's Published Writings 1600–1700." In *Women* in *English Society 1500–1800,* edited by Mary Prior, 211–82. London: Methuen, 1985.

Creasy, Maurice A. " 'Inward' and 'Outward': A Study in Early Quaker Language." *Journal of the Friends' Historical Society* Supplement 30 (1962).

Crossfield, Helen C. *Margaret Fox of Swarthmore Hall.* London: Headley Brothers, 1913.

Curran, Stuart. "Romantic Poetry: The I Altered." In *Romanticism and Feminism,* edited by Anne K. Mellor, 185–207. Bloomington: Indiana Univ. Press, 1988.

de Certeau, Michel. *Heterologies: Discourse on the Other.* Translated by Brian Massumi. Minneapolis: Univ. of Minnesota Press, 1986.

de Lauretis, Teresa, ed. *Feminist Studies/Critical Studies.* Bloomington: Indiana Univ. Press, 1986.

Dibelius, Martin. *A Fresh Approach to the New Testament and Early Christian Literature.* 1936. Reprint. Westport, Conn.: Greenwood Press, 1979.

Eagleton, Mary, ed. *Feminist Literary Theory.* Oxford: Basil Blackwell, 1986.

Eisenstein, Hester, and Alice Jardine, eds. *The Future of Difference.* New Brunswick, N.J.: Rutgers Univ. Press, 1985.

Elliott, Valerie. "Single Women in the London Marriage Market: Age, Status and Mobility, 1598–1619." In *Marriage and Society: Studies in the Social History of Marriage,* edited by R. B. Outhwaite, 81–100. London: Europa Press, 1981.

Ezell, Margaret J. M. *The Patriarch's Wife: Literary Evidence and the History of the Family.* Chapel Hill: Univ. of North Carolina Press, 1987.

———. "To Be Your Daughter in Your Pen: The Social Functions of Literature in the Writings of Lady Elizabeth Brackley and Lady Jane Cavendish." *Huntington Library Quarterly* 51 (1988): 281–96.

Ferguson, Margaret W., Maureen Quilligan, and Nancy J. Vickers, eds. *Rewriting the Renaissance: The Discourses of Sexual Difference in Early Modern Europe.* Chicago: Univ. of Chicago Press, 1986.

Ferguson, Moira, ed. *First Feminists: British Women Writers 1578–1799.* Bloomington: Indiana Univ. Press, 1985.

Finke, Laurie. "The Rhetoric of Marginality: Why I Do Feminist Theory." *Tulsa Studies in Women's Literature* 5 (1986): 251–72.

Fogelklou, Emily. *James Nayler: The Rebel Saint 1618–1660.* Translated by Lajla Yapp. London: Earnest Benn, 1931.

Gilbert, Sandra M. "Patriarchal Poetics and the Woman Reader: Reflections on Milton's Bogey." *PMLA* 93 (1978): 368–82.

———. "What Do Feminist Critics Want?" In *The New Feminist Criticism,* edited by Elaine Showalter, 29–45. New York: Pantheon, 1985.

Gilbert, Sandra M., and Susan Gubar. *The Madwoman in the Attic: The Woman Writer and the Nineteenth-Century Literary Imagination.* New Haven: Yale Univ. Press, 1979.

———, eds. *Shakespeare's Sisters: Feminist Essays on Women Poets.* Bloomington: Indiana Univ. Press, 1979.

Goldsmith, Elizabeth C. "Authority, Authenticity, and the Publication of

Letters by Women." In *Writing the Female Voice: Essays on Epistolary Literature*, edited by Goldsmith, 46–59. Boston: Northeastern Univ. Press, 1989.

Gordon, Linda. "What's New in Women's History." In *Feminist Studies/ Critical Studies*, edited by Teresa de Lauretis, 20–30. Bloomington: Indiana Univ. Press, 1986.

Goreau, Angeline. *Reconstructing Aphra: A Social Biography of Aphra Behn*. London: Oxford Univ. Press, 1980.

———, ed. *The Whole Duty of a Woman: Female Writers in Seventeenth-Century England*. New York: Dial Press, 1985.

Goulianos, Joan. *By a Woman Writt: Literature from Six Centuries by and about Women*. Baltimore: Penguin, 1973.

Greer, Germaine. "The Tulsa Center for the Study of Women's Literature: What We Are Doing and Why We Are Doing It." *Tulsa Studies in Women's Literature* 1 (1982): 5–26.

Greer, Germaine, et al., eds. *Kissing the Rod: An Anthology of Seventeenth-Century Women's Verse*. London: Virago Press, 1988.

Grubb, Isabel. *Quakers in Ireland, 1654–1900*. London: Swarthmore Press, 1927.

Halsband, Robert. "Ladies of Letters in the Eighteenth Century." In *The Lady of Letters in the Eighteenth Century*. 31–51. Los Angeles: Univ. of California Press, 1969.

Hannay, Margaret Patterson. "Lady Wroth: Mary Sidney." In *Women Writers of the Renaissance and Reformation* edited by Katharina M. Wilson, 548–65. Athens: Univ of Georgia Press, 1987.

———. *Silent but for the Word: Tudor Women as Patrons, Translators, and Writers of Religious Works*. Kent, Ohio: Kent State University Press, 1985.

Harris, Brice. "Captain Robert Julian, Secretary to the Muses." *ELH* 10 (1943): 294–309.

Harris, Stephen L. *Understanding the Bible: A Reader's Introduction*. 2d ed. Palo Alto, Calif.: Mayfield Publishing, 1985.

Harvey, T. Edmund. "Quaker Language." *Journal of the Friends' Historical Society* Supplement 15 (1928).

Hill, Bridget, ed. *The First English Feminist: Reflections on Marriage and Other Writings by Mary Astell*. New York: St. Martin's Press, 1986.

Hill, Christopher. *The World Turned Upside Down: Radical Ideas during the English Revolution*. New York: Viking Press, 1972.

Hobby, Elaine. *Virtue of Necessity: English Women's Writing 1649–88*. Ann Arbor: Univ. of Michigan Press, 1989.

Holstun, James. *A Rational Millennium: Puritan Utopias of Seventeenth-Century England and America*. New York: Oxford Univ. Press, 1987.

Homans, Margaret. *Bearing the Word: Language and Female Experience in Nineteenth-Century Women's Writing*. Chicago: Univ. of Chicago Press, 1986.

Huber, Elaine C. " 'A Woman Must Not Speak': Quaker Women in the English Left Wing." In *Women of Spirit*, edited by Ruether and Eleanor McLaughlin, 153–82. New York: Simon and Schuster, 1979.

Jacobus, Mary. "Is There a Woman in This Text?" *New Literary History* 14 (1982): 117–41.

Jardine, Alice. "Introduction to Julia Kristeva's 'Women's Time.'" *Signs* 7 (1981): 7.

———. "Prelude: The Future of Difference." In *The Future of Difference*, edited by Hester Eisenstein and Alice Jardine, xxv–xxvii. New Brunswick, N.J.: Rutgers Univ. Press, 1985.

Jordan, Constance. *Renaissance Feminism: Literary Texts and Political Models*. Ithaca, N.Y.: Cornell Univ. Press, 1990.

Kaplan, Cora, ed. *Salt and Bitter and Good: Three Centuries of English and American Women Poets*. New York: Paddington Press, 1975.

Kassmaul, Ann. *Servants in Husbandry in Early Modern England*. Cambridge: Cambridge Univ. Press, 1985.

Keeble, N. H. *The Literary Culture of Nonconformity in Later Seventeenth-Century England*. Athens: Univ. of Georgia Press, 1987.

Kolodny, Annette. "Dancing through the Minefield: Some Observations on the Theory, Practice, and Politics of a Feminist Literary Criticism." In *The New Feminist Criticism: Essays on Women, Literature, and Theory*, edited by Elaine Showalter, 144–67. New York: Pantheon, 1985.

Kunze, Bonnelyn Young. "Religious Authority and Social Status in Seventeenth-Century England: The Friendship of Margaret Fell, George Fox, and William Penn." *Church History* 57 (1988): 170–86.

Landry, Donna. *The Muses of Resistance: Laboring-Class Women's Poetry in Britain, 1739–1796*. Cambridge: Cambridge Univ. Press, 1990.

Lang, Amy Schrager. *Prophetic Woman: Anne Hutchinson and the Problem of Dissent in the Literature of New England*. Los Angeles: Univ. of California Press, 1987.

Laslett, Peter. *The World We Have Lost—Further Explored*. 3d ed., rev. London: Methuen, 1983.

Lloyd, Arnold. *Quaker Social History, 1669–1738*. London: Longmans, 1950.

Lonsdale, Roger, ed. *Eighteenth-Century Women Poets*. Oxford: Oxford Univ. Press, 1989.

Love, Harold. "Scribal Publication in Seventeenth-Century England." *Transactions of the Cambridge Bibliographical Society* 9 (1987): 130–54.

———. "Scribal Texts and Literary Communities: The Rochester Circle and Osborn b.105." *Studies in Bibliography* 17 (1989): 219–35.

Mack, Phyllis. "Gender and Spirituality in Early English Quakerism, 1659–1665." In *Witnesses for Change: Quaker Women over Three Centuries*, edited by Elisabeth Potts Brown and Susan Mosher Stuard, 31–63. New Brunswick, N.J.: Rutgers Univ. Press, 1989.

Mahl, Mary R., and Helene Koons, eds. *The Female Spectator: English Women Writers before 1800*. Bloomington: Indiana Univ. Press, 1977.

Marcus, Jane. *Art and Anger: Reading like a Woman*. Columbus: Ohio State Univ. Press, 1988.

Marks, Elaine, and Isabelle de Courtivron, eds. *New French Feminisms*. New York: Schocken Books, 1981.

Marotti, Arthur F. *John Donne, Coterie Poet*. Madison: Univ. of Wisconsin Press, 1986.

McGann, Jerome J. *The Romantic Ideology: A Critical Investigation*. Chicago: Univ. of Chicago Press, 1983.

McGregor, J. F. and Barry Reay, eds. *Radical Religion in the English Revolution*. Oxford: Oxford Univ. Press, 1984.

Mendelson, Sara Heller. *The Mental World of Stuart Women: Three Studies*. Amherst: Univ. of Massachusetts Press, 1987.

Miles, Rosalind. *The Female Form: Women Writers and the Conquest of the Novel*. New York: Routledge and Kegan Paul, 1987.

Miller, Nancy K. "Changing the Subject: Authorship, Writing, and the Reader." In *Feminist Studies/Critical Studies*, edited by Teresa de Lauretis, 102–20. Bloomington: Indiana Univ. Press, 1986.

———, ed. *The Poetics of Gender*. New York: Columbia Univ. Press, 1986.

Modleski, Tania. "Feminism and the Power of Interpretation: Some Critical Readings." In *Feminist Studies/Critical Studies*, edited by Teresa de Lauretis, 121–38. Bloomington: Indiana Univ. Press, 1986.

Moers, Ellen. *Literary Women: The Great Writers*. Garden City, N.Y.: Doubleday, 1976.

Moi, Toril. *Sexual/Textual Politics: Feminist Literary Theory*. London: Methuen, 1985.

Morgan, Fidelis, ed. *The Female Wits: Women Playwrights of the Restoration*. London: Virago Press, 1981.

Newton, Judith. "History as Usual? Feminism and the 'New Historicism.' " In *The New Historicism*, edited by H. Aram Veeser, 152–67. New York: Routledge, 1989.

———. "Making – and Remaking – History: Another Look at 'Patriarchy.' " *Tulsa Studies in Women's Literature* 3 (1984): 125-41.

The Norton Anthology of Literature by Women: The Tradition in English. Edited by Sandra M. Gilbert and Susan Gubar. New York: W. W. Norton, 1985.

Nussbaum, Felicity A. *The Autobiographical Subject: Gender and Ideology in Eighteenth-Century England*. Baltimore: Johns Hopkins Univ. Press, 1989.

———. *The Brink of All We Hate: English Satires on Women, 1660–1750*. Lexington: Univ. Press of Kentucky, 1984.

Nussbaum, Felicity A., and Laura Brown, eds. *The New Eighteenth Century: Theory, Politics, English Literature*. London: Methuen, 1987.

O'Donnell, Mary Ann. *Aphra Behn: An Annotated Bibliography of Primary and Secondary Sources*. New York: Garland Publishing, 1986.

O'Malley, Thomas F. "The Press and Quakerism, 1653–1659." *Journal of the Friends' Historical Society* 54 (1979): 167–84.

Parry, Graham. *The Golden Age Restor'd: The Culture of the Stuart Court 1603–42*. New York: St. Martin's Press, 1981.

Pearson, Jacqueline. *The Prostituted Muse: Images of Women and Women Dramatists 1642–1737*. New York: St. Martin's Press, 1988.

Perry, Ruth. *The Celebrated Mary Astell: An Early English Feminist.* Chicago: Univ. of Chicago Press, 1986.

———. "George Ballard's Biographies of Learned Ladies." In *Biography in the Eighteenth Century,* edited by J. D. Browning, 85–111. New York: Garland Publishing, 1980.

———. *Women, Letters, and the Novel.* New York: AMS Press, 1980.

Petroff, Elizabeth Alvilda. *Medieval Women's Visionary Literature.* New York: Oxford Univ. Press, 1986.

Pollard, Alfred. "Some Notes on the History of Copyright in England, 1662–1774." *Library,* 4th ser. 3 (1922): 97–114.

Poovey, Mary. *The Proper Lady and the Woman Writer: Ideology as Style in the Works of Mary Wollstonecraft, Mary Shelley, and Jane Austen.* Chicago: Univ. of Chicago Press, 1984.

———. *Uneven Developments: The Ideological Work of Gender in Mid-Victorian England.* Chicago: Univ. of Chicago Press, 1988.

Prior, Mary, ed. *Women in English Society 1500–1800.* London: Methuen, 1985.

Reay, Barry. "Quakers and Society." In *Radical Religion in the English Revolution,* edited by J. F. McGregor and Barry Reay, 141–64. Oxford: Oxford Univ. Press, 1984.

———. *The Quakers and the English Revolution.* London: Temple Smith, 1985.

Rich, Adrienne. "When We Dead Awaken: Writing as Re-Vision." In *On Lies, Secrets, and Silence,* 33–50. New York: W. W. Norton, 1979.

Roberts, Josephine. "Lady Mary Wroth's Sonnets: A Labyrinth of the Mind." *Journal of Women's Studies in Literature* 1 (1979): 319–29.

———, ed. *The Poems of Lady Mary Wroth.* Baton Rouge: Louisiana State Univ. Press, 1983.

Robinson, Lillian S. "Feminist Criticism: How Do We Know When We've Won?" *Tulsa Studies in Women's Literature* 3 (1984): 143–51.

———. "NALW: Is There a Class in This Text?" *Tulsa Studies in Women's Literature* 5 (1986): 289–302.

Rogers, Katherine M. *Before Their Time: Six Women Writers of the Eighteenth Century.* New York: Frederick Ungar, 1979.

Rose, Mary Beth, ed. *Women in the Middle Ages and the Renaissance: Literary and Historical Perspectives.* Syracuse, N.Y.: Syracuse Univ. Press, 1986.

Rosenbaum, S. P. "An Educated Man's Daughter: Leslie Stephen, Virginia Woolf and the Bloomsbury Group." In *Virginia Woolf: New Critical Essays,* edited by Patricia Clements and Isobel Grundy, 32–56. Totowa, N.J.: Barnes and Noble, 1986.

Ross, Isabel. *Margaret Fell, Mother of Quakerism.* London: Longmans, 1949.

Ruether, Rosemary, and Eleanor McLaughlin, eds. *Women of Spirit: Female Leadership in the Jewship and Christian Traditions.* New York: Simon and Schuster, 1979.

Russ, Joanna. *How to Suppress Women's Writing.* London: Women's Press, 1984.

Ruthven, K. K. *Feminist Literary Studies: An Introduction.* Cambridge: Cambridge Univ. Press, 1984.

Sasek, Lawrence A. *The Literary Temper of the English Puritans.* Baton Rouge: Louisiana State Univ. Press, 1961.

Schofield, Mary Anne. " 'Womens Speaking Justified': The Feminine Quaker Voice, 1662–1797." *Tulsa Studies in Women's Literature* 6 (1987): 61–77.

Schofield, Mary Anne, and Cecila Macheski, eds. *Fetter'd or Free? British Women Novelists 1670–1815.* Athens: Ohio Univ. Press, 1986.

Schubert, Paul. "Form and Function of the Pauline Letters." *Journal of Religion* 19 (1939): 365–77.

Showalter, Elaine. *A Literature of Their Own: British Women Novelists from Brontë to Lessing.* Princeton: Princeton Univ. Press, 1977.

———. "Women's Time, Women's Space: Writing the History of Feminist Criticism." *Tulsa Studies in Women's Literature* (1984): 29–43.

———. ed. *The New Feminist Criticism: Essays on Women, Literature, and Theory.* New York: Pantheon, 1985.

Smith, Barbara Herrnstein. "Contingencies of Value." In *Canons,* edited by Robert von Hallberg, 5–40. Chicago: Univ. of Chicago Press, 1983.

Smith, Catherine F. "Jane Lead: The Feminist Mind and Art of a Seventeenth-Century Protestant Mystic." In *Women of Spirit,* edited by Rosemary Ruether and Eleanor McLaughlin, 183–204. New York: Simon and Schuster, 1979.

Smith-Rosenberg, Carroll. "Writing History: Language, Class and Gender." In *Feminist Studies/Critical Studies,* edited by Teresa de Lauretis, 31–54. Bloomington: Indiana Univ. Press, 1986.

Snitow, Ann. "Pages from a Gender Diary: Basic Divisions in Feminism." *Dissent* (Spring 1989): 205–24.

Souden, David. "Migrants and Population Structures of Seventeenth-Century Provincial Cities and Market Towns." In *The Transformation of the English Provincial Town 1600–1800,* edited by Peter Clark. London: Hutchinson, 1984.

Spencer, Jane. *The Rise of the Woman Novelist from Aphra Behn to Jane Austen.* Oxford: Basil Blackwell, 1986.

Spender, Dale. *Man-Made Language.* London: Routledge and Kegan Paul, 1980.

———. *Mothers of the Novel: 100 Good Writers before Jane Austen.* London: Pandora, 1986.

———. *Contrasting Communities: English Villages in the Sixteenth and Seventeenth Century.* Cambridge: Cambridge Univ. Press, 1974.

Spufford, Margaret. *Small Books and Pleasant Histories: Popular Fiction and Its Readership in Seventeenth-Century England.* Athens: Univ. of Georgia Press, 1981.

Stimpson, Catharine R. "Ad/d Feminam: Women, Literature, and Society." In *Literature and Society,* edited by Edward Said, 174–92. Baltimore: Johns Hopkins Univ. Press, 1986.

Stone, Lawrence. *The Family, Sex and Marriage in England 1500–1800.* London: Weidenfeld and Nicolson, 1977.

Swift, Carolyn Ruth. "Feminine Identity in Lady Mary Wroth's *Urania.*" *English Literary Renaissance* 14 (1984): 328–46.

Thomas, Edward. *Feminine Influence on the Poets.* New York: John Lane, 1911.

Thomas, Keith. "Women in the Civil War Sects." In *Crisis in Europe 1560–1660*, edited by Trevor Aston, 317–40. London: Routledge and Kegan Paul, 1965.

Todd, Janet. *Feminist Literary History: A Defense.* Oxford: Polity Press, 1988.

———, ed. *A Dictionary of British and American Women Writers, 1660–1800.* London: Methuen, 1987.

———, ed. *Gender and Literary Voice.* New York: Holmes and Meier, 1980.

Tolles, Frederick B. *Quakers and the Atlantic Culture.* New York: Macmillan, 1960.

Travitsky, Betty, ed. *The Paradise of Women: Writings by Englishwomen of the Renaissance.* New York: Columbia Univ. Press, 1989.

Valenze, Deborah M. *Prophetic Sons and Daughters: Female Preachers and Popular Religion in Industrial England.* Princeton: Princeton Univ. Press, 1985.

Vann, Richard T. *The Social Development of English Quakerism, 1655–1755.* Cambridge: Harvard Univ. Press, 1969.

Veeser, H. Aram, ed. *The New Historicism.* New York: Routledge, 1989.

Walker, Alice. *In Search of Our Mothers' Gardens: Womanist Prose.* New York: Harcourt Brace Jovanovich, 1983.

Williamson, Marilyn L. "Toward a Feminist Literary History." *Signs* 10 (1984): 136–47.

Wilson, Katharina M., ed. *Medieval Women Writers.* Athens: Univ. of Georgia Press, 1984.

———, ed. *Women Writers of the Renaissance and Reformation.* Athens: Univ. of Georgia Press, 1987.

Woodbridge, Linda. *Women and the English Renaissance.* Urbana: Univ. of Illinois Press, 1984.

Woolf, Virginia. *A Room of One's Own.* 1929. Reprint. New York: Harcourt Brace Jovanovich, 1957.

Wright, Luella. *The Literary Life of the Early Friends, 1650–1725.* New York: Columbia Univ. Press, 1932.

———. *Literature and Education in Early Quakerism.* Univ. of Iowa Studies/Humanistic Studies Series, vol. 5, no. 2. Iowa City: Univ. of Iowa, 1933.

Wrigley, E. A. with Roger Schofield. *The Population History of England 1541–1871.* London: Edward Arnold, 1981.

Zagarelle, Sandra A. "Conceptualizing Women's Literary History: Reflections on the *NALW.*" *Tulsa Studies in Women's Literature* 5 (1986). 273–87.

Index

Authorship *(cont.)*
nineteenth-century conceptions of, 21, 22, 26, 89, 97; "public" and "private" expression and, 4, 30, 33–34, 48; Quakers and, 138–39, 159; twientieth-century conceptions of, 54, 55, 56–57
Autobiography, 35, 42
Awakening, The (Chopin), 62

Baillie, Joanna, 60–61
Baillie, Lady Griselle, 58
Baker, Daniel, 148
Ballard, Elizabeth, 79
Ballard, George, 104; as antiquarian, 79, 80–82, 83–84; influence on later historians, 78–80, 81, 86–87, 88, 91, 103; model for female authors, 79, 82, 84–89, 90, 94, 100, 101, 103, 117, 120
Barbauld, Anna Letitia, 60–61, 116
Barber, Mary, 52–53; in anthologies, 91, 112, 113–15, 116; imprisonment, 120; Swift's praise for, 73, 107
Barbour, Hugh, 135
Barker, Jane, 60–61, 107
Bauman, Richard, 139
Before Their Time (Rogers), 51
Behn, Aphra, 28, 173n.13; in anthologies, 45, 60, 70, 71, 112, 115–16; critical disparagement of, 72, 89, 93–94, 101, 104, 110; critical praise for, 74, 76, 89; excluded from literary histories, 29, 85; as "first" professional woman writer, 22, 30, 41, 47, 48; influence on later authors, 76; poetry, 107, 115–16; role in evolutionary model, 41–42, 45, 46, 47; Victorian critics and, 93–94, 101, 109, 118; Woolf on, 45, 46, 47, 53
Beilin, Elaine V., 3
Belles lettres, 44
Berners, Juliana, 121
Bernikow, Louise, 35–36, 41, 51, 52
Betham, Matilda, 80
Bethune, George Washington: anthology of women's poetry, 94, 117, 118, 120, 162; on domestic lives of authors, 97; editing of poems, 118, 119, 125; evolutionary model of women's literature, 94–95, 104;

literary criticism, 121, 122, 123, 124, 127; writings, 118–19
Bible, 141, 151; Revelation, 132, 152, 153, 155, 165
Bibliotheca (Tanner), 85
Biddle, Hester, 152, 179n.50
Biographical dictionaries, 67, 68, 69, 78, 79–80
Biographical Dictionary of Celebrated Women of Every Age and Country, A (Betham), 80
Biographium Faemineum, 78, 79–80
Biography, 6, 80–81, 84, 89
"Bird, The" (Finch), 128
Blackbarrow, Sarah, 138, 140, 152, 153–57, 158
Blackborrow, William, 153
Blecki, Catherine La Courreye, 140
Boleyn, Anne, 119, 122–23, 124
Bovey, Catherine, 86, 87
Boyle, Robert, 36
Brackley, Lady Elizabeth, 56
Bradstreet, Anne, 52, 54, 60
Braidley, Margaret, 179n.50
Brailsford, Mabel Richmond, 140, 154
Bridgewater, Elizabeth, Countess of, 84, 86
British Female Poets, The (Bethune), 94, 104, 162
British Museum, 49
Brockbank, Elisabeth, 140, 154
Brontë, Charlotte, 62
Brontë sisters, 21, 35, 48
Browning, Elizabeth Barrett, 21
Brydges, Sir Samuel Egerton, 108–9, 110, 111
Burghope, Marie, 56
Burnet, Elizabeth, 56
Burnet, Gilbert (bishop of Salisbury), 85
Byron, George Noel Gordon, Lord, 26

Caldwell, Patricia, 180n.68
"Calliope's Directions How to Deserve and Distinguish the Muses Inspiration" (Cockburn), 77
Cambridge Platonists, 85
Camm, Anne Audland, 135–36
Camm, John, 136
Campbell, Thomas, 118
Canon, 7, 163–64, 165; anthologies in formation of, 10, 40, 42, 61–62, 112,

129–30; definition of authorship and, 33, 60; feminist, 63, 64–65, 163, 165; literary hierarchies in, 44, 57, 62, 63; male tradition and, 59, 63–64; and manuscript writing, 60; nineteenth-century authors in, 105, 106; professional authorship and, 48, 49, 55, 107; silence of early authors in, 43, 44, 55, 59, 60, 104

Carew, Lady Elizabeth, 3, 51, 55, 119, 124

Carter, Eliza, 116

Carter, Elizabeth, 75–76

"Castration or Decapitation?" (Cixous), 161

Caton, William, 136

Cavaliers, 56

Cavendish, Lady Jane, 56

Cavendish, Margaret (duchess of Newcastle), 73; in anthologies, 27–28, 47, 60, 116, 119, 125–27, 128; biographies of, 78, 89; "coarseness" of language, 108, 110–11, 126; "domestic virtues," 89, 100–101; family connections, 106; as feminist, 27–28; nineteenth-century critical opinions of, 100, 101, 108–9, 110, 111; Woolf on, 45; Wordsworth and, 118

Cavendish, William, 52–53

Celebrated Mary Astell (Perry), 6

Centlivre, Susannah, 85, 87, 90

Chaine of Pearle, A (Primrose), 121

Chapone, Hester, 82

Chapone, Sarah, 82, 83, 87

Charles II (king of England), 95

Chauncey, Sir Henry, 84

Cheevers, Sarah, 136, 148–49, 158

Childbirth, 98

Chopin, Kate, 62

Christianity, 85, 87, 142, 154

Chudleigh, Lady Mary, 60, 111–12

Church History of Britain (Fuller), 85

Cibber, Colley, 89

Cibber, Theophilus, 74, 78, 89–90, 103, 104

Cicero, Marcus Tullius, 141

City of London Magazine, 119

Cixous, Hélène, "démoïsation" in reading, 17–18, 133; dismissal of the past, 14, 15, 16, 30, 72; l'écriture feminine ideal, 15, 17, 151, 156; and metalanguage, 161, 163

Clarissa (Richardson), 10–11, 87

Clark, Peter, 49

Clark, Sandra, 49

Cockburn, Catherine Trotter, 76–77, 78, 92, 111–12, 116

Collection of Some Modern Epistles (Guez), 34

Collins, Ann, 60–61

Collins, William, 118

Colman, George, 119, 125; evolutionary model of poetry, 78; literary criticism, 91, 93, 116–17; Poems by Eminent Ladies, 66, 69, 73, 90–91, 107, 112, 113, 118; Poems by the Most Eminent Ladies of Great Britain and Ireland, 112–17

Commercial authorship: dominated by males, 11, 34; in evolutionary model of women's writing, 23, 32–33, 47–49; nineteenth-century model of literature, 4, 21, 33–34, 37, 38, 49, 55

Congrave, William, 63

Contemporary literature, 62

Conway, Anne, Viscountess, 85

Cope, Jackson I., 140, 150, 157, 158

Corinna, 71

Costello, Louisa, 94, 99, 100–101

Coterie literature. See Manuscript circulation

Cotterell, Sir Charles, 36

Court Poems (Montagu), 106

Cowley, Abraham, 74, 75, 77

Crawford, Patricia, 3, 43, 58, 134, 176n.5

Creasey, Maurice, 139

Curran, Stuart, 172n.1

Cyclopedia of Female Poets (Rowton), 69

Dallaway, James, 106, 109–10, 111

"Dancing through the Minefield" (Kolodny), 17

Dancy, Elizabeth, 83

Davies, Lady Eleanor, 85

Debator, The (Rowton), 119

de Certeau, Michel, 132, 151

"Defiled is my Name" (Boleyn), 122

de Lauretis, Teresa, 13, 167n.2

"Démoïsation," 17–18, 133

de Pisan, Christine, 50
Desire and Domestic Fiction (Armstrong), 6
"Despair" (Rowe), 116
Devout Exercises of the Heart (Rowe), 105
Diaries, 34–35, 62, 63
Dictionary (Johnson), 80, 81
Dictionary of British and American Women Writers, 1660–1800 (Todd), 3
Dictionary of English Authors, 106
Dictionary of National Biography, 68, 78, 80
Domesticity, 97–98, 99, 100–101
Donne, John, 54, 63
Drama, 31, 44, 78
Dryden, John, 55, 94; death of, 112; on Elizabeth Thomas, 71–72; ode to Anne Killigrew, 72, 87, 107; on women's writing, 71, 72, 74, 92, 103, 104
Durfey, Tom, 74
Dyce, Alexander: anthology of women's poetry, 111, 117, 118, 119, 120, 125, 126; evolutionary model of women's literature, 95; literary career, 117–18; literary criticism, 121, 122, 123, 127; "tedious chase" through literature, 94; Wordsworth and, 106, 118
Dyer, Lady Katherine, 60–61

Eagleton, Mary, 46
Écriture feminine, L', 15, 16, 17, 151, 156
Education: feminist writers and, 31; limited opportunities for women, 25, 42, 135; literary canons in, 163–64; Quakers, 135–36, 159; upper- and middle-class, 87, 135; of women, men and, 56, 88
Effigies Poeticae (Procter), 99–100
Eighteenth-Century English Literature (Tillotson, Fussell, and Waingrow), 60
Electronic data bases, 3, 164
Eliot, George, 21
Elizabeth I (queen of England): anthologized writings, 50, 99, 119, 121–23; and intellectual women, 95
Elliot, Jane, 60–61
Elliott, Valerie, 49
Elstob, Elizabeth, 82–83
Elwood, Anne, 69–70, 100

Encyclopedias, 67, 68, 69
England, 143, 152; English society, 41, 44, 49
English civil war, 135
English literature, 30; colloquial language, Quakers and, 151, 159; novels, 29; poetry, evolution of, 71, 78, 92, 94, 124; women's writing in, 5, 40, 41. *See also* Anglo-American feminism
English Poetesses (Robertson), 68–69
English Verse (Peacock), 60
Englishwomen, 41–42, 50, 51, 68, 70, 98
English Women of Letters (Kavanagh), 93, 104
"Ephelia," 60–61, 76
"Epigraph to the Theme of Love" (Cavendish), 73
Epistles, 34, 55–56, 141–46. *See also* Letters
Epistle to All the Christian Magistrates, An (Gould), 142–43
"Epistle to Lady Bower" (Jones), 75
"Essentialist," 8, 17, 98
Evans, Katherine, 136, 148–49, 150, 153, 158

Fables (Gay), 113
Fage, Mary, 120
Falkland, Lady, 22
Fanshawe, Sir Richard, 54
"Farewell to France" (Mary, Queen of Scots), 122
Fell, Margaret: daughters' education, 136; epistles, 143, 144–45; on the "Inner Light," 137, 138, 144; letters to Fox, 140, 145; literary historians and, 85, 134, 140, 158, 159; pamphlet writings, 145–46, 154; on reading Scripture, 139; social origins, 135
Female Biography (Hays), 69, 80
"Female poetic," 10, 39, 40, 68, 102
Female Spectator (Mahl and Koons), 30
"Female tradition," 18–19, 39, 43, 55, 68
"Feminine poetic," 67
"Femininity," 25, 99, 103
Feminism, 23–24, 78–79, 167n.2; "anger" as defining element in, 64–65, 162–63; of early female authors, 22, 27–28, 31, 55

women's writing, 22, 23, 42, 46–47, 64; historiography of women's writing, 1, 4, 5, 45, 46, 48–50, 53, 66–68, 79, 106, 128–29; influence on later historians, 25–26, 42–43, 44, 46–47, 61; literary criticism, 25, 46; myth of Judith Shakespeare, 10, 44–45, 49, 50, 98; on poetry's exclusion of women, 33, 43, 45, 48, 62, 63, 66; on professional women writers, 23, 32–33, 47–48, 56, 86

Wooly, Hannah, 85
Wordsworth, Dorothy, 62
Wordsworth, William, 106, 118, 127, 128, 129
World Split Open, The (Bernikow), 51
Wright, Luella, 140, 158
Wrigley, E. A., 49
Writing Schoolmaster (Davies), 34
Wroth, Lady Mary, 3, 55
Wyat, Hester, 52, 53